Encouraging Early Literacy

Encouraging Early Literacy

An Integrated Approach to Reading and Writing in N–3

Judith I. Schwartz
QUEENS COLLEGE
CITY UNIVERSITY OF NEW YORK

Heinemann
Portsmouth, New Hampshire

Heinemann Educational Books, Inc.
70 Court Street   Portsmouth, NH 03801
Offices and agents throughout the world

The following have generously given permission to use quotations from copyrighted works:
Figures 1–1 through 1–5: From B. Gail Heald-Taylor, "Scribble in First Grade Writing," *The Reading Teacher*, October 1984. Reprinted with permission of B. Gail Heald-Taylor and the International Reading Association.
Page 84: Lines from *Millions of Cats* by Wanda Gag, copyright 1928 by Coward-McCann, Inc., copyright renewed © 1956 by Robert Janssen. Reprinted by permission of Coward-McCann, Inc.
Page 84: From Dr. Seuss, *The Cat in the Hat*. Copyright © 1957 by Dr. Seuss. Reprinted by permission of Random House, Inc.
Page 154: From Spike Milligan, "A Thousand Hairy Savages," *Silly Verse, For Kids*. Reprinted by permission of Spike Milligan Productions Ltd.
Page 154: "Fog" from *Chicago Poems* by Carl Sandburg, copyright 1916 by Holt, Rinehart and Winston, Inc.; renewed 1944 by Carl Sandburg. Reprinted by permission of Harcourt Brace Jovanovich, Inc.
Page 154: "Mountains" from *In My Mother's House*, by Ann Nolan Clark. Copyright 1941, Copyright © renewed 1969 by Ann Nolan Clark. Reprinted by permission of Viking Penguin, Inc.

Library of Congress Cataloging-in-Publication Data
Schwartz, Judy I.
　Encouraging early literacy.

　Bibliography: p.
　Includes index.
　1. Reading (Primary)—Language experience approach.
2. Reading—United States—History.　3. Language acquisition.　4. Reading comprehension.　5. Creative activities and seat work.　I. Title.
LB1525.34.S38　1988　　　372.4　　　86-26964
ISBN 0-435-08435-6

10　9　8　7　6　5　4　3　2　1

Front cover photo © Norvia Behling, P.O. Box 189, St. Germain, WI 54558.
Designed by Maria Szmauz.
Printed in the United States of America.

CONTENTS

PREFACE

I have written *Encouraging Early Literacy* in the sincere hope that it will provide pre- and in-service teachers with a sound, reasonable, and humane approach to helping young children learn to read and write. It is based on current theory and the findings of recent research about how children learn in general and about their acquisition of and development in language in particular. This book developed as well out of my many experiences with children and teachers in preschool and primary grade classrooms and my ongoing interactions with graduate and undergraduate students in the courses I teach. These experiences in the real world of children and teachers led to a deep concern on my part about the development of literacy, and more particularly, about how literacy is actually taught in school.

Too often, literacy instruction consists of training children to master a series of separate skills, which are presented in a fixed sequence and taught in a highly didactic style. Drill, repetition, and memorization are usually the hallmarks of this approach. It seems to me that this is a case of putting the cart before the horse. That is, it is based on the erroneous assumption that children learn language by assembling its pieces into a whole in the same way they put together the pieces of a puzzle. On the contrary, children first apprehend both the spoken and the written aspects of language as a whole, undifferentiated medium that is deeply contextualized in the reality of their everyday lives. This understanding of children's learning has three implications for teaching:

1. Children make sense of things when there is much support from the context. Whole language is more meaningful, and thus easier to learn, than are isolated pieces of language, which is why children master phoneme/grapheme (sound/letter) relationships in the process of reading, not before it.

2. Children are motivated to learn both spoken and written forms of language because they need to get something done; they want to communicate. (For example, children learn standard spellings so that they can communicate to an audience through writing.) Thus real contexts and whole language make more sense in teaching children because they allow for *function*.

3. Children's knowledge of the world, their experience in general, influences their success in reading and writing. This experience is the source of the meanings children construct in spoken and written texts.

Encouraging Early Literacy is not a survey text on the methodology of teaching literacy, nor is it designed to present a broad and balanced coverage of many different approaches. Rather, its purpose is to provide an in-depth view of a particular approach to the teaching of reading and writing, its rationale, and its application. It says that children are apt to be successful in becoming literate if they have contact with whole and meaningful language used with real purpose to satisfy real needs. Will every teacher want to implement the plan discussed here? Probably not. Are all children likely to experience failure in school unless they are taught in the ways described here? Again, probably not, because many children already have preschool and out-of-school experiences of this kind. But I think that many teachers and soon-to-be teachers will want to try this approach, perhaps beginning slowly, because of its inherent effectiveness and because it is described in this book with sufficient detail and guidance to make it workable. I believe, as well, that most children would profit greatly from an approach that fits their way of learning, engages rather than ignores their interests, and makes reading and writing enjoyable and functional activities instead of tedious skills for which they can see no real purpose.

The book is divided into three sections. The first, "Foundations of Instruction," gathers the research and theory that underlie the approach to teaching literacy presented here. Chapter 1, "Knowing Children," outlines important developmental trends in children's learning and language acquisition, and the significance of knowing children as unique and individual beings. Chapter 2, "Understanding the Written Code," takes a close look at the nature of language and its characteristics and how these affect the teaching of reading and writing.

The second section, which could be considered the heart of the book, is called "The Program in Action." It describes in concrete and practical detail how the program operates from the preschool through the third grade. The chapters in this section concentrate on school programs for different developmental levels. Chapter 3, "Emergent Literacy," shows how to initiate the literacy program with children as young as three years. Chapter 4, "Reading and Writing More Conventionally," describes how children can be effectively engaged in more formal and sustained experiences with the written aspect of language, as would typically occur in the first grade. Chapter 5, "Becoming Proficient in Reading and Writing," illustrates the different ways children's developing abilities in reading and writing take shape in the later primary grades. I have used these grade-level designations for organizational efficiency, but as I will suggest throughout the book, children's actual needs rather than their grade level should determine instructional strategies and materials.

The title of the last section of the book, "Specifics of Instruction," may be somewhat misleading because many important instructional specifics are incorporated into the program descriptions in chapters 3, 4, and 5. The third section, however, gives more attention to topics of particular concern. Chapter 6 concentrates on "Comprehension," the central yet often undervalued purpose of reading. Finally, chapter 7, "Assessment," shows how the teacher can use careful observation and documentation to diagnose children's performance and modify the teaching plan, if necessary, to meet their needs more effectively.

Each chapter is preceded by a preview to help you anticipate, organize, and remember what you read. Because I believe it is essential to tie reading *about* teaching reading and writing to the actual *practice* of teaching reading and writing, I have included several child-centered activities at the end of each chapter. I hope you will read this book while you have actual contact with children in schools. Finally, I have carefully selected the suggestions for further reading (and in some cases viewing) at the close of each chapter, and they are fully worth your time and attention.

So many individuals helped to make this book a reality. Earlier I noted how significant interactions with my students, and through them, with their students, have been. But there are a special few whose suggestions and comments on the manuscript in preparation were particularly useful: Alvina Treut Burrows, one of my own teachers; three former students, Melanie Bigman, Christine Haffner, and Roseanne Silverstein; several anonymous reviewers; and most especially, Steven Heller, my husband, whose continued support and invaluable assistance have helped me through good times and bad.

In the final analysis, it is those things that have held personal significance for us that we recall and act on. The writing of this book has demanded hard work, but it has also offered me the chance to struggle with competing ideas, to think through and to clarify ambiguities, and in the process, to understand more fully. I hope this book will also help other teachers and prospective teachers to think about how and what to teach and to grow in the process. For both author and reader, I dedicate *Encouraging Early Literacy* to the goal of becoming better teachers.

BIgBIrdelis.time you Bal
Hey! Whats going for yo
Oscar the Grouch going on
Nant to to you asBar

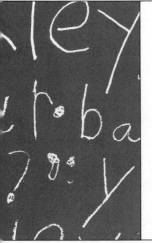

Foundations of Instruction

The two chapters comprising this section explain the theory and research behind the approach to literacy instruction described in this book. It is an approach based on a sociocognitive view of language learning[1] and is drawn primarily from the work of Jean Piaget on cognitive development and the research of psycho- and sociolinguists on the nature and development of language and its relation to thinking. According to the sociocognitive view, language learning is a higher order thinking process in which the learner's construction of meaning is central. It is a process that is deeply affected by the learner's environment and his transactions with significant others within that social context. The implications of this view of language learning for encouraging young children to read and write will be described in detail in sections II and III.

Chapter 1

Knowing
Children

Preview

Human intelligence, a splendid accomplishment of evolution, allows children to make rapid advances in early childhood. Through exploration of their environment and interaction with others, children learn about life. The order, continuity, and consistency children experience in their own lives enable them to derive meaning from all that surrounds them. They are ready to learn about everything, including language in its oral and written aspects.

This chapter discusses the importance of knowing about how children learn and of knowing children as individuals. It focuses on how children's language and thinking develop from birth to about eight years of age. Here are some of the topics that will be discussed in this chapter:

1. *Why Piaget's theory of cognitive development is called a "genetic" psychology.*
2. *What is needed to trigger the natural development of logical thought.*
3. *The most significant developments of the sensorimotor, preoperational, and concrete operational periods.*
4. *Teaching implications of Piaget's theory.*
5. *Basic principles of language development.*
6. *What probably accounts for how children learn language structure.*
7. *Possible reasons for some children's difficulty in learning to read and write.*
8. *Sound practices teachers can apply in teaching literacy, based on current understanding of how children learn.*
9. *The importance of knowing children as individuals and some helpful suggestions.*

Knowing About Children

This is a book about teaching children to read and write. But, as all good teachers (or prospective teachers) know, quality teaching requires *knowing your students*—knowing them personally and directly, and knowing about them in a more general way. When you meet a new class, you have expectations about the abilities and interests of children of that age level that shape the character and direction of your instruction. For this reason, we will consider first the development of young children. Our most immediate concern is children's cognitive development, with particular emphasis on language. This section considers Piaget's theory of cognitive development and the characteristics of language development during early childhood.

Piaget's Theory of Cognitive Development

Cognition means the process of knowing, and cognitive development refers to the intellectual aspect of growth.[1] Swiss psychologist Jean Piaget's theory of cognitive development is considered by many to be the foremost statement of how children learn.

The impact of Piaget's early work in biology is very clear in his theory. His work is sometimes called a "genetic" psychology, because he considered the development of intelligence to be genetically specified. All human beings proceed through the same stages of cognitive development, although they do so at different rates.[2] Piaget noted that in order to survive, an organism must adapt to its environment. He found, for example, that the typically elongated shape of an aquatic mollusk (a kind of shellfish) had become more rounded as an adaptation to the movement of the waters in its particular environment.

Three kinds of knowledge.   Piaget identified three kinds of knowledge: social, physical, and logico-mathematical. He was most interested in the development of logico-mathematical knowledge. To illustrate the distinctions among the three, let us say that there is a red and a blue chip. On the one hand, the labels (words) applied to them (*red chip*, *blue chip*) are fundamentally arbitrary social conventions; they are part of the *social* knowledge associated with the chips. On the other hand, the chips are actually observable; they exist in time and space. This knowledge of the chips can be said, therefore, to be *physical*. Relationships *between* the chips, however, are not observable; they do not exist outside the mind of the observer. That the chips are the same (or a different) size or color is part of the *logico-mathematical* system of knowledge constructed by each person. The relationship of one chip to another does not exist in either chip or in external reality but in the mind of the person who constructed it.[3]

Piaget traced the development of logico-mathematical knowledge from earliest infancy by collecting detailed, longitudinal observations of his own three children. He concluded that intelligence develops as the child adapts to its environment. According to Piaget, psychological adaptation has two components:

1. Assimilation—new information is transformed and incorporated into already existing structures.
2. Accommodation—already existing structures are modified to adjust to new information.

Initially, for example, a child may call all vehicles "cars." Buses, motorcycles, even trains are *assimilated* into the child's concept of "car." Later, as the child begins to draw distinctions among different kinds of vehicles, she calls some vehicles cars but refers to others as buses, motorcycles, or trains. She has *accommodated* her cognitive structure to include different labels for different classes of vehicles.

The *schema* is a major construct of Jean Piaget's theory of cognitive development. A *schema* (*schemata* in the plural) is a cognitive or mental structure through which an individual intellectually adapts to and organizes the environment. Schemata are created through interaction with the environment, and an individual actively seeks to organize experiences and information into schemata according to common characteristics. On seeing a rabbit for the first time, a young child may call it a kitten, because the rabbit and kitten have some features in common: they are both soft, cuddly, and small, and they both have whiskers and four legs. But schemata are continually being changed and refined as the child assimilates and accommodates new experiences. When a stimulus or experience cannot be assimilated into an already existing schema, the child accommodates by either modifying an already existing schema or creating a new one.[4] In the previous example, the child would ultimately develop a new schema for rabbits that encompassed both rabbits and kittens.

According to Piaget, growth is genetically influenced and develops through internal transformations such as accommodation and assimilation. Susan Isaacs's description of the young child's mind as prehensile and exploratory reflects this biological predisposition to learn.[5] Through her active interaction with the environment, then, the child *creates* knowledge.

Periods of cognitive development.   Piaget defined four major periods of cognitive development and their approximate age levels:[6]

- *Sensorimotor:* birth to twenty-four months.
- *Preoperational:* two to seven years.
- *Concrete operational:* seven to eleven years.
- *Formal operational:* eleven years and beyond.

Sensorimotor period.   Piaget's description of infant intelligence as sensorimotor indicates that the child's mental activity is focused on organizing sensations and controlling muscular activity. That is, the child has no way of symbolizing an action mentally. Not until the final stage of the sensorimotor period is there any representation. To "think" an act, the child must actually perform it. A toddler, for example, in order to think about lifting and throwing a block, must actually do it, until one day as he does so, he bends down and "pretends" to take hold of another block and throw that one too. In this last instance, the child has thrown an imaginary block. The beginning of imagination and speech in the sensorimotor period marks its transition to the next level of cognitive development, that of preoperational thought.[7]

Preoperational period.   The highlight of preoperational thought, when compared with sensorimotor intelligence, is *symbolic representation*. Whereas the infant (in the sensorimotor period) needed to manipulate objects to understand them, the preoperational child can substitute a mental image for overt action. Preoperational thought involves manipulation of symbols. It is the ability to think without simultaneously having to act. Consider a child at a form box. A child at the sensorimotor stage fits each piece into each hole by trial and error and only gets the piece in by acting out. A preoperational child, on the other hand, *looks* at the forms, looks at the holes, and imagines how they relate. She runs the action through in her head. She has insight. She can grasp several thoughts simultaneously, anticipate outcomes, and connect past, present, and future. An example is the four-year-old who was scrubbing some doll clothes against a washboard in her bathtub. "This is the way we wash our clothes, wash our clothes, wash our clothes. This is the way we wash our clothes, so early in the morning," she sang as she worked. When a neighbor saw her so engrossed, she asked, "What are you doing, Toni?" "Washing clothes, like Mommy." "Does your Mommy use a washboard?" "Uh-huh, sometimes. But she uses the washing machine too. These are special clothes here. I'm gonna hang them on the line later on. Mommy don't like when I make the floor wet."

In this brief exchange, it is easy to see the symbolic representation in Toni's thinking: she has connected a symbolic (play) sequence with a real one (Mommy washing); she has thought about previous episodes like it (Mommy washing); and she has anticipated future events (hanging the clothes up to dry, wetting the floor).

Another feature of preoperational thought is that it does not depend on concrete action. Now, the child can think *before* acting rather than only *through* acting. The four-year-old Toni can recall what happened the last time she washed some doll clothes in the bathtub. She can anticipate the consequences of wetting the tile floor (her mother's annoyance) and make changes in her current actions to prevent this from happening again.

The cognitive changes that occur during the preoperational period are very significant for the attainment of literacy. The referent of a written word is not usually present when the word is read; and in order to handle this degree of abstraction from reality, a child must be capable of the symbolic representation that is characteristic of preoperational thought. Another characteristic of preoperational thinking is *centration*. Centration refers to the child's tendency to fix her attention on a single aspect of a relationship. Despite the preoperational child's many advances in thinking, she is still far from mature. For example, I once observed a child of about six, articulate and doing well in schoolwork, who was working on a typical Piagetian task in which two sets of the same number of blue and red pencils were lined up, one-to-one. The interviewer asked if there were as many blue pencils as red ones. "Yes," she answered. As he chatted with her, the interviewer grouped the blue pencils together. He then asked again if there were as many blue pencils as red ones, to which she responded, "No." This child had centered her attention on the lengths of the two sets of pencils and ignored the difference in the density with which the two sets of pencils were spaced. The child's thinking was still limited by her reliance on perception rather than logic.

Concrete operational period.   By the time the child is in the second or third grade, the concrete operational period of development, she is able to coordinate several aspects of a relationship. The hallmark of the concrete operational period is the construction of *logical* operations and their application to the solution of concrete problems. When faced with the kind of conservation problem the preoperational child described above was unable to solve, the concrete operational child applies logical operations that supersede conceptual constraints. She can decenter her perceptions from just a single aspect of a problem and attend to several aspects at once.

One of the child's new logical operations is *reversibility*. Piaget offers this example of inversion to illustrate simple reversibility.[8] The child is shown three balls of the same size but different colors. First, the balls are placed in a cylinder in a given sequence—A (red), B (blue), C (yellow). When they are left in this order, the preoperational child will correctly predict that they will leave the cylinder in the sequence C–B–A. When the cylinder is rotated 180°, however, the preoperational child persists in this same prediction. In contrast, the concrete operational child is able to predict correctly that the balls will leave in the reverse order—A–B–C. Although logical operations are clearly present in this period, the child only uses them in the solution of problems that involve real, observable objects and events in the immediate present. It is not until the final period of cognitive development, that of formal operations, that the child's thought is no longer bound by direct experience.

Recent reassessment of Piagetian theory.   Since the 1970s, Piaget's theory has undergone reassessment.[9] One of the major criticisms to emerge during this period of reinterpretation is based on the view that young children are generally more skillful than Piaget concluded. Piaget stated that preoperational thought is highly *egocentric*, particularly in its earlier stages. When Piaget explained a very simple experiment to a preoperational child, warning the child in advance that he would have to explain the same experiment to someone else, the child simply repeated what he remembered of the directions without taking the listener's needs into account at all. However, more recent research does not support this conclusion. Even very young children have been found to show empathy for their peers, and some three-year-olds have been shown to adopt the special speech register called baby talk when speaking to infants.

In addition, Piaget did not believe that language is necessary for the development of intelligence, although he did acknowledge that it provides a useful medium for the symbolic function; representational skills, of which language is one, enable a child to think more quickly and efficiently. According to Piaget, language and thought are separate, and not until the period of formal operations (beginning at about eleven years of age) does language have a direct role in the acquisition of knowledge. Language is never the source of logico-mathematical knowledge.

Today, many theorists and researchers who believe that there is a closer relationship between language and thought than Piaget acknowledged often refer to the work of the Russian linguist Lev Vygotsky for a theoretical rationale on the language/thought relationship.[10] Vygotsky saw an interactive relationship between language and thinking. While language and thought arise independently, it is not until the two systems fuse with the development of *inner speech* that logical reasoning develops. Moreover, young children use language not only to communicate, according to Vygotsky, but also to plan and guide their behavior in a self-regulatory manner. In addition, the highly social approach to learning language supported by recent research contradicts Piaget's explanations. Learning to speak is firmly embedded in the child's social life. The work of Harste, Burke, and Woodward, for example, finds that the interpretive rules of language use are acquired through social interaction at a very early age.[11] Gordon Wells and Jerome Bruner emphasize mutuality and reciprocity in the meanings that are communicated via talk between adult and young child.[12]

Implications of Piaget's theory for teaching.   Jean Piaget was not an educator. He considered his work in developmental psychology *epistemological*, part of the branch of philosophy concerned with the nature and origin of knowledge. There is very little in his many books and papers that directly addresses teaching, although what does appear has been significant. In the foreword to Almy's *Young Children's Thinking*, Piaget says: ". . . school children and students should be allowed a *maximum* of activity of their own, directed by means of materials which permit their activities to be cognitively useful."[13] He reminds us that children have a real understanding only of what they verify themselves. Each time we try to teach children too quickly, we prevent them from constructing or reinventing knowledge.

Children as active processors of experience.   At the beginning of the twentieth century, researchers believed that the world was a great, buzzing confusion to the infant, who, passive and helpless, lay waiting to be imprinted. We now know that the infant takes an active role in its own development, influencing its environment as well as being influenced by it. According to Piaget, the origins of intelligence lie in the sensorimotor period, in the child's interaction with the environment and her observation of the effects of these interactions. We would add the significant interactions between infant and caregivers. By the time she enters preschool, the child has acquired quite a range of knowledge about the world and the necessary tools to help her solve new problems. She knows that her actions bring results and that causes have effects. She has observed regularities or patterns in the world and has deduced hypotheses about them. The young child has had many experiences with means-ends relationships: she throws her bottle off the high chair tray, and down it goes to the floor; she pulls a string on her pull toy and, lo and behold, the toy moves; or she pulls on her blanket, and a favorite toy atop it moves closer. Learning goes on all the time in the child's life as she explores and acts on her environment.

One of the most significant features of that environment is the language that surrounds the child, and she applies the same problem-solving tools to language that she uses on the rest of the environment. The child learns first about the world, perceives that language is an important aspect of that world, and then maps her knowledge of the world onto language. The same search for patterns, for meaning and rules, that goes on in learning about other things also goes on in learning about language. This amusing exchange between a linguist and her preschooler illustrates much of what Piaget tells us:

Child: My teacher holded the baby rabbits and we patted them.

Adult: Did you say your teacher held the baby rabbits?

Child: Yes.
Adult: What did you say she did?
Child: She holded the baby rabbits and we patted them.
Adult: Did you say she held them tightly?
Child: No, she holded them loosely.[14]

From her many experiences of hearing the past tense marker *-ed* this child has nonconsciously induced that the past tense of verbs is indicated by *-ed*, so she pronounces all verbs—regular and irregular—with the past tense marker: *walked*, *jumped*, *singed*, and *holded*. We will look more closely at the child's grammar in the next section; here it is important to note that:

1. The child actively processes the language around her.
2. Rule induction accounts for most of the child's grasp of language (e.g., no one taught the child the rule about past tense markers).
3. Direct teaching has minimal effect (e.g., "Did you say she *held* them tightly?" "No, she *holded* them loosely.")

According to Wadsworth, the child approaches learning to read and write in the same way that he intuitively approaches any problem.[15] Confronted with graphic symbols that he does not understand, he tries to assimilate and accommodate those symbols in an attempt to make sense out of written language. Making sense out of written symbols is a problem to be solved.

What can we apply from all this to encourage beginning literacy? First, surround the child with an environment rich in purposeful language experiences. Children learn how to read and write by reading and writing, by hearing stories read aloud and reading along themselves, by drawing up lists and making party invitations. Ensure that reading and writing are an essential part of all activities, fully integrated into the total teaching plan. Emphasize the crucial place of meaning: how children *bring* meaning *to* reading as well as to writing and likewise, how children *take* meaning *from* writing as well as from reading. Make certain that learning to read and write will be necessary for the children's full participation in the life of their class, where they will use reading and writing as tools to accomplish real tasks. Emphasize that reading and writing are *thinking* processes requiring the same kinds of problem-solving skills used in other aspects of life. Integrate reading and writing with listening and speaking, and help children use their mastery of oral language in learning the written form. Learning to read and write requires experiences in language that enhance the operation of children's natural adaptive intelligence—experiences that are whole, meaningful, integrated, and functional.

Language Development

Language constitutes a highly significant feature of the child's environment. From birth the child is immersed in a sea of language through which he interacts with people and things. Because language helps him make sense of, and master, his world, it is intimately and interactively related to cognition. In the last section, we reviewed Piaget's theory of cognitive development. Now let us take a closer look at how language develops.

All human cultures use language (at least in its spoken form) as a highly organized and systematic way of symbolically representing experience. Undoubtedly, language enhances and refines intellectual development and is necessary for higher abstract reasoning. But the child's understanding of the world also affects his development in language.

Language is present from the very beginning of a child's life. Adults use language to communicate with infants for various purposes: to make contact, give comfort, and direct behavior. Adults relate language to a meaningful context; Snow found that even with a three-month-old, adults used language that concerned something the child could see or do, or was attending to.[16] Therefore, right from the onset of communication, language is both meaningful and useful.

Language comprehension and production.   The young infant can comprehend differences among speech sounds long before he can produce them.[17] Throughout our lives, language comprehension surpasses language production. That is why our understanding vocabulary always remains larger than our speaking and writing vocabularies, particularly when we learn a second language. I often hear complaints from exasperated teachers about the apparent absence of language in their non-English-speaking children. "Julio doesn't talk at all. I can't get him to say a word to me. What am I supposed to do? How am I expected to teach a child to read if he can't speak?" A bit of probing almost always reveals that a) Julio *does* use language, usually his native language, in informal settings such as dramatic play, block building, on the playground, and in the lunchroom, and that b) Julio *understands* a great deal of English, even if he is not yet ready to produce it.

Interrelatedness of language modes.   The *language arts* constitute a traditional division of the production and comprehension aspects of language. Because in both speaking and writing meaning is *expressed* symbolically through language, they are called the *expressive modes*. In listening and reading, meaning is *received* symbolically through language; thus, they are called the *receptive modes*.

Typically, the language arts are presented in the sequence listening, speaking, reading, and writing because this is considered the progression of stages in language development. In infancy, children begin to listen to language with comprehension; as toddlers, they start to produce meaningful speech; later on in school, they are taught to read and write. However, there are two difficulties with this sequence. First, we know that some children write before they read. Durkin's studies of children who read before they start school found many involved in pre-writing and writing activities before they could actually read conventionally.[18] A child might ask her parent how to spell a word, trace over the parent's model, write the word herself, and later recognize the word on sight in a different context. Of course, these children do much unconventional reading too: for example, they remember the names of fast-food chains and can read their signs when seen in context ("That says McDonald's"). Such children can also "read" favorite stories they recall by heart from many readings.

Another problem with the listening, speaking, reading, and writing sequence is that it gives the incorrect impression that the language arts are totally independent units, which develop in a rigidly fixed sequence. This is simply not so. Natural language is whole and integrated. Children do not learn language in small bits, nor are they exposed to language as separate modes. On the contrary, children experience language in which giving and receiving meaning is the essence. It is language in which listening, speaking, reading, and writing occur as a dynamic flow. Consider this episode:

Tina, three and a half, is sitting at the kitchen table while her mother stands nearby sorting clothes for the wash. With a new set of fine-line felt-tip markers, Tina is engrossed in drawing and writing on some paper.

Mother: Tina, how do you like your new magic markers?

Tina: I love 'em. I'm writing letters.

Mother: Oh, who are you writing to?

Tina: Gramps. Wanna see?

Tina gets off her chair and brings her paper over for her mother's admiration.

Mother: Oh, Tina, that's lovely. Gramps will be so happy to get your letter. Will you read it to me?

Tina reads her letter, which consists of alphabet letters, numerals, and pictures, plus TINA, spelled in wobbly upper case near the bottom:

"Dear Gramps. Mommy got me new magic markers. I'm writing letters. Love, Tina. I love you."

Tina: Mommy, can you write the envelope?

Mother: Of course, sweetie, after we finish the wash. Okay? Now, get me the new box of Tide.

Tina runs to the laundry room and selects the correct detergent from assorted cleaning products arranged on a low shelf.

Although only three and a half years old, Tina is already engaged in all aspects of language. She listens to and understands her mother. She knows that meaning can be encoded in written symbols. She can even correctly read the name of a familiar product. Tina is a typical example of the way children learn language as a natural, functional, and meaningful part of their everyday lives. Indeed, it is not until children enter school that they may experience language artificially fragmented and devoid of purpose.

Now let us trace the development of language from infancy through the primary grades.

Infancy

Purpose of early vocalizations. An infant's prespeech vocalizations exert a powerful influence on his caregivers. Crying, for instance, will bring an adult to the infant to check on whether he is ill, or needs to be fed or changed or simply comforted. With his needs met, the infant stops crying, and the adult is reassured of the baby's well-being. Prespeech appears to have three stages. The *crying* stage begins with the birth cry, whose purpose is to help establish normal respiration and promote oxygenation of the blood. About the end of the first month, the infant enters the *cooing* stage, using the organs of articulation (i.e., mouth, lips, tongue) to produce more varied vocalizations than the cry. The vocalizations sound like "cooing" because they are produced at the back of the mouth with the lips in a rounded position. *Babbling* begins about the middle of the first year. It sounds more like conventional speech than do earlier vocalizations because it consists of consonant-vowel combinations (e.g., *la la la*, *da da da*, *ga ga ga*). The distinctive pitch contour of a baby's native language shows up very early in his babbling. Weir has reported that five- to eight-month-old babies, of Chinese-speaking and American English-speaking parents, had different intonation patterns in their babbling.[19] The Chinese infants, even at this early age, could already be identified by their distinctive pitch patterns.

From birth, infants engage in the reciprocal play of communication. In a frame-by-frame analysis of films of the movements made by newborn babies in the presence of adult speech, Condon and Sander found a correspondence of ninety percent between the body movement of babies as young as one day old and the articulatory segments of adult speech.[20] The word *over*, for instance, was accompanied by segments of infant movement exactly synchronous with the word's three articulatory segments *oooo*, *vv*, and *iririr*. Infants employ systematic ways of expressing various intentions—they gesture, point, and use supports to pull objects nearer. What is more, their "conversations" with adults are even characterized by turn-taking. Thus, the communicative function of language is present in a baby's earliest vocalizations. Language develops in the service of fulfilling varied needs: predicting the environment, interacting with others, and reaching goals with someone's help.

One-word stage.   Language develops by a process through which the young child maps or translates it to his rapidly growing store of facts and concepts about the world. At about a year old, the child begins to use one-word utterances, called *holophrases*, to represent an entire thought. Holophrases are an accompaniment to action; the child uses them to demand, declare, question, or describe a relationship. Bruner says that the initial use of language probably supports and is closely linked to action.[21] Language and action share a similar structure: agent-action-object (for example, baby drops the ball). Adults may have difficulty in interpreting holophrases because they are entirely context-bound. Thus, if a child said, "Teddy," without specific clues from the environment, it would be impossible to know if he meant "I see my teddy bear," or "Give me my teddy bear," or something else entirely.

Overextensions.   Frequent overextensions of a word to inappropriate categories is another characteristic of the very young child's speech. We have all been amused when a child calls any male person "Daddy." This occurs because children begin to use words before they have acquired an adult sense of their full meaning. *Semantics* is the study of meaning in language forms. According to Eve Clark's *semantic feature theory*, the meaning of each word is comprised of a bundle of features.[22] A child gradually adds more features of a word's meaning to her understanding of the word until her combination of features for the word approximates that of an adult. Semantic features acquired first are the most general. Initially a toddler may label all hairy, four-legged creatures, "doggy." Later, as she adds more specific features to her concept of "doggy," she will discriminate among dogs, cats, cows, and horses. Still later, the child will associate "dog" with larger categories such as pet, companion, and hunter. Some researchers believe that perceptual features such as shape, size, or movement account for much of a child's early semantic development.

Toddlerhood to preschool

Telegraphic speech.   Usually between eighteen months and two years, the child begins to combine words into two-word utterances. This is quite a major achievement, since it marks the beginning of the use of language to express relations and intentions. Between two and three years of age, children speak sentences that consist mainly of nouns and verbs, with some adjectives and adverbs. Prepositions, conjunctions, articles, and auxiliary verbs are usually absent. Speech at this stage is called *telegraphic*, because it has the characteristic abbreviated form of the telegram.

Rule-governed and systematic development.   Children process the speech that surrounds them and induce from this a latent language structure of their own. The errors in young children's speech are not random but rather consistent with the grammar they have created at their particular stage of language development. One common error children make is the application of the plural *-s* to irregular nouns, which produces such forms as *mans* and *sheeps*. It is highly unlikely that the child has actually heard and imitated these forms. Instead, from the many examples she has heard in which *-s* is the marker of the plural in regular nouns (*hats*, *dogs*, etc.) she has probably nonconsciously overgeneralized to irregular nouns. What she has actually done is to *regularize* the language.[23]

Imitation and reinforcement cannot account for the child's mastery of the structure of language. If they did, why would a child produce forms she has never heard an adult use, such as irregular noun plurals? Ervin analyzed tape recordings of the spontaneous speech of children twenty-two to thirty-six months old over several months.[24] She compared the frequency of their spontaneous imitations with their freely generated sentences and found that only five to twenty percent of the sentences were imitations. The structure of children's language is different from the adult version and appears to develop in a systematic and consistent way.

Biological predisposition for language.   Noam Chomsky attributes language development to biological factors that exist specifically in the human being.[25] He believes that specific language structures are built into the human nervous system. According to this view, language develops through a process of maturation, which is stimulated by experience. This view contrasts with that of Piaget, who believed that sensorimotor intelligence formed the basis for language development.

Support for Chomsky's view that human beings are biologically predisposed for language development comes from various kinds of indirect evidence: a) that children proceed through the same stages in the mastery of language structure across different languages; b) that despite the magnitude of the task, children acquire language with great speed; c) that all languages are based upon the same principles; and d) that the kinds of errors children produce indicate a need to construct and follow rules in their speech.

Primary grades.   By the time he enters school, the child speaks relatively as well as the adults in his immediate environment. He has mastered a good part of English grammar and is even quite adept at the social conventions of communication, such as taking turns and knowing when to respond and when not to. These are remarkable achievements, considering the complexity of language and the short span of time (five to six years) in which all of this is accomplished.

Differences in mastering the written and spoken aspects of language.   The apparent ease with which children master spoken language contrasts sharply with what many of them experience with the written form of language in the primary grades. Learning to read and write is often a highly frustrating task, in which failure, rather than success, is the outcome. Why is this so? No one knows the answer in the way that one knows the sum of a set of numbers or the solution to an algebraic equation. There can be no simple answer to a problem as complex as this one. It seems to me, however, that the factors associated with failure in literacy cluster around three areas: a) differences between spoken and written language; b) differences among children; c) ways in which literacy is taught. Let us consider each of these.

Differences between the written and spoken aspects of language.   We have seen that language is a form of symbolic representation. A spoken word represents, among other things, an object, a thought, a feeling, or a relationship, but it achieves a level of abstraction beyond the actual object, thought, feeling, or relationship. To the child, however, a written word is a still less familiar abstraction of the actual object (thought, feeling, or relationship). A child can see a real chair; he can sit on it, stand on it, even fall off it. The child's experience with the real chair is direct and immediate. But when he hears the word *chair* spoken, he must think back to the original chair and associate all the real features of the chair with the spoken word. Later on, he will recognize the word *chair* in its written form. The beginning reader may associate the written symbols *c-h-a-i-r* with the spoken word *chair*, which in turn will conjure up all his direct associations with a real chair. Much of this occurs at a nonconscious level, and the skilled reader usually omits this intermediate step entirely.

Mastering the written form of language requires an ability to attend consciously to the language forms themselves, rather than focusing on what the language is communicating. Cazden, among others, has called this ability *metalinguistic awareness*, an awareness of language.[26] Thus, to understand the concept "word," a child must be able to separate words from the continuous flow of speech he hears and perceive them as discrete units of sound. For the moment, word meaning becomes less important than word function. Likewise, in order to learn how to spell, a child must think about, analyze, and isolate the sounds of words. Learning to read and write requires a higher level of consciousness about language than mastery of speaking and listening. Hiebert found that three- to five-year-olds were aware of the fact that print is meaningful and is associated with the processes of reading and writing.[27] Yet some children in this age group do not generally understand what a word is; they may label a single letter a word and they cannot, generally, identify single words from the flow of speech.[28] One of the consequences of learning to read and write is increased awareness and understanding of the nature and function of print.

In oral language, the child can use all sorts of cues—the speaker's facial expressions and gestures, the objects in the immediate surroundings, and changes in the speaker's pitch, stress, and juncture—to help figure out what the speaker means. Written language, too, contains paralinguistic features of its own, such as punctuation, changes in typographical style (italics, boldface), illustrations, headings and underlining, and the like, all of which signal meaning. In both oral and written language, meaning resides not only in the words themselves but also in how they are said or written. Although the paralinguistic cues to meaning are generally considered more potent in oral than in written language, written-language cues do have some advantages. The reader of a message can alter his reading speed to suit his purpose for reading and the difficulty of the reading material. He also has the option of rereading the message. Unless it is audiotaped, a spoken message does not permit these accommodations.

Differences among children.   Even though ours is a literate society, most children do not experience written language as continuously and pervasively as they experience spoken language. Although some children come from families where printed material and reading are an important part of their lives, many others experience written language in a more sporadic and less personal way. They may see words on TV and labels at the supermarket, but perhaps no one ever reads or writes at home. In addition, studies by sociolinguists and anthropologists such as Basil Bernstein and Shirley Brice Heath have found important differences in the way language is used by different groups within a given culture.[29] When a child's ways of communicating differ significantly from what is expected in school, he may experience problems in learning to read and write. If because of his particular cultural background a child's way of answering questions and raising questions of his own is at variance with the teacher's expectations, which are conditioned by her own background, it can create the kind of communication dissonance that may interfere with the child's progress.

Teaching reading and writing in schools.   There may be more reading and writing programs than, in the words of an old phrase, you can shake a stick at. However, in my own experience as a teacher and a teacher of teachers, and in that of my students and colleagues, I have observed certain practices that may actually hinder rather than help children in learning to read and write. These practices can impede the operation of the child's native ability, break the natural bridge from listening and speaking to reading and writing, and undermine the internal coherence of the language arts. Some examples: reading instruction may be isolated in a separate period. Reading and writing instruction may consist of mastery of a hierarchy of skills. Meaning in writing may be subordinated to form. Word identification may be emphasized while comprehension is neglected, and reading and writing may be completely dissociated from useful, meaningful tasks.

Development of writing.   Writing activity can begin as early as eighteen months, or even earlier, with the toddler's handling of writing instruments and scribbling. The scribbling may then continue for several years. The following examples from first graders illustrate several kinds of scribbling: precommunicative, which conveys no message but has qualities of writing such as correct directionality (Figure 1–1); story matching, in which a child is able to reread scribble after an interval of time, matching her retelling of the story to a particular segment of scribble (Figure 1–2); sentence and word matching, in which the child matches a line of scribble to a complete thought or puts spaces between scribbles to match each scribble to a word (Figure 1–3); letter and consonant spelling, in which the child combines letters with scribbles (Figure 1–4); and scribble integration, which integrates the child's knowledge of letter/sound relationships, words, syntax, and punctuation with scribbling (Figure 1–5). One child will not usually display all these varieties of scribbling. Moreover, children vary in how long they employ a particular variety.[30]

Although the child's early writing may seem to bear little relationship to conventional writing, close inspection reveals a number of characteristics that indicate growth toward print. For example, rather than being randomly drawn, the scribbles may display such important features of print as linearity (horizontal and vertical movement) and horizontal arrangement on the page, and consist of similar segments (Figure 1–6).[31] When the child starts to experiment with the combination of lines to form letters, his writing will show less scribble and more of what Clay labels *mock writing*, letterlike forms together with conventional letters (Figure 1–7).[32]

The way in which the child uses space when he writes provides still another index of his growth toward conventional print. The child begins by writing words

Figure 1–1   Precommunicative scribble (from Gail Heald-Taylor, "Scribble in First-Grade Writing," *The Reading Teacher*, October 1984, Figure 2)

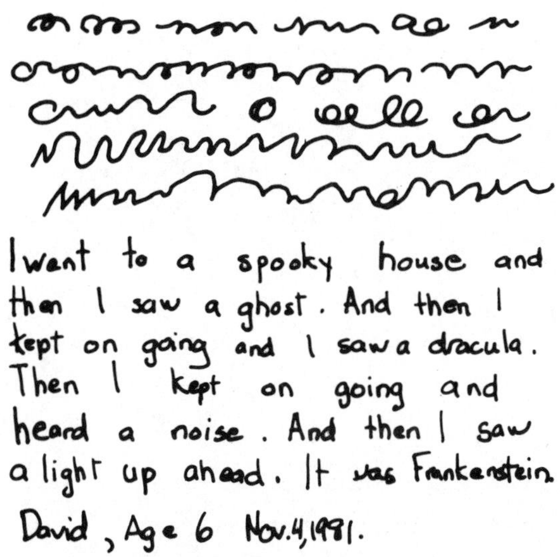

I went to a spooky house and then I saw a ghost. And then I kept on going and I saw a dracula. Then I kept on going and heard a noise. And then I saw a light up ahead. It was Frankenstein.

David, Age 6 Nov. 4, 1981.

Figure 1–2   Story-matching scribble (from Gail Heald-Taylor, "Scribble in First-Grade Writing," *The Reading Teacher*, October 1984, Figure 3)

as continuous strings of letters with no spaces between. Later, as he comes to understand that words are discrete entities, the child may begin to use dots or some other kind of mark to separate the words (Figure 1–8).

As with spoken language, the mastery of writing requires an understanding of the purpose and nature of symbolic representation. Initially, children use writing to symbolize known objects directly rather than to represent speech. At this point, they interpret letters as direct representations of objects.[33] They are probably more interested in creating a message than in communicating it. This process- rather than product-orientation is also evident in their play with tempera, sand, clay, and other media. Some time between three and five years of age, when they become aware of the existence of print as a representation of language, preschoolers start to accompany their drawings with a special scribble they call "writing." King and Rentel found that while some children read only a general message from their print and do not understand that each symbol or symbol cluster represents a specific

Me and my friend are skipping.
Karen, Age 6.

Figure 1–3   Word-matching scribble (from Gail Heald-Taylor, "Scribble in First-Grade Writing," *The Reading Teacher*, October 1984, Figure 4)

FGRF

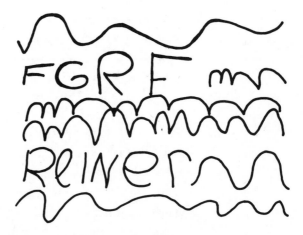

Figure 1–4 Letters and scribbles combined (from Gail Heald-Taylor, "Scribble in First-Grade Writing," *The Reading Teacher*, October 1984, Figure 5)

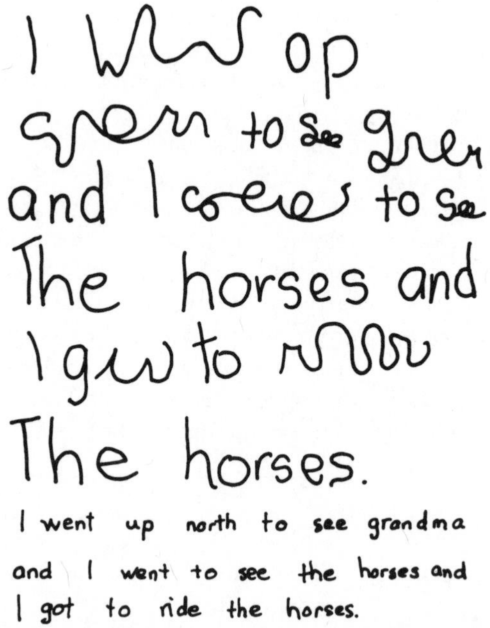
The horses and
The horses.
I went up north to see grandma
and I went to see the horses and
I got to ride the horses.

Figure 1–5 Scribble integration (from Gail Heald-Taylor, "Scribble in First-Grade Writing," *The Reading Teacher*, October 1984, Figure 6)

Figure 1–6   Scribble showing linearity, horizontal arrangement, and similar segments

word, others read a specific message from their writing and are able to match their written symbols to words.[34] Researchers are finding that rather than proceeding through a fixed series of stages, children move back and forth between various levels of writing and drawing.[35]

The oral and written aspects of language develop in a parallel rather than a strictly serial fashion. Moreover, they interact upon each other, each feeding into and enriching the other. Lamme and Childers found that the three young children they studied continually shared or read aloud what they composed, or, when they could not understand a message, asked the author for an interpretation.[36] In England, Britton and Tough also observed that oral language was an integral part of early writing.[37] The content of children's writing often evolved in the talk that preceded the writing.

Marie Clay's observations of the drawing and writing done by five-year-olds in New Zealand at home and school revealed a number of consistent features, which she identified as principles and concepts of early writing.[38] Most fundamental is the *sign concept*, in which children learn that marks on paper are purposeful. When children acquire the *message concept*, they understand that writing is meaningful. Some other characteristics of early writing are described in Clay's principles: the *recurring principle*—children repeat the same marks over and over as a form of practice play; the *flexibility principle*—children create new symbols by rearranging or decorating standard forms; the *inventory principle*—children write lists of familiar symbols such as numerals and letters; the *directional principle*—children learn that English writing proceeds from left to right and from top to bottom; and the *linear principle*—children learn that the identity of written letters may change

| Figure 1–7 | Mock writing |

with direction (e.g., *b, d, p, q*). How many of Clay's concepts and principles can you identify in Figure 1–9?

Spelling.   Just as with spoken language, development in written language is rule-governed and systematic. This is particularly obvious in the development of children's ability to spell. Children *invent spelling* in much the same way they invent words in oral language development. They are sensitive to rules but then over-extend them. They understand the relationship between speech and print and that letters represent speech sounds, but they think that writing consists of recording these speech sounds as precisely as possible in the order in which they are heard. Of course, written words are not so precise phonemically; there are other rules that also govern spelling, and many exceptions.

Although from the point of view of consistent sound/symbol relationships English spelling may appear unpredictable, it actually is not.[39] Our writing system usually preserves the relationship between words with similar meanings. For example, the words *muscle* and *muscular* are related by their meaning. A completely phonemic spelling system might create dissimilar spellings for the two words— *mussel* or *mussle*, and *muscular*—but then the visual cue to the relationship between the meaning of the words would be obscured.

Figure 1–8   Using dots to separate words

This kind of visual representation of meaning is particularly obvious in *homophones*—words that are pronounced alike but have different spellings and meanings. In this set of homophones, *pear*, *pare*, and *pair*, the meaning is triggered not by sound but by spelling. Of course, meaning is usually unambiguous when a suitable context allows for distinguishing among the homophones. The visual signaling of meaning probably leads to greater reading speed.[40] However, this kind of writing system is more complex than one based on consistent sound/symbol relationships and probably takes children longer to master.

Stages in spelling development.   Until children's acquaintance with print grows and their familiarity with print increases, they will use invented spellings in their writing. As exposure to print continues, invented spellings gradually yield to standard forms. Gentry has identified several distinct stages of spelling development.[41] The first stage is called the *precommunicative stage* because the child writes random sequences of any letters she is able to recall. That is, there is no relationship between the letters chosen and the sounds they represent. A child might say that "MRT" spells "people," for example. The second stage is called the *semi-phonetic stage* because children produce one- to three-letter spellings that indicate a primitive understanding of the relationship between sounds and symbols. Thus, "MSR" might represent "monster." Researchers such as Read, Beers, and Henderson have all concluded that young children appear to recognize implicitly letter/sound relationships and to represent these in their writing.[42] One of the commonly seen spelling strategies is called the *letter name strategy*. When a child spells the word

Figure 1–9   Five writing samples

are as "R," or *you* as "U," she is using a *letter name strategy* in which sounds, syllables, or entire words are represented with letters that match their names.

From observing the way young children represent vowels in writing, Read concluded that they concentrate on how these sounds are formed in the mouth. Thus, since *feel* and *fill* are formed similarly in the mouth, they might both be written as "*FEL.*" *Like* and *lock* might be spelled "*LIK*" for the same reason. In each of these pairs, the long vowel sound is actually comprised of two sounds. For long /e/, the two sounds are /ĭ/ + /y/; long /a/ is made up of /ĕ/ + /y/; and long /i/ is comprised of /ah/ + /y/. Read's subjects heard the first part of the vowel blend and then used the letter associated with that part when they wrote. Thus, in their writing, they used

- *e* for /ĭ/ (*bet* for *bit*).
- *a* for /ĕ/ (*pat* for *pet*).
- *i* for /ah/ (*click* for *clock*).

Another letter/sound relationship strategy is the affrication of *d* and *t* before *r*, which explains why spellings such as "*JREM*" for *dream* and "*CHRAN*" for *train* appear so frequently in young children's writing.[43] In addition, children often omit nasal sounds before consonants ("*ED*" for *end* and "*NUBRS*" for *numbers*).

The *phonetic stage* follows the semi-phonetic. The child now represents with a letter each sound that he hears in a word. At first, in the transitional substage, the child includes vowels in every syllable and begins to incorporate familiar patterns:

- *tode*   for   *toad.*
- *thes*   for   *this.*
- *faktores*   for   *factories.*

Later, in the *standard spelling stage*, the child spells most words correctly.[44]

Making meaning explicit.   Children's writing undergoes other interesting changes as it develops. For one thing, it becomes less egocentric, that is, more concerned with audience. Bissex suggests that this is due to *decentration*, a phenomenon we discussed earlier, in which the child is able to focus on more than one aspect of a relationship at a time.[45] While the egocentric child writes as if he alone will read the piece, the child who can decenter asks, "Will this make sense to someone else?" He writes so that the reader can also understand his message.

The degree of development of decentration in children's writing can be gauged by their use of various devices to make meaning more or less explicit. *Reference* is one type of integrative element that builds cohesion. Beginning writers frequently use *exophoric reference*, in which items refer to something entirely outside the message. A beginner might write "They ate and ate and ate" and simply assume that the reader knows who "They" refers to. But, with experience and development, children use less exophoric and more *endophoric reference* (reference to items within the message). In addition, they show greater competence in the use of two other cohesive devices: *lexical ties*, in which either the same words are repeated or similar words are used; and *conjunction*, in which connective words such as *and*, *but*, and *then* relate sentences to each other.[46]

Sense of story. As he develops, the child is able to make his meanings more explicit in writing; at the same time, the stories he tells and writes reveal a growing understanding of story structure. Children as young as two or three use a primitive structure or schema that heightens the coherence of their stories. Even the youngest storyteller employs *centering*—maintaining some central element throughout the story and tying other story elements to it. Young storytellers also use *chaining*—linking each event to the next one[47]—and often organize their stories around basic pairs of actions, such as chase and escape, elements that can recur in a story repeatedly. Older children likewise incorporate several pairs of actions with supporting elements, but their stories generally contain more elaborate plot structure and accompanying details, such as characters' motivations, attributes, and reactions.[48]

The following stories told by a prekindergarten, a first- and a fourth-grade child in response to a wordless picture book illustrate the development of children's sense of story and cohesion. The book, *The Good Bird*, by Peter Wezel, tells of a bird who befriends a sad fish swimming in a bowl. When the bird finds a worm in an apple, he returns to share it with the fish.

There was a bird and there was a fish in the house. He looked at the fish very close and then the fish looked at him. And then he flied off. And then he found a worm in an apple. And then he flied back with the worm to the fish. And the fish smiled. And then they cutted it. And then they pulled. And they got half. And then they sleeped. Good end.

Prekindergarten child

There once was a good bird. (I hate pine trees.) It flew over to the window to see what was the matter with a fish. He hopped on the table, and then he flew away. There was this pumpkin that was in trouble with a worm inside. And the bird got the worm out and flew back to the house. And the fish was happy because he came back. (That fish likes eating *worms*?) Then the bird knocked on the cage again, and the fish came over and was happy again. Then they shared the worm until it broke. (I hate worms!) Then they ate the worm. (I don't think fish like worms.) Then at nighttime they went to sleep. The end.

First-grade child

Once there was a bird by a farm who saw a fish in a fish tank who was hungry. So the bird flew to the window to see the fish. Then the fish and the bird looked at each other. This bird went out and left the fish. And then the bird went to a worm's hole, caught a worm, and brought it back to the fish. Then the bird split the worm in half, and gave half to the fish, and the bird took the other half. And then they ate the worm, and lived happily and went to bed.

Fourth-grade child
(Samples courtesy of E. Sommers)

Recognizing words. Another important aspect of the young child's growing understanding of written language is the ability to recognize words. Many children can read their own first names and other words, such as familiar brand names, long before they enter first grade. In a literate society that uses an alphabetic writing system (a writing system in which there is a relationship between individual sounds and symbols), young children acquire a fund of knowledge about letters, words, and books. They gain some insight into the nature of words, and they become aware that some words sound the same at their beginnings or ends.

Learning to recognize words at this point involves a process of *decontextualization* of familiar print. The first words a child identifies are often highly contextualized—words such as *Cheerios* on the familiar cereal box, or *STOP* from the ubiquitous traffic sign. In remembering these words, the child probably uses cues from the *physical* context in which they appear—the red background and octagonal shape of the *STOP* sign, for example. Later, *historical* context plays an increasingly important role.[49] The child's memory provides cues for words he has previously encountered in familiar and frequently read books, particularly those with highly patterned and repetitive language. Increasing familiarity with print and opportunities for experimentation with print lead the child to insights she uses to identify words:

1. There is an arbitrary set of letters.
2. Letters serve a particular function (primarily to represent sounds within words).
3. Letters are associated with parts of words.
4. The spelling system is rule-governed.
5. There is a relationship between the sounds and meanings of words and word order in oral language and between their equivalents in written language.

Of course, language is never really decontextualized, since it always functions in a particular social and cognitive environment. Upon hearing good news, saying "Great" would probably be meant to convey genuine pleasure. A disappointment, on the other hand, might also be greeted with the word "Great," but with the very opposite meaning.

Progression in literacy, then, involves active and systematic learning, which depends on opportunities to experiment with print. It requires a functional and meaningful context in which the child's natural inclination for problem-solving can flourish.

Knowing Children as Individuals

The bulk of this chapter has been devoted to a discussion of how children develop during the early childhood years, information important in setting appropriate expectations and developing suitable experiences for your class. However, quality teaching also requires *knowing your students as individuals*—knowing them personally and directly as well as knowing about them in a more general way.

The first weeks of a new school year provide a valuable opportunity to meet and get to know the children in your class, and, while you will revise and update your "knowing" all through the coming months, this initial impression is essential for planning the specific experiences needed to assist each child's learning. You cannot do this effectively without really knowing each child. Interestingly but not surprisingly, students at all educational levels note this special, personal quality in describing outstanding learning experiences. Think, for example, about a favorite teacher who made you feel special, who really listened, and somehow reached out to you alone. Do you recall how this special teacher made you want to try, work hard, and learn?

Let me cite one example from my own teaching experience, which, although negative, nonetheless points up the importance of getting to know your children well, early in the year. Lisa appeared in my first-grade class as a quiet, sweet child, acquiescent and intelligent and not at all what we anticipate in a "difficult" child. Indeed, she was anything but difficult until I was out with a cold for several days. To my astonishment, during my absence Lisa turned into a little hellion—crying, refusing to do anything she was asked, developing stomachaches each morning before school, and generally acting entirely miserable. The school psychologist diagnosed a case of "incipient school phobia." Perhaps she was scared of, or at the very least unhappy with, school, but the question remained: *Why?* A little investigating on my part gave me some answers. Lisa, though just six herself, had several younger brothers and sisters at home; she held the responsibility and pride of the oldest child. She was smart, and she was going to read. Her parents expected that Lisa would do well; maybe they even pressured her somewhat. Lisa expected to learn to read when she went to school. Instead, what she found was an inexperienced teacher (me), clinging to the lockstep regimen of a highly programmed reading approach, which required that the children receive several weeks of "readiness" work before they started formal reading instruction. (Here, I plead guilty, by reason of ignorance, to the charge of poor teaching.) Lisa was bored, angry, and frightened. She was supposed to learn to read. Instead, all she had been doing for an awfully long time (by her calculations, at least) were things such as finding likenesses and differences in pictures and practicing left-to-right eye progression. Maybe she would *never* learn to read. What would that mean to her parents, sisters, and brothers, and most important, to herself? So Lisa took steps to remedy the situation. She protested loudly and long to her teacher (me). It took months to get Lisa to where she might well have been much earlier if I had known her well enough to respond to what *she* needed instead of blindly following a program.

The lesson I learned, and the one I hope to convey is, first of all, get to know the children in your new class as human beings. I found that the rewards were far greater if I took the time to get to know my children than if I rushed them into some program in a desperate, often fruitless attempt to keep up with the curriculum. Although Lisa was the most obvious victim of this lockstep regime, the rest of the children suffered too, because their needs were also being ignored.

Observing Children Carefully

How can you get to know your students, right from the beginning? First, observe them. Coupled with insight and understanding, such observations of their behavior can help you find answers to the problems you face: how to get Jimmy interested in reading; why Armand is so angry; whether to separate Maria and Shareen; how to extend Mario's reading interests. Good observation not only helps teachers get to know their children better and to meet their needs better, but it also adds to their own effectiveness as teachers. A third-grade teacher who had planned a social studies unit about the surrounding community found on a class trip that the class was far more interested in the Hudson River, which was only a few blocks away from the school. The river became the focus of a several-month-long project, which spanned all curriculum areas and led the children to many important discoveries.

You can monitor your own teaching methods and modify them as needed; then observe the patterns of change in the children's behavior. In the revised edition of *Ways of Studying Children*, Milly Almy and Celia Genishi offer many suggestions for a humane and holistic approach to classroom observation. Like the third-grade teacher noted above, you will discover many specific opportunities to change your teaching tactics based on your firsthand knowledge of the children's needs and interests. (See the activities at the end of this chapter for some specific ideas on observing young children.)

Talking to Children

Second, talk to the children. Find out what games they enjoy playing, if they have any favorite stories, who their TV heroes are, whether they have taken any trips, if they have pets. In other words, get them to talk to you about themselves and their lives. With most children, you will have no trouble—they are delighted to have the ear of a really interested adult. For the more reticent, you will need to provide more time and gentle encouragement. Then take the information you have collected about the children's interests and make it the basis of your instruction. If you find that some children are interested in computers, they can become a focus for class study. Some children may have computers at home and many may have used them for games or seen their parents use them for more practical purposes, such as home banking. The children's own information can form the nucleus of an extended investigation. The children might suggest a visit to a computer store or write an invitation to a representative of a computer company, such as Apple Computer, to speak to the class. If your school has a computer lab, it will undoubtedly offer a number of opportunities to expand the children's knowledge. Encouraging children to investigate this or any similar topic of interest will engage them in all the processes of language.

Listening to Children and Telling Them About Yourself

Third in this list but at the top in importance is to really listen attentively to each child—and respond with genuine interest and concern. (Isn't this something we require of a really good friend? Why not of a really good teacher?) In addition, talk about yourself. Children need to know you as a real person, someone with a family and a home, a life away from school. I remember when I was in school, in the early grades at least, how most of us believed the teacher somehow "lodged" in the school, perhaps in the cloakroom, from which she appeared each morning to greet us. What a shock it was when we actually saw her outside school, shopping or driving! (There is an amusing storybook on this very subject you might want to share with the children early in the school year: *My Teacher Sleeps in School*, by L. Weiss [New York: Frederick Warne, 1984].)

Getting to Know the Child's Family

Fourth, make every effort to get to know the child's family. From those hurried, spontaneous chats when parents bring their children to school in the morning and pick them up in the afternoon, to formal, planned conferences, each exchange between you and a member of the child's family is a valuable opportunity for sharing ideas, feelings, and information. Emphasize interaction and keep the lines of communication open between the participants. If you share information about the child's behavior at school in a caring way, the parent is more likely to share information about the child at home. This kind of cooperation can give you significant background about the child, and help both you and the parent work together toward improving the child's development.

These suggestions do not exhaust all the possibilities, but they do represent the foundation, the most basic things you need to do to meet and know the children in your class.

Summary

This chapter suggested that effective teachers know children well, both as unique and individual personalities, and more generally as children. Children learn in a certain way and their thinking has particular characteristics. Here are the main points covered in the chapter:

- Logico-mathematical knowledge, as described by Piaget, develops in a series of stages as a result of internal transformations. The child's active manipulation of the environment enables learning to occur. Children's interactions with significant others and with language are also essential for cognitive development.

- Language develops as a result of the child's active processing of his environment. From the meaningful and useful language that surrounds him, the child induces rules about language. He maps language to his growing knowledge of the world.

- Literacy development requires an environment rich in real language experiences that challenge children's natural adaptive intelligence.

- The first few weeks of school are especially valuable for the opportunities they provide in getting to know the children in your class. Suggestions include careful observation, talking with children, listening to children, and interacting with their parents.

Activities

1. Engage a familiar toddler in this imaginary play sequence. Pretend to set a table for tea. Serve the child and yourself each an imaginary cup; add milk and sugar. Invest the scene with a sense of the real by a show of enthusiasm and expression. Does the child: join in the play; pretend to drink the tea; contribute to the scene?

2. Tape-record three children from three different grade levels telling a story based on the same wordless picture book. (One example is *Bubble, Bubble* by Mercer Mayer.) Transcribe your tape. Compare the three different story-tellings for complexity of grammar and meaning, fluency, inclusion of detail, and explicitness.

3. Collect a variety of items, such as buttons, shells, bottle caps, and seeds. In separate sessions, have kindergarten and fourth-grade children sort the items. Ask the children to describe what they are doing as they sort. What differences do you note between the two age groups in their classification systems and descriptive language?

4. Tape-record about thirty minutes of speech from a child who is learning a second language when he or she is engaged in an informal play activity with one or more children who speak the second language (the language the child is learning). Suitable settings would be the dramatic play or block area of a classroom. Observe and describe:

   a) How the child uses language and other means to become and remain part of the social group. For example, does the child use some pat formulas in the second language ("hi," "can I play," "me too")? Does the child watch and copy the actions of the others (if one child picks up a dish and pretends to wash it, does the subject child do the same)? Does the child use whatever devices he or she has in the second language to express new ideas? How? Does the child pantomime? If so, what and how?

   b) How the other children adapt their behavior for the child's benefit. Do they use simpler structures and vocabulary? Do they repeat and/or para-phrase? Do they accompany their words with extra gestures that help to make their meaning clear? Do they ever guide the child physically through an appropriate action sequence?

5. Administer these two tasks adapted from Jean Berko (a) and Carol Chomsky (b) to at least two children, one four to five years old and the other nine to ten years old:[50]

   a) Draw a single nonrepresentational figure on a sheet of paper. On an-other sheet, draw two of these same figures. Say to the child:
      First picture   This is a wug.
      Second picture   Now there are two of them.
      Elicit child's response   There are two ——.

b) Blindfold a doll. Ask the doll if it is easy or hard to see. Then, depending upon the response, ask the child to make the doll easy (or hard) to see. Is there any difference in the ability of the children in the different age categories to complete the tasks successfully? What developmental differences do you observe?

Further Reading and Viewing

Printed Materials

Bissex, G. L., *Gnys at Wrk: A Child Learns to Write and Read.* Cambridge, Mass.: Harvard University Press, 1980.

Cohen, D. H., and Stern, V., with Balaban, N. *Observing and Recording the Behavior of Young Children.* 3d ed. New York: Teachers College Press, 1983.

Ferreiro, E., and Teberosky, A. *Literacy Before Schooling.* Portsmouth, N.H.: Heinemann, 1982.

Isaacs, S., *Intellectual Growth in Young Children.* London: Routledge & Kegan Paul, 1930.

Piaget, J., *The Language and Thought of the Child.* London: Routledge & Kegan Paul, 1959. (Or, for a simplified treatment, see B. J. Wadsworth, *Piaget's Theory of Cognitive and Affective Development.* 3d ed. New York: Longman, 1984.)

Films

How Babies Learn. 16mm. New York: New York University Film Library.

Out of the Mouths of Babes. 16mm. Toronto: Canadian Broadcasting System.

Chapter 2

Understanding the Written Code

Preview

Knowing how to read and write is very important. School performance in all subjects hinges on literacy skills, and later, getting a good job and enjoying many of the benefits of a literate society. Thus, it is not surprising that methods of helping children to become literate are controversial. When reports of declining achievement in literacy appear, some react by putting pressure on schools and teachers to teach literacy skills in a specific, cut-and-dried way. Yet, this approach may not serve children very well.

In this chapter, we will look at the nature of written language for guidance in teaching children to read and write. This information, combined with the survey of child development in chapter 1, will help us to design truly effective approaches to encouraging beginning literacy.

The major topics discussed in this chapter include:

1. *Changes in literacy programs in the United States from the seventeenth century to the present.*

2. *The major characteristics of language.*

3. *The function of each of the three systems of language.*

4. *The difference between traditional school grammar, structural linguistic grammar, and transformational grammar.*

5. *The difference between deep structure and surface structure.*

6. *What cognitive, behavioral, and interactive psycholinguistic models of reading each emphasize about the reading process.*

7. *How each of the three cue systems of written language work.*

8. *How redundancy enables cue systems to operate.*

9. *How children's schemata affect their reading.*

10. *How the characteristics of short-term and long-term memory affect the reading process.*

11. *Good teaching strategies for working with children of diverse linguistic backgrounds.*

12. *What the nature of language implies about stimulating children to read and write.*

The Controversy over How to Teach Reading

In 1967, Jeanne Chall published *Learning to Read: The Great Debate*, in which she reviewed more than fifty years of research on the teaching of reading. Rather than helping to settle the controversy surrounding the question of *how* to teach reading, Chall added fuel to the fire. Although the results of her careful and thorough analysis were inconclusive, Chall, nonetheless, supported a phonics or decoding approach as the best one to use!

The debate continues, and it is often heated and irrational. Literacy remains a *political* issue today, as it has always been. People believe that there is power in the written word and that teaching someone to read and write gives access to that power. To deny someone access violates the egalitarian principles of a democracy. If you were to go out on the street and ask the first adult who came by, "Why is it important to know how to read and write?" your respondent would no doubt tell you (probably annoyed at so obvious a question) that you need these skills to *survive* in our world, to do well in school, to get and keep a decent job, and to enjoy the benefits of our society. That is why news of declining achievement is inevitably received with alarm. Recently, falling SAT scores were met with calls to go "Back to Basics": to teach reading, writing and 'rithmetic the "old fashioned" way, and to drop "soft" subjects such as the arts. Such a reaction to declining achievement is typical. In the late 1950s, similar alarm was registered when the USSR launched the first space satellite. If children could learn to read earlier, popular reasoning went, they could master science and math earlier, and the earlier they mastered science and math, the more they would learn in the long run. The more they learned, the better America's chance to become preeminent in the space race.

But it is not simple to decide how best to teach children to read and write. Everyone wants children to acquire literacy skills, but they disagree on how to go about it because they disagree on the nature of the reading process and learning to read. Is reading simply a matter of deciphering the written code? Or is it something more than recognition of the words? Is it comprehension of the meaning intended by the writer? Does it end there, or does reading involve bringing the reader's *own* meaning to the encoded symbols?

The various approaches to teaching reading in the United States since the seventeenth century reflect changing views of the reading process and the purposes of reading.

Teaching Reading in the United States

In colonial America, one read in order to acquire religious information and inspiration from the Bible and from prayer books. A justification for the famous Act of 1647 (the "Old Deluder Satan Law"), which required every town of the Massachusetts Bay Colony to provide elementary education for its children, was to foil Satan, whose goal was to keep men from knowledge of the Scriptures.[1] Although the purpose of reading was comprehension, the teaching method emphasized word recognition, instructing children to *sound out* first single letters, then word fragments, and finally entire words.

Early in the nineteenth century, Horace Mann substituted a *whole-word* approach for the previously used phonics method. Children memorized entire words before they analyzed their letter/sound relationships. Mann believed that this approach resulted in better comprehension of written material. Reading texts in the nineteenth century continued to emphasize morality, but under a less religious guise. Their parables, moral lessons, and patriotic stories were designed to teach children of the young republic industry, sobriety, thrift, propriety, modesty, punctuality, conformity, and love of country. The famous *McGuffey's Readers* made their appearance in the 1830s. The page from the second reader in Figure 2–1 illustrates the nineteenth-century belief that the purpose of education was primarily moral.

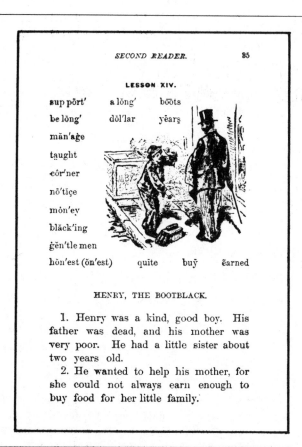

Figure 2–1   A page from *McGuffey's Second Reader*

Another characteristic of reading instruction in the nineteenth century was the development of reading material according to an organized plan of sequential steps. In a one-hundred-and-eighty-degree turn from a century before, phonics instruction had become popular again by the late 1800s.[2] Both sequential planning of instruction and emphasis on phonics were to find full expression in the programmed instruction and basal readers of the twentieth century, although their content is no longer morally didactic.

Since the 1970s, basal readers have undergone some changes. Various attempts to upgrade them sociologically have resulted in a shift away from their former countrylike settings inhabited by all-white characters. Today, more of the neighborhoods are urban, the people are of differing ethnic groups, males and females are depicted less stereotypically, and the aged and handicapped occasionally appear as story characters. The readers have changed somewhat in methodology, too: there has been an increase in the number of new words introduced,[3] a decrease in the number of repetitions of words,[4] and a heavier emphasis on phonics instruction than in comparable texts published in the 1950s and 1960s.[5] In addition, some basal reader series today incorporate many more literary selections than did readers of twenty or thirty years ago.

One's approach to the question of how to teach reading and writing depends on one's view of how children learn. Chapter 1 outlined a sociocognitive view of learning. Another important consideration is the nature of the written code itself, which is the topic of this chapter. We will first look at the nature of language and then consider reading and writing as psycholinguistic processes.

Nature of Language

Britton describes language as a highly organized, systematic means of representing and symbolizing experience.[6] Because language *is* systematic, it can be described and predicted.

Characteristics of Language

All languages share certain features:

1. *Language is a medium of communication.* From the very beginning of life, infants use their vocal repertoire to attract and hold attention and to communicate their needs. A crying baby, for example, may be demanding to be fed. Throughout life, an individual uses language (speaking, writing, signing) to convey thoughts and emotions, although people do communicate, of course, through the arts and through actions.

2. *Language is a system of symbols.* In spoken language, the symbols are auditory and exist in a time continuum. In written language, the symbols are visual and exist in a space continuum. Language originated as an *oral* medium and only later developed a written form. Even today, only a few oral languages have a written counterpart. The symbols of a language are intended to represent experience, but symbols in themselves are not neces-

sarily linked to what they represent. Language symbols are, in this sense, arbitrary. Neither the letters nor sounds of the word *dog*, for example, bear any relationship to the furry, four-legged canine companion that we know. In contrast, a picture of a dog does resemble a dog. Communicating through art is not necessarily as arbitrary as communicating through language.

3. *Language is an organized, coherent system.* All languages are bound by rules that govern the way meaningful units are put together to form the language. Although the rules vary from language to language, their presence is a universal characteristic of language. These rules determine how the major systems of a language, its sound system (*phonology*), its grammatical system (*syntax*), and its meaning system (*semantics*) work. For example, all languages denote gender but not necessarily in the same manner. In English, the gender of a noun is defined only by its pronoun substitute, *he, she,* or *it.* In other languages, gender may be denoted by changing the form of an article to match the gender of its noun (*el* or *la* in Spanish, for example), or by changing the ending of the noun itself (*alumnus* or *alumna* in Latin).

4. *Language has many functions.* It can be used to inform, persuade, amuse, intimidate, or confuse. Halliday describes seven functions of language for the child: (1) *instrumental* (to get something the child wants); (2) *regulatory* (to control behavior); (3) *interactional* (to mediate and maintain personal relationships); (4) *personal* (to represent the child's individuality); (5) *heuristic* (to find out about things); (6) *imaginative* (to create new images); and (7) *representational* (to communicate information or ideas).[7] (See chapter 4 for further elaboration of Halliday's functions.) Basic to all the separate functions of language is its role in reflection. As Suzanne Langer points out, language makes experience amenable to the workings of thought and imagination.[8]

5. *Language varies according to the social context.* Popular belief holds that there is one right way to speak and that each language has a standard, invariant form, which should be used by everyone under all circumstances. This simply is not the case. People use language in many social contexts, perhaps in a job interview, in a telephone conversation with a close friend, in playing with an infant, in making love, in a speech before a large audience, or in religious confession. Language use varies according to the constraints and demands of the social context. People shift styles to suit the occasion.[9] Linguists employ the term *speech register* to denote different styles of speaking, depending on context. *Pragmatics* is that branch of language study concerned with how and when language is used. Researchers who study pragmatics look very carefully at the effect of social context on communication.

Although on the surface languages differ, each one bears these five characteristics, and thus has the potential to express any experience its users can understand. In helping to organize and classify experience, language gives its speakers a measure of control over their lives.

Language Systems

Language has three broad systems, a *phonological*, or sound system, a *syntactic*, or grammatical system, and a *semantic*, or meaning system.

Phonological system.   Although there is disagreement about the exact number, most authorities say that English has between forty-four and forty-six sounds, or *phonemes. Phonemes* are the smallest units of sound in a language. They are divided into two categories: consonants, which are produced when the breath is altered as it is being emitted by an action of the speech organs (e.g., lips, tongue, teeth, vocal cords); and vowels, which are produced when the breath is allowed unobstructed vocal passage. None of the speech organs has speech as its primary function, however. Differences in vocal sounds are created by changes in the position of the tongue and the shape of the mouth and oral cavity. The intonational pattern of English includes *pitch*, *stress*, and *juncture*, and meaning can be triggered directly by changes in these features. Read the following samples aloud.

1. Pitch (relative level)
   Falling pitch (declarative sentence):
     We're going to the movies.
   Rising pitch (interrogative sentence):
     We're going to the movies?

2. Stress (relative loudness)
   Change from noun to verb:
     an´nex → an nex´
     re´cord → re cord´

3. Juncture (pause)
   Changes in word meaning:
     nitrate
     night rate
     Nye trait

Written language can be mapped to oral language in three different ways: through an alphabet, a syllabary, or ideograms. Written English is primarily an *alphabetic* system. This means that there is a relationship between the spoken symbols (phonemes) and the graphic symbols (graphemes) used to represent them in writing. Thus, the word *cat* consists of three phonemes, /c/, /a/, and /t/, which are represented by three graphemes, c, a, and t. To distinguish them from graphemes, phonemes are printed between diagonal lines.

The relationship between sound symbols and written symbols is called *phoneme/grapheme correspondence*. Languages differ in terms of the degree to which there is a one-to-one correspondence between sound and symbol. The phoneme/grapheme correspondence in English is not as high as that of Spanish or Russian. But even English is not as irregular in its phoneme/grapheme correspondence as some believe.

Languages have different ways of representing meaning in written form. Chinese, for example, has three different kinds of characters: *pictograms*, which are pictures of objects; *ideograms*, which are composite symbols representing abstract ideas; and *phonograms*, which are compound characters in which the more important element represents a spoken sound. The Japanese writing system consists of two *syllabaries* (one symbol for each syllable), called the *Katakana* and the *Hiragana* systems. Another part of the Japanese writing system is made up of ideograms, known as *Kanji*. One study found that Japanese who were beginning readers learned ideograms more quickly than they learned the syllabary.[10] Of course, the children had only a limited number of the symbols to learn for the purposes of the investigation, rather than the great many they actually need to learn to master Japanese. However, the researchers concluded that meaningfulness is much more important than perceptual complexity in learning writing symbols. An important point to remember is that ideograms represent meaning more directly than do alphabetic systems such as English, in which the written symbols represent spoken language and are therefore related to meaning more indirectly. But English also employs ideograms. Arabic numerals are ideograms. No numeral bears any relationship to the sound of the corresponding number word. Others are $, %, and #. Sometimes, these symbols are called *logograms*. A very popular logogram has been the heart symbol which resulted in a proliferation of bumper stickers with a slogan like *I ♡ my dog*.

Syntax.   *Syntax* refers to the rules that govern how words are combined to form meaningful phrases and sentences. Sometimes the word *grammar* is used interchangeably with syntax. Many people think of grammar as a prescriptive set of rules on usage: *don't* use double negatives; *do* use the nominative after any form of the verb *to be*; etc. In this sense, grammar and syntax are *not* synonymous. This popular notion of grammar refers to *traditional school grammar*, a set of rules that prescribes how language *ought to be* used. Much of traditional school grammar is based on Latin, a language with many significant differences from English. For instance, because word order is not important in Latin, it receives little attention in traditional school grammar. Yet word order is a highly significant feature of English syntax. Mismatches of this kind greatly reduce the usefulness of traditional school grammar. Studies of the effect of teaching children grammatical rules in isolation show that they have little or no impact on children's writing.

A second type of grammar is called *structural linguistic grammar*. This kind of grammar describes the features of a language as they actually are, rather than as they ought to be. Structural linguistics divides words into two classes: *content words* (nouns, verbs, adjectives, adverbs) that usually carry the meaning of the sentence, have referents in the world, and are almost infinite in number; and *function words* (prepositions, conjunctions, relative pronouns and adjectives, auxiliary and linking verbs, and articles) that usually have no meaning in themselves, but connect and show relationships among other words, and are limited to about three hundred. All languages in use are changing. One way they change is in their content words. Function words, however, show relatively little change, even over hundreds of years. English syntax has three components: word order, which is most important; function words; and *affixes*, meaningful word elements that are attached to nouns and verbs and indicate person, number, and tense.

Finally, there is *transformational grammar*. Transformational grammar has no interest in how language ought to be, and unlike structural linguistic grammar it is much more than descriptive. It is considered a *generative* grammar, because it attempts to explain how speakers of a language can produce or generate all the sentences of their language. Transformational grammar is concerned with language process rather than product, the process of language generation. According to Noam Chomsky, every sentence has two structures: a *deep structure* that represents its underlying meaning and a *surface structure* that represents the sentence in either its spoken or written form.[11] Deep structure is translated into surface structure through formal operations called transformational rules. The following two sentences have the same surface structure but each has a different deep structure (meaning):

- The man was bitten by the dog.
- The dog was bitten by the man.

In this next set, both sentences have the same deep structure but different surface structures:

- The man was bitten by the dog.
- The dog bit the man.

According to transformational grammar, an infinite number of sentences can be generated through the application of a limited set of transformational rules. Transformational grammar depicts language production as a highly creative process.

Semantics.   *Semantics* is concerned with meaning and, as such, it is the most complex and least understood language system. Dissatisfaction with Chomsky's theory because of its emphasis on grammar over meaning has increased since the 1970s. This dissatisfaction has inspired a new interdisciplinary field, *generative semantics*, that investigates how meaning generates language forms. According to generative semantics, it is meaning that determines the form sentences take.

The term *parts of speech* refers to the function words take on according to their position in a sentence. This means that when the form of a content word changes according to its function in a sentence, it signals a change in meaning as well: for example, *education* is the noun form, *educational* the adjective, and *educate* the transitive verb. Thus, a word's form is a clue to its function in the sentence.

A *morpheme* is the smallest unit of meaning in a language. English has two kinds of morphemes, free and bound. *Free morphemes* can both stand by themselves and signal meaning by themselves: *cat*, *jump*, and *old* are free morphemes. *Bound morphemes* must be affixed to free morphemes or to other bound morphemes in order to indicate meaning: *-s*, which designates the plural form in nouns (*boys*) as well as tense in some verbs (*plays*), and *-ed*, which designates the past tense in verbs (*played*), are examples of bound morphemes.

Although semantics includes the denotative and connotative meanings of words,[12] it refers to much more than a set of definable words or morphemes. As Goodman observes, pragmatic meaning is also part of this system.[13] People usually concentrate on the meaning of a message or written text; rather than remembering specific words, they will recall its semantic and pragmatic aspects. People are sensitive to pragmatic cues in dialogue and social context. Imagine this scene: You have just arrived at a dinner party. Suddenly a friend, looking very concerned, comes up and quickly ushers you into another room, where she begins talking in a hushed voice. Even before you hear one word of what she has to say, various pragmatic cues have triggered possible meanings. Perhaps she is about to tell you about a phone call from one of your neighbors describing some disaster at home. Much of your interpretation depends on your friend's demeanor. If instead of looking concerned she appears happy, then your interpretation will be quite different. Perhaps she wants to tell you about a surprise that the guests have planned for the host. Nonverbal cues such as posture, gesture, facial expression, eye contact, and distance between speakers also signal meaning. People are capable of conveying highly complex social and personal meanings through an elaborate network of verbal and nonverbal cues.

Reading and Writing as Psycholinguistic Processes

Psycholinguistics is the scientific study of the relationship between thought and language. The term is derived from *psyche*, meaning "mind," and *linguistics*, meaning "pertaining to language." Much of the information we now have about young children's language development is the result of the psycholinguistic research carried out since the 1960s (see chapter 1). Psycholinguistics views reading and writing as *language-based* processes requiring the same kind of problem-solving strategies and having a similar pattern of development as listening and speaking. A psycholinguistic perspective on the processing of written language emphasizes the interaction between the mind of the reader/writer and the language of the text.[14] All four language modalities (reading, writing, speaking, listening) have as their prime function the processing of meaning through symbols. In reading and writing, meaning is processed through written symbols. In speaking and listening, the symbols are oral.

Psycholinguistic Models of Reading

Models of reading are theoretical frameworks created to explain what occurs during the reading process and how a learner learns. *Psycholinguistic models of reading*, which began to be formulated in the 1960s and 1970s, are based on insights from psycholinguistic research. Before that, most reading specialists espoused a behavioral view of the reading process, in which the learner played the passive role of receiver of knowledge, and viewed the reading process itself as the accumulation of a hierarchy of separate skills. In contrast, psycholinguistic models consider reading and writing as continuous and integrated with all language processes, and the learner as an active participant in the construction of knowledge.

Most models of reading can be classified as one of three kinds:

1. *Behavioral* or *reading occurs in the eye* models, which put most emphasis upon decoding graphic symbols. This school of thought claims that reading starts with the synthesis of letters into words and then words into sentences, until finally the reader has decoded a large enough chunk of text to comprehend the author's message.

2. *Cognitive* or *reading occurs in the brain* models, which emphasize the reader's own cognitive structures and involve the strategies of sampling, predicting, confirming, anticipating, and correcting. Comprehension of a text depends on what the reader has in her mind, what she brings *to* the text. Therefore, reading requires some prior understanding on the part of the reader, who is reconstructing the author's message.

3. *Interactive* or *reading occurs in both the eye and the brain* models, which say that both visual and cognitive data are used in the reading process.[15]

Upon close inspection, many reading models actually turn out to be interactive. Where they vary is in the *degree* of emphasis they give to decoding versus understanding.

Recently, L. M. Rosenblatt has described a *transactional* view of language,[16] which considers reading as a receptive written process, one of the four language modalities in literate cultures (listening, reading, speaking, writing). In the productive generative processes (speaking and writing), a text is constructed to represent meaning. In the receptive processes (listening and reading), meaning is constructed through direct transactions with the text and thus, indirectly, with the writer.[17] Research conducted since the 1970s has found that unless readers relate a text to their own background, they are unable to understand the structure of a story or draw inferences from it.[18] According to this view, all the language processes are active, constructive, and transactional. Meaning resides in both the author and the reader. While the text has the potential to evoke meaning, it has no meaning in itself. A reader's understanding of a text will be affected by how well the author constructs it and how well the reader reconstructs it, thereby constructing its meaning.[19]

Cognitive, interactive, and transactional models view the reading process as a construction of meaning from text. Rumelhart's interactive model of reading illustrates the transactions between a proficient reader and a text.[20] The reader uses both perceptual and cognitive cues in reading print, which appear in six forms: semantic, syntactic, lexical (vocabulary), letter cluster, letter, and letter feature. The proficient reader uses information from these sources as he needs them, and they can vary in importance at different times. In trying to understand the word *acrimony* in a sentence, for example, the reader might first try to determine the word's meaning based on context cues. He notices that the surrounding text deals with an angry discussion, so perhaps *acrimony* has a negative connotation. Still unsure, he analyzes the word's graphemes, and notices its resemblance to *acrid*. Syntax indicates that the word must be a noun. He concludes that it probably means "bitterness."

Cue Systems

To relate theory to practice and to become more conscious of what the reading process entails (and heighten your metalingual awareness of reading), read the following four passages. After you read each one, write one sentence summarizing what it says.

First, from a fire insurance policy:

In consideration of the provisions and stipulations herein or added hereto and of the premium above specified, The Stock Insurance Company indicated above by X, herein called "The Company," for the term of years specified above from inception date shown above At Noon (Standard Time) to expiration date shown above At Noon (Standard Time) at location of property invalued, to an amount not exceeding the amount(s) above specified, does insure the insured named above and legal representations, to the extent of the actual cash value of the property at the time of loss, but not exceeding the amount which it would cost to repair or replace the property with material of like kind and quality within a reasonable time after such loss, without allowance for any increased cost of repair or reconstruction by reason of any ordinance or law regulating construction or repair, and without compensation for loss resulting from interruption of business or manufacture, nor in any event for more than the interest of the insured, against all direct loss by fire, lightning and by removal from premises endangered by the perils insured against in this policy except as hereinafter provided, to the property described herein while located or contained as described in this policy, or pro rata for five days at each proper place to which any of the property shall necessarily be removed for preservation from the perils insured against in this policy, but not elsewhere.

Second, a passage of Gregg shorthand:

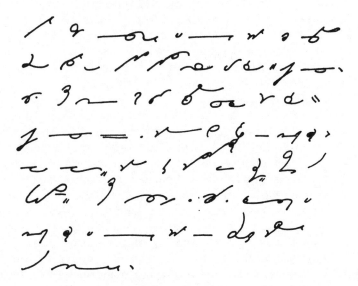

Next, an account of Montessori procedures:

Maria Montessori's didactic materials are designed so that the child's correct and incorrect responses are, typically, self-evident. That is to say, a child can correct her own mistakes by making modifications in her responses to the materials. In essence, this is a trial-and-error (or success) process in which the probability of error is low. Thus, the necessity for evaluative feedback from the teacher to the child is reduced. (Adapted from E. D. Evans, *Contemporary Influences in Early Childhood Education* [N.Y.: Holt, Rinehart and Winston, 1971].)

And finally, an extract from a poem by Edmund Spenser:

By this, the northern wagoner had set
His sevenfold team behind the steadfast star
That was in ocean waves yet never wet,
But firm is fixed, and sendeth light from far
To all that in the wide deep wandering are;
And cheerful Chanticleer with his note shrill
Had warnèd once that Phoebus' fiery car
In haste was climbing up the eastern hill,
Full envious that night so long his room did fill;

Were you able to read the four passages? If reading meant only saying words, then for at least three of the passages, the answer would be yes. But were you able to summarize the passages in your own words? One was probably impossible and two others were likely very difficult to paraphrase. Obviously, reading involves much more than just saying words. As you have just observed in going over the above passages, without understanding there is no real reading.

Now, let us look at the four passages more closely to find out what was operating in them that affected your understanding or comprehension. If you were to rank the passages from easiest to comprehend to hardest, this would probably be the order: number three (Montessori); number one (fire insurance policy); number four (Spenser, *The Faerie Queen*); and number two (Gregg shorthand). Or, given the density of "legalese," you might rank the passage by Spenser as easier than the excerpt from a fire insurance policy. Why did you rank the passages in the order you did? Are some intrinsically more difficult than others? How do these passages differ for you?

To answer these questions, we will look at the ways in which language signals meaning. To do this, we will consider the cue systems involved in reading.

According to Kenneth Goodman, written language has three *cue systems*.[21] There are *graphophonic cues*, in the relationship between graphemes (the written or graphic symbols) and phonemes (the sound symbols). There are *syntactic cues*, in the patterning and order of words. And there are *semantic cues*, in the meaning and concepts represented by printed words. Although these three cue systems were present in each of the preceding passages, they were not always available to you. Unless you already know Gregg shorthand, passage number two is meaningless, because the unfamiliar orthography (written symbols) of the Gregg shorthand system precludes knowing which graphemes represent which phonemes. And without other available cues, the passage is simply incomprehensible.

Because the passage from Spenser's *The Faerie Queen* and the fire insurance policy excerpt are written in English orthography, you *were* able to use their graphophonic cues, although Spenser's unfamiliar spelling might have made this somewhat difficult. However, even with available graphophonic cues, the meaning of these two passages still may have eluded you. The rather archaic poetic form of *The Faerie Queen* probably interfered with your ability to use syntactic cues, that is, information from the arrangement and pattern of words in the poem. And although the fire insurance policy excerpt is written in modern English, it is so wordy and weighted down with embedded phrases, it was probably very difficult for you to extract much meaning from its syntactic cues.

This leaves passage three, a description of Montessori methods. You probably found this passage easiest to comprehend *not* because its content is any easier than the others, but because you were able to use all three cue systems. Its graphophonic cues are based on modern English orthography, a familiar system; you could use information from the patterning and order of the words, because the passage is written in a clear, straightforward style; finally, you could draw on semantic cues, despite the fact that the passage is technical. Your own background of familiar experiences could allow you to tap into the concepts and meanings represented here. What the reader brings to the text helps in understanding its meaning.

Goodman has defined reading as the partial reconstruction of meaning represented in written symbols by a writer.[22] The reconstruction is partial because unless the written passage is designed to be understood in a *strictly literal* fashion (a recipe, for example), it is probably not possible to deduce all of the meanings and interpretations the writer intended.

Reread the Montessori passage, and this time, try to make a conscious effort to note which cue systems you use (graphophonic, syntactic, semantic). Did you use all three? Probably not. In most cases, a proficient reader does not have to translate written symbols into oral symbols to understand what he reads. Ordinarily, print represents meaning directly. Your strategy as a reader is to search only for enough clues to permit you to draw reasonable hypotheses about the probable meaning of the passage. If the hypotheses make sense syntactically and semantically, then you do not need to search for additional clues. A proficient reader can extract meaning directly from the visual features of the text without having to go through a process of mediated word identification.[23]

Although as a proficient reader, you do not have to translate written symbols into oral symbols before you can understand what you have read, try reading the following sentence aloud to see what happens when normal spelling-to-meaning associations are upset.

The none tolled hymn that she had scene a pare of bear feat in hour rheum.

If you identified words solely by first associating sounds with letters, then in hearing the sounds of the above sentence, you would have experienced no difficulty in identifying the meaning of the words. However, the spelling-to-meaning associations that were triggered when you read the words interfered with the smooth, immediate comprehension of the sentence.

Now read this brief passage silently:

Last evening Mary and Hal went to
to the movies to see "Raiders of the Lost

Ark." They loved it. Oh well, there's no
accounting for taste!

Although you were reading carefully, you still may not have spotted the redundant
to at the beginning of the second line. Although proficient readers may sample
graphic cues fully, they use fewer resources and devote less attention to them than
less proficient readers. It is a more efficient process. Thus, because the second *to*
was an irrelevant cue, you probably ignored it. Ask a less proficient reader to read
this passage and see what happens. Actually, some professional proofreaders are
trained to read backward, right to left. In this way, they break the grip of meaning
in connected discourse. They are forced to read one word at a time and spot errors
much more effectively than if they were reading left to right.

A proficient reader can normally go directly from print to meaning. But what
about the beginning reader? Beginners usually need to *recode* written symbols
into oral symbols before they can extract meaning from them.[24] They may do this
through overt vocalizing. Older children who are having difficulty learning how
to read often use this recoding procedure too. Sometimes they are labeled "word-
callers." The problem with recoding is that the reader often forgets what he has
read because the procedure is so time-consuming it overloads short-term memory
capacity.[25] Most of us are able to recall for up to fifteen seconds about seven
unrelated items of information (e.g., the digits of a telephone number). By the
time a child has recoded the graphemes in a sentence, however, he may be unable
to recall what he read earlier in the same sentence. Beginning readers rely more
heavily on graphophonic cues than proficient readers do. In essence, beginners
deduce meaning from the surface structure of written language, and this process
requires a maximum amount of visual information. However, this may be difficult
for some five- and six-year-olds, who may still be relatively unskilled in visual
exploratory behavior. They may not scan systematically, fixate accurately, or sample
as widely as the task requires.[26]

Redundancy

Language has a particular feature—redundancy—that enables us to use the cue
systems effectively. Redundancy helps to make language predictable. It reduces
uncertainty in reading because it limits what items can appear in a language.[27] The
reader knows what to expect and can therefore make reasonable predictions about
what he will find in the text. Redundancy also refers to the fact that a sentence in
written English contains more information than is absolutely necessary for the
reader to ascertain its meaning under ideal conditions. This allows the reader to
understand the sentence even if parts of it are unavailable. Consider the following:

One bedroom cooperative apartment for sale. It has large rooms and is three minutes
from the Long Island Rail Road. It has new wall-to-wall carpeting. The monthly mainte-
nance fee is $332, and the purchase price is $79,000. You may call on weekends or after
9 PM, Monday through Friday, at the following number: 555–9122.

This is a very redundant passage, as you can see from the following condensed version as it might appear in a classified advertisement:

1BR,lrg rms,3 min fr LIRR,new w-w crptg,mt $332,$79K. Wknds or aft 9 PM,M–F:555–9122.

Since this ad would be listed under "Co-operative Apartments for Sale," the extremely abbreviated spelling and syntax would not prevent a reader from reconstructing most of its meaning. The meaning of "LIRR," however, could not be deduced unless the reader was already aware of the existence of the Long Island Rail Road. The less redundancy present in a text, the more prior knowledge is needed to comprehend it.

Written language contains orthographic, syntactic, and semantic redundancies. *Orthographic redundancy* means that certain letter combinations are much more probable than others. In English, consonant-vowel-consonant is a very common sequence (*cat*, *hit*, *top*). Advertisers often use orthographic redundancy in inventing new names for products: *Fab*, *Duz*, *Lux*. Can you imagine a new detergent called *Gna*? Definitely not in English! *Syntactic redundancy* in languages such as English, where word order is significant, controls which word classes (noun, verb, etc.) can appear in certain positions. For example, in English, the word following the article *the* could not be a verb in its infinitive form (e.g., to go), but it could be a noun. *Semantic redundancy* imposes psychological limitations on what does or does not make sense in a given context. Although the sentence *The man bit the dog* is orthographically and syntactically acceptable, it represents an unlikely reality, and thus would not be expected by a reader. A proficient reader, reading quickly, might even transpose it to read *The dog bit the man*, since this makes better sense. By using these redundancies, the proficient reader moves directly from print to meaning in a process of immediate word recognition. Because of the redundancy of language, the reader can draw inferences and make predictions. He can hypothesize about the text, test his hypotheses out, and then either accept or reject them. In other words, he can play what Goodman has called a psycholinguistic guessing game.[28]

Rapid readers who comprehend well take excellent advantage of redundancy. Although it may seem that your eyes move steadily along each line of print as you read, this is definitely not the case. Oculomotor studies have found that reading consists of a series of *fixations*, extremely brief pauses in eye movements during which you see words and reading actually occurs. The rest of the time the eyes *sweep* back to the left margin and *regress* right to left to recheck on missed or misunderstood words. Proficient silent reading involves a minimum number of fixations and regressions, and fixations that are very brief. By good scanning, proficient readers make use of the redundant cues in language that signal meaning and are able to reconstruct the text very efficiently.

Schema Theory

Schema theory, which is based on the Piagetian construct of schemata (the plural form of schema), attempts to explain the significance of the reader's background in understanding written text. As you will recall from chapter 1, a schema is Piaget's term for the cognitive structure an individual constructs in intellectually adapting to and organizing his environment. According to schema theory, a spoken or written text has no meaning in itself. Meaning is bestowed on the text by the reader or listener.[29] Perhaps an example will help to illustrate this idea. Recently, I was driving with a companion when he observed a license plate on a nearby car that said, "FOR US–7." The tragic accident on the space shuttle *Challenger*, in which seven people had perished, had occurred just a week earlier. He commented, "That was fast," meaning that this commemorative license plate had been issued very quickly. Of course, the license plate, in all probability, had nothing to do with this event, and had meaning only to the driver of the car. Yet my companion had constructed his own meaning based on the recent event. In predicting the meaning of a written text, a reader summons alternative schemata that she can use to interpret the incoming information. As she continues to read, confirming some predictions and rejecting others, her schemata interact with and shape what she is reading. Earlier in this chapter, you saw how relatively easy it was to read a passage describing some of Maria Montessori's teaching methods. Because the material was familiar, you could easily assimilate it into existing schemata.

Schema theory is also concerned with how information is retained in memory. Generally, memory is described as being of two kinds: *short-term memory*, in which up to approximately seven unrelated items of information can be retained for about fifteen seconds; and *long-term memory*, which is relatively permanent and which stores an individual's knowledge and beliefs. Short-term memory is especially important in those types of literacy instruction that require the child to learn and recall new information by rote. These practices may be detrimental if the task is too difficult. Sometimes children are expected to memorize words taught in isolation, totally separate from any meaningful context. Most of us were taught to spell in this fashion. Some reading programs do not permit the child to read any connected discourse until he has mastered a prescribed number of phoneme/grapheme correspondences and can identify words that contain these correspondences.

The possible effect of such practices can be seen if you try to memorize each of the following lists in the precise order in which it appears. Take up to five minutes for each list. You might enjoy doing this activity with two acquaintances, each of you memorizing one list:

List 1	List 2	List 3
gleb	go	is
flum	girl	rose
mib	see	are
zob	house	the
ruz	light	me
hab	book	off
nom	where	or
blik	down	white
dup	put	jump
tus	you	bee

Most likely, list 2 was the easiest to memorize and list 1 the hardest, because nonsense syllables are exceedingly difficult to relate to any context. List 1 provides no semantic network that could provide a meaningful context for triggering recall. Just the opposite condition exists in list 2. It contains real words, which can be strung together to resemble a meaningful sentence. You probably created phrases by varying the juncture and pitch of the words as you tried to memorize them: go girl, see house light, book where down, put you. You may even have been impelled to invert the order of *house* and *light* to create another meaningful word, *lighthouse*. The point is that our minds are driven to impose order and seek meaning in experience. These are strengths of human cognition, and teaching practices ought to build on, rather than subvert them. Children learn words more quickly and remember them longer when they are embedded in meaningful contexts rather than in lists or in isolation.[30] Schema theory reminds us that when information is embedded in an integrated and meaningful context, we retain much more of it than when it is learned as unrelated items. It would probably be impossible for you to recall the exact words of the sentence before this one, yet you could probably paraphrase the content of this section or the entire page with little difficulty.

Language Diversity

The United States is rich in ethnic diversity. Its citizens come from every country in the world, and many of them speak the language of their native land. No matter where you teach in the United States, it is likely that some of your students will be bilingual and that others will speak a native American English dialect that is considered nonstandard. What are the consequences of this language diversity for learning how to read and write?

Bilingualism.   Most of the children who speak a native language other than English are not strictly bilingual. A bilingual person has skill roughly equal in both languages. It is the goal of many bilingual education programs to achieve this dual proficiency. The "bilingual" children in your class may range from totally monolingual in their native language to any point along a bilingual continuum—competent in their native language and becoming more competent in English.

The same language does not necessarily mean the same culture. Spanish is now the most frequent non-English native language of American schoolchildren. However, the cultural background of Hispanic children varies. Some come from the islands of the Caribbean, others are from Mexico or Central and South America, and only a very few come from Spain.

Bilingual-bicultural education programs aim to promote bilingualism. They are neither compensatory nor remedial in nature. Many of these programs were developed as a result of requirements imposed by legal decisions. In New York City, for example, bilingual education programs are required to meet the following criteria: intensive instruction in English as a second language, major subject area instruction in the native language, and language arts instruction in the native language. As the child demonstrates more competence in English, more of his instruction is conducted in English.

There is some evidence that children who learned to read in their native language before they learned to read in English are more successful than those who had to read English first.[31] We have seen that reading involves actively using an already internalized knowledge of language to reconstruct the meaning encoded in written symbols. If the child's native language is Spanish, then it is his internalized knowledge of *Spanish*, not English, that he will bring to the reading and writing task. His growing competence in English, plus his knowledge of written language acquired through learning to read in Spanish, can combine to make learning to read English a simpler task.

There are basically two models of second-language acquisition. The older *interference model* takes a behavioral view, while the newer *creative construction model* is a sociocognitive view. The interference model has traditionally been used to explain second-language learning. According to the interference model, difficulty in learning a second language arises because of the mismatch between the two languages. The learner makes errors in the new language by trying to make it conform to the phonological, syntactic, and semantic rules of his native language. Thus, a native speaker of Spanish might say *the dress red*, *the dog big*, *my hat pretty* because in Spanish adjectives occur after the noun. Teaching the second language, therefore, might involve the use of audiolingual drills on specific points of interference between the first and second languages.

However, most of the errors made by Spanish-speaking children do not seem to be caused by this kind of interference. Rodrigues and White report a study in which almost 90 percent of the errors made by five- to eight-year-old Spanish-speaking children who were learning English as a second language reflected the same developmental structures used by children learning English as a first language. Only 4.7 percent of their errors were attributed to interference between the two languages, and 8.2 percent were idiosyncratic.[32] This finding is consistent with a *creative construction view* of second-language learning.

According to the creative construction model, children acquire a second language in the same way they do a first. They discern the underlying rules of language structure and use in the second language. They continually hypothesize, test, and revise as they learn and interact in the new language environment. There are strong similarities in the processes children use in first- and second-language learning: they move from shorter utterances comprised primarily of content words to longer utterances containing function words; they overgeneralize, regularizing exceptional forms (e.g., *sheeps*); and they overextend semantic classes, including in them items that native adult speakers would not include.[33] According to this view, children can be helped to master the second language if they are in classrooms where they are actively involved in meaningful interactions with speakers of the second language. In such situations, children will want and need to acquire mastery over the second language.

Finally, bilingual education is a political as well as an educational issue. In the mid-1980s, the pendulum may be swinging away from bilingual education. Semanticist and former Senator S. I. Hayakawa sponsored *U.S. English*, an organization whose purpose has been to restore an English-only ballot in California, and to limit bilingual education to a "transitional role." Politics aside, however, what we know about language learning and development tells us that we should build on a child's strengths in his native language in helping him to acquire his second language; and that we should provide every opportunity for the child to use his second language in meaningful situations to accomplish real purposes.

Nonstandard dialect. Do you speak a dialect? When I ask my students this question, usually about half of them say they do. The others, believing that dialect means substandard speech, are convinced that they do not. Actually, we all speak a dialect of American English. According to Webster's *Third New International Dictionary*, *dialect* is a variety of language used by one group of people whose vocabulary, grammar, and pronunciation distinguish it from other varieties used by other groups. In American English, almost all dialects can be understood by speakers of other American dialects, though imperfectly at first. In some languages, such as Italian, dialects are so different that speakers of other dialects cannot understand each other at all.

Dialects develop when members of one group communicate among themselves more than they do with speakers of another group. These communication groups exist along different dimensions. Occupational or professional groups frequently use a specialized jargon (e.g., the words *software* and *debugging* from computers). So do hobbyists (e.g., CB radio buffs). People of different generations may use different terms for the same concept—*icebox* for *refrigerator* or *beau* for *boyfriend*. Traveling in the United States provides firsthand experience of regional dialect differences. I remember ordering a cherry soda when I was visiting southern Florida as a child. When I complained about the cherry ice-cream soda I was given, the waitress said, "Oh, you mean a cherry *phosphate*!" Dialects also signal social class. The notorious "Brooklynese," for instance, inevitably conjures up a picture of a working- or lower-class New Yorker.

Regardless of the dialect in question, context or social setting affects how we speak. William Labov's concept of style shifting emphasizes this point.[34] He uses the example of "r-lessness" in the speech of some New Yorkers to illustrate style shifting. In relaxed, informal situations, New Yorkers may not pronounce the final /r/ in some words, saying /ca/ for /car/, for example. In more formal circumstances, such as a job interview, they may become more self-conscious about their speech and make a point of pronouncing all the /r/s in words; for the moment, *r-lessness* disappears.

Dialect is one way people show kinship or community. For example, I am a frequent bus rider in New York City. Stalled in traffic jams, buses going in opposite directions sit next to one another, allowing the bus drivers the chance to chat. The dialect they use seems to be dependent upon whether both drivers are of the same or different ethnic groups.

Although no one standard dialect is used throughout the United States, there are several such dialects spoken in different geographical areas by the educated citizens of those regions. Schools in each region use the standard dialect for their region. Likewise, there are many nonstandard dialects in the United States, dialects whose usage is not considered acceptable. Nonstandard dialects are not inferior intrinsically to standard dialects. A nonstandard dialect is not "sloppy," "lazy," or "bad" speech. The most significant difference between a nonstandard and a standard dialect is that the nonstandard dialect is *socially disapproved*. It is a *non*-prestigious way to speak. If you have command of only a nonstandard dialect, your chances of doing well in school, getting a good job, and making a decent life for yourself may be jeopardized.

Black Vernacular English.   The most extensively studied nonstandard dialect in the United States is black vernacular English (BVE). BVE is used by a substantial number of low-income black people all over the United States. Remember, however, that dialect is *learned*. Many black people do not use BVE, while some white people do. BVE has phonological, semantic, and syntactic features that distinguish it from standard English. Some of its features are shared with other nonstandard dialects of the rural South, such as the pronunciation of the short /e/ and /i/ sounds (*pin* for *pen*). Some of the words that have become part of mainstream American English are borrowed from the lexicon of BVE, especially from the community of black musicians: *hip, cool, man, jazz*. The features of BVE that are probably the most disapproved of are syntactic, such as omitting the forms *is* and *are* from the verb *to be*: *He tired; They with us*. You will find a description of the major characteristics of BVE in appendix A.

The question of concern here is how BVE affects literacy. We know that achievement in reading and writing among children who use BVE falls below national norms. But this does not mean that there is a *causal* relationship between the two conditions. In fact, extensive reviews of the research in this area have *not* found a causal relationship.[35] Perhaps something much more fundamental and pervasive in the lives of children who use BVE is responsible. Some researchers have hypothesized that the critical factor in the poor school achievement of these children is the negative attitude of many school personnel toward BVE.[36]

The impact of BVE on school achievement and the question of how the school ought to work with children who speak it are issues that have aroused much controversy and even some litigation. In 1977, three mothers filed a lawsuit on behalf of their children, who attended the Martin Luther King, Jr. Elementary School in Ann Arbor, Michigan. The controversial Ann Arbor decision required teachers at the school to attend five training sessions in BVE. The suit was brought by the mothers because they contended that school personnel viewed pupils who use BVE as being learning disabled, often erroneously assigning them to special education classes.

It is *not* necessary for teachers of children who use BVE to be able to speak BVE themselves. It *is* necessary, however, for them to know the features of BVE and be sensitive to the needs of children whose dialect is nonstandard. Nonstandard dialect should be considered different, not deficient.

A teacher's goal should not be to replace the child's native dialect, just as it should not be to replace her native language. The teacher should build upon and add to the child's native dialect by being a good language model and by providing many opportunities for enjoying standard English through such activities as reading aloud, singing songs, and playing games.

Teachers should acknowledge a child's native language with appreciation by recording it precisely as she dictates it in her own stories. Later, the child can be helped to learn that ideas can be expressed in different ways, as she is shown how to rewrite her thoughts in standard English. Dialogue and play with peers who use standard English themselves should be encouraged. In every way, teachers should show children that they value them for who they are.

Teaching Implications

In this chapter, we have seen that the nature of language and how children learn language have a direct bearing on how we teach children to read and write. We know that meaning is central to the reading process. A child's own background—his experiences and understanding—is just as significant in determining what meaning he will impose on a reading passage as it is in determining what he will create in writing a passage himself. Both reading and writing are active processes of meaning construction that require the same creative problem-solving strategies the child used earlier to decipher spoken language.

Our instructional practices should capitalize on the linguistic and cognitive abilities the child brings quite naturally to the literacy task. What we do should complement the child's abilities and thereby extend his linguistic competence from the oral to the written mode. Our program of literacy instruction should, therefore, have these features:

- It should build a foundation of real and meaningful experiences that can be drawn upon in reading and writing.
- It should emphasize from the very beginning that meaning and understanding are the essence of the literacy process.
- It should use real, whole language as instructional material from which the child can learn the rules of written language.
- It should encourage the purposeful use of reading and writing as tools to complete real tasks and to solve real problems.

The remainder of this book describes in detail how to incorporate these features into an early literacy program.

Summary

This chapter has looked at the nature of written language for what it could reveal about how to teach reading and writing. We have seen that all languages are used to communicate, are composed of symbols, are organized as coherent systems, serve many functions, and are variable according to the demands of the situation. How literacy is taught is affected by the prevailing conception of what the reading and writing process entails, as well as by the more general educational goals of the time. Psycholinguistics considers reading and writing as whole language processes that have much in common with listening and speaking. All four are dependent on the processing of meaning through symbols. This psycholinguistic perspective on literacy indicates that:

- Reading involves both visual and cognitive strategies.

- Reading and writing are active processes of meaning construction.
- Written language has graphophonic, syntactic, and semantic cues that are used to make predictions about what is being read.
- Beginning readers must often recode from written to oral symbols to get meaning from a text and, thus, rely more on visual information than proficient readers who can go directly from written symbols to meaning.
- Meaning is bestowed upon a text by a listener or reader.
- Learning to read and write words that are embedded within a meaningful context is easier than learning them in isolation.
- Building on the native language strengths of children who are bilingual or whose dialect is nonstandard will help them learn to read and write.

Activities

1. Ask two children who know you (one in first grade, the other in fourth grade) to read aloud from their school reader or language arts textbook. Tape-record their reading. Then compare their oral reading with the actual texts. What strategies did each child use in reading aloud? What differences in their oral reading did you find?

2. Read an unfamiliar yet appropriate story to a kindergarten or first-grade child. Ask the child if she enjoyed the story and why. Then ask her to tell you what happened in the story. How much of the story did the child recall? Then tell the child you are going to play a game in which she has to remember some of the "secrets" in the story. The secrets are five to ten single words that you select from the child's retelling of the story. Tell the child the words (secrets). Now, ask her to repeat them herself. How many was she able to recall? How would you compare her recollection of the whole story and the separate words? What accounts for the difference?

3. Draw up a list of adjectives that describe language, based on the discussion in the first section of this chapter. Give the list to three adults and ask them to indicate which terms best describe *language*. Which terms are most frequently selected? What does this tell you about people's concept of language?

4. There are different levels of reading. With a partner, discuss what each of the following kinds of reading entails:

   Read the map.
   Read the sheet of music.
   Read the poem.
   Read your palm.
   Read your mind.
   Read the handwriting on the wall.
                    (Courtesy of J. K. Mott)

5. Select a passage from the King James version of the New Testament and compare it to the same passage in a present-day translation. How does the difference in language affect the meaning of the passage? How does the difference in language affect the emotional impact of the passage? How would you describe the quality of the language in the two different versions?

Further Reading and Viewing

Printed Materials

Goodman, K. S., and Niles, O. S. *Reading: Process and Program*. Champaign, Ill.: National Council of Teachers of English, 1970.

Huey, E. B. *The Psychology and Pedagogy of Reading*. Cambridge, Mass.: MIT Press, 1968. First published in 1908.

Smith, F. *Reading Without Nonsense*. 2d ed. New York: Teachers College Press, 1985.

Vygotsky, L. S. *Thought and Language*. Cambridge, Mass.: MIT Press, 1962.

Weaver, C. *Reading Process and Practice: From Socio-Psycholinguistics to Whole Language*. Portsmouth, N.H.: Heinemann, 1988.

Videotape Cassette

American Tongues. Videotape. New York: Center for New American Media.

SECTION TWO

The Program in Action

The next three chapters will discuss language learning in classes for children of about three to eight years old from a sociocognitive perspective. In some instances, the application is immediate; for example, Piaget's notion of decentering is directly associated with a growing sense of audience in children's writing in the later primary grades. Usually, however, the classroom application is more general and consists of experiences and attitudes supporting a sociocognitive view of language learning that emphasizes integrated, meaningful, and functional language experiences embedded within the social context of the child's life.

Chapter 3

Emergent Literacy

Preview

In a literate culture, children are surrounded by written language from earliest infancy. Regardless of family income, ethnic background, or geographical locale, print from TV, movie marquees, store signs, boxes of breakfast cereal, newspapers, and name tags sewn or pasted on their possessions impinges upon children's experience. This chapter describes ways in which teachers in the nursery school and kindergarten can help turn children's implicit knowledge of print into an active ability to read and write by building on their competence in spoken language and spurring their native curiosity and problem-solving strategies to explore written language. The following list of topics will serve as a guide to your reading.

1. *Characteristics of out-of-school learning that can be used in teaching.*
2. *The use of everyday printed material in the classroom, in the school building, and outside the school to foster beginning literacy.*
3. *Ways to encourage writing in the nursery school and kindergarten child.*
4. *The advantages of story dictation in learning how to read and write.*
5. *Some possible problems in story dictation and ways of handling them.*
6. *Conditions necessary for successful story dictation.*
7. *Why teachers should read aloud to children.*
8. *Why teachers should encourage children to play with books in readinglike ways and appreciate their successive approximations at reading independently.*
9. *How listening to the emotionally charged and patterned language of good children's literature can help children learn how to read.*
10. *Why the expressive arts are important in the process of becoming literate and how the expressive arts can help to promote literacy.*

Learning Before School

Have you ever watched as an adult helps a baby learn to walk? The interaction is alive with encouragement for the child and delight in his accomplishments. The adult urges the baby to take his first, uncertain steps: "Come on, Bobby. Come to Daddy." (Bobby takes a tentative step or two. He looks at his father, whose beaming smile acts as a magnet to try again.) "Come on Bobby, come to Daddy." (Bobby starts again, this time with a burst of energy that sends him in a stumbling rush to his father's arms.) "Great! You did it! You walked! Good for you!" (Bobby squeals with delight, as his father lifts him high into the air.) "Let's find Mommy. Let's show Mommy how you can walk."

Have you ever listened to the dialogue between a parent and a very young child? James is fourteen months old, the first child born to his parents. The setting for this dialogue is the den and kitchen in his home (M = Mother, J = James):

[J carries the Poppin' Pals toy he is playing with and walks away from mother.]

M   *[points to the toy]*: Let's do pop.

J: Pop.

M: Let's pop the numbers, 1, 2, 3, 4, 5.

[J looks and points to the toy.]

M: Pop the yellow one.

[J pops the yellow one.]

M: Pop the blue one.

J: Pop, pop. *[Pops the blue and red ones.]*

M: Hurray!

[J claps his hands.]

M: Get the cottage.

[J turns toward mother.]

M: Look James, look at the man go down the chute.

[J looks and laughs.]

M: Do you want some milk?

J: Ba, ba.

M: Okay.

[J follows his mother to kitchen.]

M: Let's warm the bottle.

J: Eh, eh. *[He starts to cry and points to the bottle.]*

M: It will be warm soon, don't cry.

[J continues to cry louder.]

M: Here is the bottle.

[J drinks milk eagerly. M walks back to the living room. J follows with bottle.]

M: Sit here and drink your bottle. *[J drinks half a bottle of milk and throws the bottle on the floor. M picks up bottle and places it on the table.]* Go get your horse.

[J points to horse.]

M: Let's go for a ride.

[J walks to shelf and gets teddy bear.]

M: Can mommy have the teddy?

[J gives his mother the teddy bear. M turns on the TV to "Sesame Street."]

J: Deet.

M: Look at Big Bird!

J   *[points to TV]*: Bir.

M: They're counting now.

J: Daw.

M: One, two, three.

J: Ta.

M: One.

J: Ta.

M: Three.

J: Tee

M: Hurray!

J   *[gets bottle from table and holds it out]*: Ba, ba.

M: There's the Grouch in the garbage can. See his eyes.

J: Eye. *[Points to his eye; M smiles.]* Eye.

M: There's the telephone.

[J points to the telephone.]

M: Hello!

J: Hi!

[M talks to someone on the phone. J climbs on couch to get his mother's attention.]

M: Get down!

J: Din. *[J continues to walk on couch.]*

M: Get down!

[J laughs. M ends conversation and takes James off the couch.]

J: Din.

(Sample courtesy of M. Torcasso)

In this typical sequence, the adult focuses on the meaning conveyed in the child's language. James's mother was not concerned with his immature speech. She did not correct or drill him. Studies indicate that adults intervene to correct some error in the child's *understanding*, some aspect of meaning, particularly of a true-false distinction, which doesn't jibe with reality:

Child: See doggy. See.

Mother: No, Debbie, that's a kitten, not a doggie. See her whiskers. Here, kitty, kitty.

These episodes exemplify the kind of learning that occurs before school. What are some characteristics of this learning?

First, it is concrete and immediate. It is tied to the important activities of day-to-day living—eating and playing and sleeping, getting in and out of clothes, and meeting new people.

Second, it is infused with acceptance of the inadequacies of immature performance. The bumbling approximations of a child learning to walk or to talk are encouraged and appreciated as milestones in his growth toward maturity.

Third, it is highly charged emotionally and much of the emotion is positive. The smiles and caresses, the words of glowing praise and delight from parents and other loved ones, act as powerful reinforcement of the child's accomplishments.

Fourth, it is unpressured and unhurried. There is lots of time for the child to practice each new skill as it is learned until he refines and fully masters it.

Fifth, it is intrinsically rewarding. Children seem to take lots of pleasure in learning. Ruth Weir taped her two-and-a-half-year-old son Anthony's presleep monologues and found that he spent a great deal of time playing with word sounds and structures.[1]

Sixth, it is really used. Each accomplishment allows the child to expand his access to the world of people and things: with the ability to grasp, he can bring the world closer; with walking, he can get closer to the world; and with speech, he can do these and more.

Finally, it is highly successful. With the exception of those who have serious physical or emotional handicaps, all children master the major developmental tasks of the period from birth to four or five years of age.

Learning in School

When they enter school, however, many children may experience learning that is very different. They may be age graded and ability grouped. They may learn about things that are remote from the context of their own lives. The books they are given to read may reflect stilted and unnatural language. They may be urged to compete with their peers for their teacher's approval or some other externally imposed reward. With perfection as the goal of performance, they may experience intolerance for the shortcomings of their emergent abilities. This is quite a dramatic contrast with learning before school entry. Even those children who fare pretty well might do even better in a more congenial environment. And children who do not do well at all may respond to school with anger or apathy and take the earliest opportunity to escape.

Facilitative Environments for Learning

It is possible to avoid these negative consequences. Learning does not need to be so limiting or punishing. There are ways to create schools where children have a better experience while learning. The first principle in teaching beginning reading and writing is to establish the kind of positive atmosphere that will promote learning. Because the preschool is still not as tightly bound by the constraints of a formal curriculum as are the later grades, it is usually compatible with a positive environment for learning. Reasonably flexible scheduling, informal activity areas (e.g., block building, dramatic play), a lower pupil-to-teacher ratio, extra teaching personnel (e.g., aides, volunteers), and the relatively relaxed atmosphere of the preschool or kindergarten make creating a natural environment for learning an attainable goal.

This natural environment for learning provides the broad context in which specific procedures for launching children into reading and writing can be carried out. Let us look closely at these specific procedures: exploiting everyday print, emergent writing, dictating stories, reading aloud, and using the expressive arts.

Exploiting Everyday Print

As we have noted, print is everywhere. For the baby plunked in front of a TV, the preschooler on a shopping excursion, the toddler riding in a car, *print is everywhere*. However, there is wide variation in the degree to which children are consciously made aware of print and actively explore it.

Here is part of what I overheard when I followed a child of about four as she shopped with her mother in a supermarket. Although in this sample her mother appears primarily concerned with helping Jane identify words, Jane's behavior reveals that she already understands the purpose and composition of a shopping list (*M* = Mother, *C* = Child):

M: Mmmm, now let's see. *[Consults her shopping list.]* Yes, we need bread, and maybe some rolls, too.

C: Lemme see, Mommy, please. *[Looks at shopping list.]*

M: Can you read the list? Show me *bread*—B-R-E-A-D. *[Emphasizes /BR/ sound. Child studies list with look of concentration.]* Jane, it's this one. See—bread. *[Spells out b-r-e-a-d.]*

C: Let's get Brannola, Mommy. Okay?

M: Okay, Jane. How about oatmeal?

C: Goodie. I'll get it. *[Child runs off to collect a loaf of Brannola Oatmeal Bread.]*

On another occasion, I was sitting across from two brothers, one about five, the other eight or nine, and their mother, on a subway (*M* = Mother, *YC* = younger child, *OC* = older child):

OC: Let's play a game, okay?

YC: Okay.

OC: Okay. See that sign over there? *[Points to an advertisement. YC nods.]* I'm gonna pick out a letter. Then you're gonna hafta find the same letter in another word. Like, if I say *t*, then you hafta find another *t*. Understand?

YC: Yeah.

M: Shhh! *[With some irritation.]* Stop making so much noise, will you.

OC: Find a . . . *b*.

YC *[Excited, gets up to have a closer look at the advertisement]*: Here, I can find it. Here's a *b*. *[Points to letter b.]*

M: Now just stop all of this. Sit down and BE QUIET!

The natural inclination of the child's mind is to be exploratory, bent on solving problems such as discovering the meaning behind the curious marks on signs and labels and the like. This natural urge is reinforced and stimulated in some children (such as the little girl in the supermarket), while in others (for example, the two brothers in the subway), it may not be. The inclination is there in *all* children, however, as is the exposure to written language. The teacher's task is to use familiar everyday printed matter to trigger children's natural curiosity about written language.

Kinds of Familiar Print

There are several kinds of print the child may already be familiar with when she first enters a preschool or kindergarten class. First, there is her name. "Cindy Lou, Cindy Lou. My name is Cindy Lou. If my name is Cindy Lou, who are you?" Cindy Lou introduced herself to her preschool class with this simple chant when she entered in late November. Soon, most of the other four-year-olds were inventing rhymes around their own names:

Larry, Larry, my name is Larry.
If my name is Larry, you must be Harry.
Tracy, Tracy, my name is Tracy.
My name is Tracy, and you are Bacy.

With nonsense or real words, the children were enjoying play with word sounds using the most immediate and personal example of written language—their own names. In addition, this word play was alerting them to the phenomenon of rhyming sounds. Their astute teacher saw this activity as a chance to familiarize them with the look and sound of words. She asked them if they would like her to write out their "name chants," and they said yes. The children dictated their own name chants, which were recorded on a chart by the teacher and then illustrated by the children. Subsequently, the chart was hung at eye level and reread by the teacher and children many times over the next weeks and months. Not only did many children learn to recognize the names of some of their classmates, they became intrigued with rhyme and sound play. The teacher extended this interest with lots of poetry reading and many other opportunities for the children to concoct rhymes of their own. These were audiotaped and then written down for further savoring. In addition to sound play, this experience also gave the children a chance to experiment with language structure. Note how they altered the second line of the original chant without changing the basic meaning:

_____, who are you?
_____, you must be _____.
_____, and you are _____.

The nursery school and kindergarten abound with opportunities to write and read children's names. Parents are usually asked to identify possessions with name tags. Cubbyholes and other storage areas can be labeled with names along with an additional identifying symbol, such as a flower or animal decal. Names can also be used in carrying out routines and job assignments. For example, you can construct a chart such as the one in Figure 3–1, in which each child's name is hung

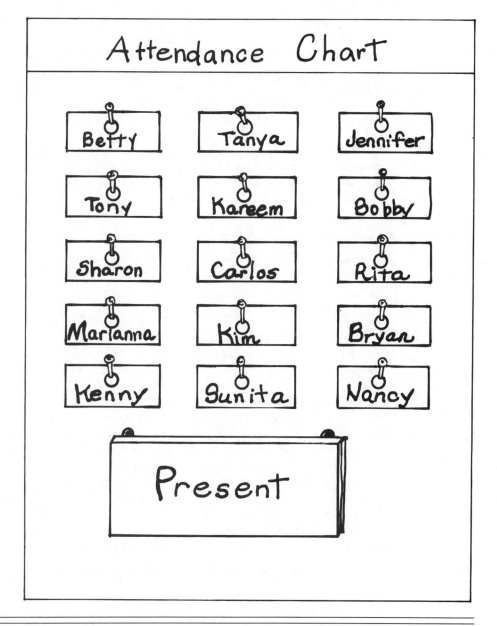

Figure 3–1   Attendance chart

on a hook. At the bottom of the chart is an envelope labeled "*PRESENT*." One of the child's routine tasks on arriving at school is to check this attendance chart, locate his name tag, and put it in the envelope. Later on, when the children gather around the teacher for sharing time, someone can read aloud the name tags of those children who are absent. These will be the ones left hanging on the chart.

In addition to using an attendance chart, children can gain familiarity with their names if they are encouraged to sign all of their work. You may also want to provide models of names for tracing over for those children who seem interested. The models can be made on a gradient of difficulty.

Labels, signs, names of TV shows, and advertising slogans and logos are other kinds of everyday print that you can use to familiarize children with written language. The dramatic play (often called housekeeping) and blockbuilding areas provide ideal settings for doing this. Familiar signs such as the STOP sign are common additions to the blockbuilding equipment, and empty boxes of cereal and other food products with familiar brand names are usually included among the housekeeping supplies. Play associated with different occupations and activities can be stimulated by adding job- or activity-related props. For example, to simulate a doctor's office in the dramatic play area, you would have a white jacket, doctor's bag, stethoscope, eye chart, and the like. You can also add symbolic props such as these to extend the play:

- "Doctor Is In," "Doctor Is Out," and "Thank You for Not Smoking" signs.
- An appointment book for the receptionist to use and the children to write their names in.
- Books and magazines for the patients to read in the waiting room.
- Pencils and paper for the doctor and receptionist to use.

Try playing the familiar "What's Missing" game, only use the empty food boxes from the dramatic play area. Are the children able to identify which box has been removed from the set of three or four in front of them? Do they identify the missing item by brand name ("The box of Wheaties is gone"), or product type (cereal)? Those children who seem able to identify product names out of context might enjoy a matching game in which they try to locate a pair of identical product names from a collection of several. Putting a picture of the product on the back of the cards on which the names are written is a good self-checking device.

In addition to making everyday print a part of the classroom, similar attention should be directed to print whenever the children go outside. There are plenty of signs to know about in the school building: "Director," "Principal," "Girls," "Boys," "Boiler Room," "Exit." You can read labels and signs on bulletin boards with the children, and make connections between them and the writing that is already familiar to the children, as this teacher did with her kindergarten class:

T: This bulletin board was prepared by class 2–1. It says, "How American Indians Lived Long Ago." *[Points to each word as it is read.]* Read this label with me, children.

C   *[Children chime in]*: How American Indians lived long ago.

T: Look at this *[pointing to the Ls in "Lived" and "Long"]*. Two Ls. Whose name begins like *Lived* and *Long?* *[Two children raise their hands, Libby and Liana.]* Good for you, Libby and Liana. Let's see how many *L*s we can find before we go back to our room. Raise your hand when you see one. *[Class goes off carefully scrutinizing the environment for more Ls.]*

Excursions beyond the school grounds should likewise be used to exploit and extend the children's knowledge of print. For example, imagine all the fine opportunities provided by a trip to the grocery store or supermarket to buy ingredients for making cranberry sauce for Thanksgiving:

- Observing the street signs along the way.
- Noting the store name.
- Looking for specific ingredients.
- Checking prices.
- Identifying familiar products and brand names.
- Checking off items on the shopping list.
- Watching as the prices are rung up on the cash register, or are recorded on the cash register.

Children's recognition of print in the environment can be enhanced by sharing books that feature this kind of print with them. *Signs*, by Ron and Nancy Gorr (New York: Crowell, 1983) contains clear photographs of signs in their familiar contexts so that a child can identify them easily. Tana Hoban's *I Walk and Read* (New York: Greenwillow, 1984) is another fine example of this kind of book.

Parents may not appreciate how valuable this contact with environmental print is for learning how to read and write. Because most of the experience children have with everyday print occurs outside of school, you may want to encourage parents to value its importance in conferences and informal contacts, and on open school nights. In addition, you can easily prepare and distribute to parents a short flyer on "Ways to Help Your Child Learn to Read and Write." The International Reading Association (800 Barksdale Road, P.O. Box 8139, Newark, DE 19711) publishes several helpful pamphlets for parents on this topic. Finally, some parents might enjoy reading books on the subject that are well written and rich in lively anecdotes. These are particularly useful:

- Marcia Baghban's *Our Daughter Learns to Read and Write* (Newark, Del.: International Reading Association, 1984).
- Jean Carew and others' *Observing Intelligence in Young Children* (Englewood Cliffs, N.J.: Prentice-Hall, 1976).
- Dolores Durkin's *Children Who Read Early* (New York: Teachers College Press, 1966).
- Linda Leonard Lamme's *Growing Up Reading* and *Growing Up Writing* (Washington, D.C.: Acropolis Books, 1985).
- Denny Taylor's *Family Literacy: Young Children Learning to Read and Write* (Portsmouth, N.H.: Heinemann, 1983).

- Denny Taylor and Dorothy Strickland's *Family Storybook Reading* (Portsmouth, N.H.: Heinemann, 1986).
- Jim Trelease's *The Read-Aloud Handbook* (New York: Penguin Books, 1982).

Emergent Writing

How old must a child be before he can write? Not very old at all, as we saw in chapter 1. Yet, most people would probably answer that a child would have to be at least six years old to be able to write. Most people, of course, would be thinking about writing conventionally, that is, using standard English orthography to encode meaning in written symbols. Our definition of writing is broader than this. We include under the category of emergent writing all the frequent writing activities that we find among three-, four-, and five-year-old children and those even younger than this. What distinguishes their writing from that of older children is that it usually involves *nonconventional* symbols—scribbles, for example. Melissa, at two years and four months, took the message in Figure 3–2 for her mother when she answered the phone. It says, "Grandma was calling."

Figure 3–2   Melissa's note: "Grandma was calling"

Nursery schools and kindergarten classrooms are rich with opportunities for children to write. In the dramatic play area, for example, a group of three-year-olds check the cupboard to see what supplies are running low. Figure 3–3 shows MaryJo's shopping list: Buy ketchup, milk, chicken, mayonnaise, a box of rice. One not quite four-year-old decided to make a list of all of her friends. Figure 3–4 shows what she wrote.

To encourage this kind of activity, writing materials should be placed in the various centers throughout the room with writing implements in clearly marked containers and paper of different kinds stored for easy accessibility to the children.

Lists of this kind and other writing that contains no discernable conventional symbols reveal, nonetheless, that the child has understood very important concepts about writing. Children who write in this way show an understanding of the sign concept, for example (see chapter 1). They understand that their written symbols are meant to represent, or stand for, some meaningful message. In his letter to Santa, Robert, a four-year-old, reveals some understanding of the letter format. His lines go across the page, and he may even have finished by signing off, as we usually do when writing letters. His letter (shown in Figure 3–5) says,

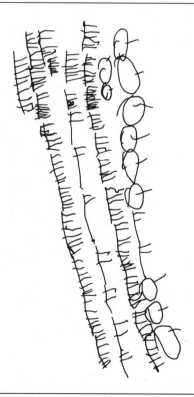

Figure 3–3   MaryJo's shopping list

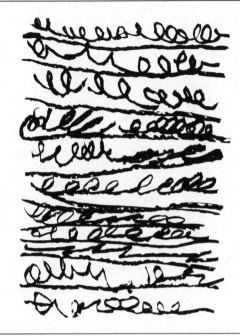

Figure 3–4   A list of friends

Figure 3–5   Robert's letter to Santa

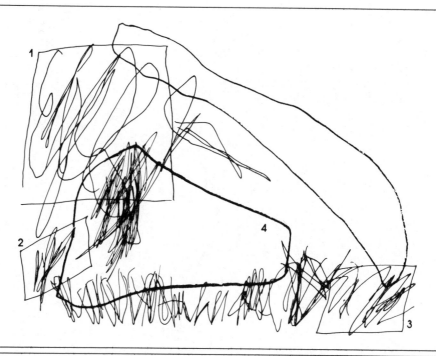

Figure 3–6   Drawing as writing

Dear Santa,

For Christmas, I want: He-Man, a train, a Donald Duck, and the Mickey Mouse.

Love,
Robert

A few of the children in a group of four-year-olds were invited to the birthday party of one of the class members. Among the party favors distributed to the children were pencils and small pads. The next day, the teacher found several of them role-playing waiters and waitresses taking orders from patrons of their restaurant.

The nursery school child may think of his drawings as writing. One three-and-a-half-year-old told his teacher that the part of his drawing marked configuration number 4 in Figure 3–6 said, "rock." He said rock is a big word, because the rock (configuration) is big. This is similar to what Ferreiro and Teberosky found in their study of young children's writing.[2] They observed that some young children saw a link between the length of a word and the size of the actual object it represented. Thus, they felt the word *train* would be a long word because a train is long.

Another common feature of the preschooler's writing is that it frequently accompanies a drawing or painting. The scribbles next to the picture in Figure 3–7 say, "It's a monster."

Art work is often signed. Many four-year-olds are already writing their names in conventional print. Even if the preschooler cannot write her name convention-

Figure 3–7   "It's a monster"

ally, however, she should be encouraged to "sign" her name. Opportunities for children three and older to sign in do not occur only in their art work. For example, they can "sign" in each morning on attendance and job charts. Figure 3–8 shows how Laura, a three-year-old, wrote her own name, followed by the names of her mommy, daddy, and brother Joseph. Note how the scribble changes in each case.

Five-year-olds often incorporate alphabetic and nonalphabetic symbols in their drawings (Figure 3–9). Of course, some five-year-olds have begun to write conventionally. The kindergartner who produced the picture and accompanying label in Figure 3–10 is clearly operating at the phonetic stage in spelling.

Observations of three-, four-, and five-year-olds both at home and at school reveal that much self-initiated writing is going on *if* this kind of activity is approved of and encouraged. Children want to write when they see others around them writing and when they are given the opportunity and the materials they need. Teachers and parents are apt to encourage emergent writing if they appreciate these two important considerations: that writing nonconventionally represents a legitimate and important part of the child's progress toward literacy; and that growth toward literacy requires the opportunity to experiment and practice with written symbols in an unpressured and responsive environment.

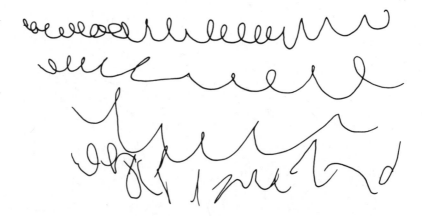

Figure 3–8   Laura's list of family members

Figure 3–9   Alphabetic and nonalphabetic symbols in drawings

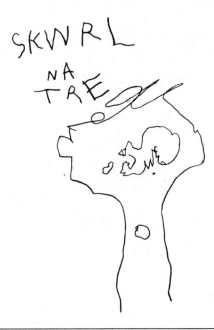

Figure 3–10   Phonetic stage

Dictating Stories

Value of Story Dictation

One of the most important things for children to understand in learning to read and write is the relationship between speaking and writing. By the time they are ready for school, children understand that the oral symbols that come to them via speech have meaning. They need to learn, however, that the same meaning can also be encoded in written language. There is no better way to make this connection than through story dictation. Earlier, we noted how a trip to the store to buy the ingredients for making cranberry sauce could provide many opportunities for reading. Once back in the classroom, the children might also want to dictate a story about the shopping trip, a list of ingredients, and the recipe for making cranberry sauce. All of this firsthand experience with written language could then be integrated with what the children are learning vicariously about Thanksgiving through storytelling and reading, poetry and songs.

When children dictate stories individually or in groups, they can observe immediately the direct translation of their spoken words into written symbols. The implicit understanding of the link between speaking and writing that children acquire via story dictation is extended by the teacher's occasional direct comments as he records the child's words:

T: What happened when you went into the Funhouse?

C: I got real scared.

T   *[Pronounces each word aloud as he writes it out]*: I ... got ... real ... scared. How many words is that, Billy?

C: Four.

T: Can you *hear* four words? *[Repeats "I got real scared."]*

C: Yeah.

T: See that? Okay, so you were real scared when you got into the Funhouse. What did you do then?

C: I took my Daddy's hand and looked into big, funny mirrors.

Do not assume that children understand the vocabulary of literacy. John Downing and Peter Oliver have found that up until age six or seven, children confuse nonverbal signs, phrases, and sentences with words.[3] Therefore, remember to use terms such as *word, letter, title,* and *sentence* casually, but consistently in story reading and writing.

Potential Problems in Story Dictation

Dictating stories is also important because it uses material that is the child's very own. A child dictating about his recent adventure on a trip to an amusement park is apt to be highly motivated to read the resulting story. Because the content of dictated stories is fresh and personal, the stories are very meaningful for the child. The language tends to be vivid and the subject matter exciting. Sometimes, however, a teacher encounters some knotty problems when taking dictation. For example, the teacher may consider the child's topic inappropriate.

I once observed a lively three-year-old bound over to the teacher's aide, pop himself into her lap, and launch into an excited description of a neighborhood rumble the evening before. She listened to him without making much comment and, after several minutes, suggested some block play. Later on, when I had a chance to talk to her, I asked whether she had considered having the boy dictate a story about his neighborhood ruckus. She answered no, and said that it would not be right for the school to condone antisocial behavior. This is a valid consideration, but it raises two questions. First, does the school actually condone inappropriate behavior by encouraging children to express what is most meaningful to them? Second, aren't children apt to read and remember the material that is most meaningful to them? Sylvia Ashton-Warner's work with Maori children in New Zealand revealed that it was the most meaning-laden words, such as *kill, knife,* and *born,* that the children learned to read most easily and remembered longest.[4]

A second knotty problem with story dictation may occur when teachers are faced with recording a child's nonstandard or immature grammar. Here is a story dictated by a five-year-old in a central city school:

Tom

My dog, he be named Tom.
He big and brown.
He real strong, too.

I love Tom.
We have lots of adventure.
            The End

The story was accompanied by a wonderful picture of a large brown dog and a small brown boy. In this case, the teacher decided to record the child's words exactly as he dictated them, making changes only to conform to standard spelling. When I asked her why, she told me that not altering the dictation made it easier for the child to read, since it was his *own* language that was taken down. Indeed, two advantages of story dictation (linking speaking and writing, and motivating content) are best met by unedited material.

Yet, you must be prepared to answer the concerns of parents and supervisors that unedited stories may reinforce "poor" grammar in the child, cause other children to acquire "poor" grammar, and interfere with reading standard English in books. Parents and others may be reassured to learn that there is no research evidence to indicate that any of these problems result from reading unedited stories. In addition to explaining the purpose behind story dictation, you may want to reserve unedited dictation for children's individual stories and edit the stories that are dictated by groups and displayed around the room. Later on, as children begin to be more proficient in reading and writing, you can show the child that it is possible to write the very same story in a different way. It is most important that this be done without in any way denigrating the child's original version. The purpose of this procedure is to demonstrate that the same meaning can be conveyed in different ways, something the children will see when poems and stories are read aloud. A sensitive teacher would rewrite "Tom" as follows:

My dog is named Tom.
He is big and brown.
He is really strong, too.
I love Tom.
We have lots of adventures.
            The End

Then both versions could be placed next to each other in the child's folder, each to be reread and enjoyed later.

Procedures for Story Dictation

Reserve time every day for dictating stories. You need no more equipment than lined paper and felt-tip markers or pencils. You might sit at a table in a quiet corner and invite children to come to you. As a child sits at the table, gently engage her in conversation. Here is how you might proceed with Kate, a kindergartner:

T: Hi, Kate. My, that's a pretty bow. Is it new?
C: Uh huh. You know, Mommy said we can get a puppy if Daddy says it's okay.
T: Do you want a puppy?
C: Uh huh.

T: What kind of puppy do you want? What would he look like?

C: A Lhasa Aps . . . , Lhasa Aps . . .

T: A Lhasa Apso?

C: Yeah.

T: What would he look like?

C: Soft and white and small. I'm gonna call her Penny.

T: What would you do with Penny?

C: Play and feed her, and go on walks, and to the vet.

T: Sounds like fun. I love dogs.

C: Me too.

T: Shall we write a story about Penny?

C: Okay.

T *[titles page "Penny"]:* How shall we start?

C: I have a new puppy and her name is Penny.

[T take the child's dictation exactly as it is given.]

Here is the resulting story:

Penny

I have a new puppy and her name is Penny.
She eats a lot and plays.
She's roly-poly.
Mommy says I can take her for a walk when I'm older.
Penny is my friend.
I take care of her.

The End

Print the story in highly legible manuscript style with a dark felt-tip marker or pencil. Each sentence begins on a new line. Use lined paper with empty space at the top for the child's illustration. After the child has finished dictating, you would invite the child to join you in rereading the story. Point to the words as they are pronounced. After you have read the story once, you might say, "Let's try it again," or "Would you like to try reading it alone," or you may simply stop right there, depending upon the child's inclination and skill. Some children are decidedly eager to proceed, while others are ready to go off and illustrate their story after the first reading. Of course, the younger preschool child will typically draw or paint first, and then dictate a label or story about the picture.

Children keep individually dictated stories in their own folders. They take them out and reread them frequently, with the teacher's help as needed. Children remember longest high-impact words, usually nouns and verbs. If a child can recognize a word on sight, it is a good idea to highlight this accomplishment by writing the word on a separate card, which the child can keep in a folder labeled "My Own Words." These are the child's special words, which she takes out and reads with pride. She will probably want to write them herself too. Be especially appreciative when you find these words on drawings and papers; it is an important accomplishment in writing. Occasionally, a four- or five-year-old may start combining word cards to make sentences of his own. This is when those small words that have no dictionary meaning of their own but serve the essential grammatical function of connecting language make their presence felt. For instance, when Kate of the Lhasa Apso story puts these cards out:

Penny   pretty

she is confronted by the need for the word *is*. Of course, her teacher prints it on a card, and Kate proudly displays:

Penny   is   pretty.

Kate will probably want to copy this sentence herself on a separate sheet of paper and illustrate it. Other children in Kate's kindergarten class and most preschoolers will not be as ready as she is to write conventionally. But their own less conventional styles of writing, which include features such as drawing and scribbling, represent important steps in the process of emerging writing and should be encouraged as well.

Because group stories reflect a collective rather than a unique experience, they usually do not have the impact of those that are individually dictated. Nonetheless, group dictation is valuable for several reasons: it underscores the integral role of writing and reading in everyday matters; it is based on the children's real experience; it provides a good medium for unison reading, in which the individual child is supported by the voices of his classmates as they all read aloud together; like individual dictation it illustrates the translation of speech into writing; and it provides enjoyable and easily available material for the child to read.

There are some pitfalls to avoid when conducting story dictation. One of these is the mistake of turning every class experience into an opportunity for dictating a story, which can make group dictation so routine it becomes boring. Class experiences that have real significance for the children—that are enjoyed a great deal or that stimulate a lot of emotion—are prime candidates for dictation, because children will remember best the language associated with such experiences.

In addition, children should not be rushed into dictation. A day or so should be allowed to pass to enable them to ruminate and reflect on an experience. In the interim, discuss the experience with the class to get a sense of their feelings about it and stimulate their thinking. When you sense enthusiasm, select a quiet time when children are rested to take the dictation. You might start like this:

T: You really enjoyed our trip Tuesday to the noodle factory.
C   *[Class chimes in]*: Yeah!
T: What was so interesting about it? Tanya?
C: Oh, the way the man made the noodles from the dough.
T: Do you remember what he did to the dough? Sounds like *knitted*.
C   *[puzzles over this]*: Nnn . . .
C   *[Another child blurts out]*: "Neeted."

T: Right . . . he *kneaded* the dough. *[Writes the word* kneaded *on the chalkboard.]* What did the man do when he *kneaded* the dough?

C: *[Second child, who remembered the word]*: Like with Silly Putty. *[Children giggle.]* He squashed it and made shapes.

T: Right. What else do you remember about the noodle factory? Luis?

C: They made all different kinds of noodles. They call it . . . They call it . . . I know, *pasta*!

T: Terrific! *[Writes* pasta *on chalkboard.]* Another new word, *pasta.* How many of you like to eat pasta? Umm . . . Me, too. Do you remember the *green* spaghetti? What did he use to make *green* spaghetti? *[No one responds.] Spinach. [Writes on chalkboard.]* Spinach is green, isn't it?

C: Spinach is yucky! *[Several others add their own versions of disapproval.]*

T: What did you like best about our trip to the noodle factory?

[Several children chime in here.]

C: The noodles he gave us to take home.

C: The subway.

C: Green spaghetti. Yuck!

C: The funny-shaped noodles.

T: Let's write a story about our trip to the noodle factory.

Seated next to an easel on which she has pinned a large piece of lined chart paper, the teacher writes the title of the story, "The Noodle Factory," with a black felt-tip marker. With skillfully posed questions, she guides the children's thinking and elicits their responses. As part of the process, the children learn about the logical structure of a story.

T: How did we get to the noodle factory?

C: Subway.

T *[writes and reads words]*: "We took a subway to the noodle factory." Do you remember what the factory looked like?

C: Old.

T *[writes and reads*: "It was in an old building." What did the man there show you?

C: How to make noodles.

T: Do you remember the special word for different kinds of noodles? *[She points to the word* pasta *on the chalkboard behind her.]*

C: Pasta, pasta.

T: Yes, pasta. *[Writes and reads]* "A man showed us how to make *pasta.*" What else did he do?

C: He made green spaghetti.

T: Uh-huh. *[Writes and reads]* "He made green spaghetti." Anything else?

C: He kneaded dough.

T: Right! *[Writes and reads]* "He *kneaded* dough." Did you like the noodle factory?

C *[together]*: Yeah!

T *[Writes and reads]*: "We liked the noodle factory."

The Noodle Factory

We took a subway to the noodle factory.
It was in an old building.
A man showed us how to make *pasta*.
He made green spaghetti.
He *kneaded* dough.
We liked the noodle factory.

Immediately after the class finishes dictating the story, the teacher invites them to read it with her. They reread it together three more times. After that, a couple of children are probably eager to read the story all alone. Each child does so, with the teacher's assistance, and receives the enthusiastic reaction of both teacher and classmates. The story is placed on public display in the room and reread many times. Some children even begin to make their own copies of the chart. The words *pasta*, *kneaded*, and *dough* are spoken frequently and are added to a few of the children's "special words" list. Varied, even exotic vocabulary and sentence structure that departs from simple Subject-Verb-Object do not impede the ability of these kindergartners to read and remember the story.

Group-dictated stories, often called *experience charts*, are a familiar feature of early childhood classes. It may seem obvious, but to be useful the charts must be physically and visually accessible to the children. This means that they should be hung at the *children's* eye level, preferably on a chart rack the children can handle easily. A dark felt-tip marker should be used, and the manuscript style print should be large, so that the chart can be read from any point in the room. In addition to rereading the charts with the children, the teacher should encourage every solo attempt. She should also be certain to point out words on the charts when the children encounter them elsewhere. For example, when Anthony, a child in the class that dictated the noodle factory story, reported that his Grandma had made pasta for the big family get-together, his teacher drew the children's attention to the word *pasta* in their story. Children might add a small illustration at the end of some sentences as an aid to recall. Ultimately group stories derive their energy from the rich and interesting activities the children experience firsthand:

- Trips around the school and away from it.
- Science experiments.
- Projects such as caring for a class pet.
- Visits to the class—by a local firefighter, for example.
- Exciting, unanticipated events, such as an electrical blackout.

Reading Aloud

Reasons for Reading Aloud

As immediate and meaningful as dictated stories are, alone they are insufficient for initiating children into the world of print. Recorded precisely as they are dictated, they have the freshness and vitality of speech but few or none of the conventions of writing. Since children have to learn how to read and write language that has all the stylistic qualities of writing, they need to be read to from books and other kinds of printed material. Written language uses punctuation and various typographical changes to express pitch, stress, and juncture (e.g., "*Stop!* she cried as she ran from the car.") It is more formal than speech and contains various peculiarities, such as inversion in word order (e.g., "Flushed with panic, she tore her way through the crowd.") Certain figures of speech, metaphors, and similes also appear more frequently in writing than in speech.

Children should also have the opportunity to savor the power and elegance of the language in good poetry and prose for purely aesthetic reasons. Reading aloud helps children to learn about story structure, something they will use later when they compose on their own. The strongly emotional and repetitive language of favorite stories makes it easy for children to predict the language and remember what happens. Even after only the first reading, preschoolers are ready to chant with the Troll (from *The Three Billy Goats Gruff*):

Trip, Trap! Trip, Trap! Trip, Trap! went the bridge. "Who's that tripping over my bridge?" roared the Troll.[5]

Children identify reading books as a grown-up activity, and they want to do it themselves. They delight in having the chance to select the book that the teacher has read aloud. Invariably, at any given time I have found that the most popular book is the one I have most recently read to the class. Finally, studies of children who read early and of those who are successful in learning how to read often find that these children have had many experiences with books at home. For all these reasons, the teacher will want to read aloud to the class every day, and to encourage individual children's attempts to read by themselves.

How and When to Read

In my visits to early-childhood classes, the most common arrangement for reading aloud I have observed has the teacher seated on a low chair in front of the children, who are seated facing her in a semi-circle on the floor. Her chair is high enough so that all the children can easily see the book she is holding, but not so high that they have to crane their necks to get a look. The teacher holds the book so that it faces the children and reads the words either by peeking over (reading upside-down) or occasionally turning the book to herself to glance quickly at the words. It seems that this is the preferred arrangement for reading aloud, because it enables all the children to see and hear the book at once. Don Holdaway suggests that rewriting favorite stories and poems in oversized versions can help recreate the trusting, secure, and expectant atmosphere of the bedtime story. Oversized versions of familiar stories are now available commercially (*Bill Martin's Big Books*, published by Holt, Rhinehart, and Winston). This Big Books notion has three phases: first, introducing the book for the primary purpose of enjoyment; second, rereading it frequently with the children (the enlarged print permits the children to see the text clearly as the teacher reads from it and points to focus attention on various features of the print); and third, encouraging the children to read the book independently and incorporating it into related expressive arts and writing activities.[6]

I support the idea of group story reading once or twice each day; however, I think teachers should supplement this plan by reading to individual children or to groups of two or three. In this arrangement, the teacher or assistant can create a more homelike atmosphere by sitting on a scatter rug or small couch with the child (or children) next to her. In addition to the more relaxed feeling of this style of reading aloud, its closer vantage point allows the child to get a better look at what real reading is all about. Seated next to the teacher, the child can actually see her reading. He can follow along while she quickly points to words as she reads, and he can chime in and read along himself. He has the teacher's full attention and is free of all the distractions caused when she has to turn the book to look at it herself and of the occasional confusion that arises out of her different left-to-right orientation when she is seated in front of rather than next to the children.

Children's Emergent Reading

If books are part of their environment, children begin to "read" from them when they are very young. If they are read to frequently, even toddlers simulate the sound of story reading before they know any of the story's words, so that their "La la la la la laaa la la laaa la" (book babbling) actually sounds like "Once upon a time there were three bears. . . ." Studies of nursery school and kindergarten children have found such simulations to be quite valuable.[7] First, book play allows children to model reading behavior—how to hold a book, turn pages, look at illustrations. Second, it familiarizes them with the features of a book—starting at the beginning of the book, looking at the pages in succession, and finishing at the end. Third, it helps to reinforce their understanding of the arrangement of English print—that it starts at the upper left, proceeds across the page, and then moves down to the next line. Fourth, it shows them that print has meaning—the marks on the page actually tell a story.

Anyone who reads aloud to children has heard the "Read it again, please" request that seems to follow every story reading. Some parents may find this irritating and wonder why children do not get as bored as they do with all-too-familiar stories. Children, however, revel in hearing their favorite stories again and again. What is more, the repetition helps them anticipate the words and action and familiarizes them with story content and language, until they reach the point where they can read it almost word for word. What they master first is the story's meaning.

At four, Aviva enjoys reading a great deal, and *The Three Bears* is one of her favorite tales. Though not apparent in this transcript, her oral retelling quite clearly reflected the character and size of each of the three bears. Her re-enactment captures the plot as well as much of the actual text. Note how the more repetitive passages are rendered most accurately.

Actual text	Re-enactment
Once upon a time there were Three Bears who lived together in a house of their own in the woods.	Once upon a time there were Three Bears who lived in a house in the woods.

Actual text	Re-enactment
One of them was a Little Wee Bear, and one was a Middle-Sized Bear, and the other was a Great Big Bear.	One was a Wee Little Bear, and one was a Middle-Sized Bear, and one was a Great Big Bear.
They each had a bowl for their porridge. The Little Wee Bear had a little wee bowl, the Middle-Sized Bear had a middle-sized bowl, and the Great Big Bear had a great big bowl.	The Wee Little Bear had a wee little bowl for his porridge, and the Middle-Sized Bear had a middle-sized bowl, and the Great Big Bear had a great big bowl.
They each had a chair to sit in. The Little Wee Bear had a little wee chair, the Middle-Sized Bear had a middle-sized chair, and the Great Big Bear had a great big chair.	The Wee Little Bear had a little chair, and the Middle-Sized Bear had a middle-sized chair, and the Great Big Bear had a great big chair.
One morning, the Three Bears made porridge for breakfast, and poured it into their bowls. But it was too hot to eat. So they decided to go for a walk in the woods until it cooled.	One morning, the Three Bears made porridge for breakfast, but it was too hot to eat, so they went for a walk in the woods until it cooled off.
While the Three Bears were walking, a little girl named Goldilocks came to their house.	Then Goldilocks came to their house.
First she looked in at the window, and then she peeped through the keyhole. Of course, there was nobody inside. Goldilocks turned the handle of the door.	Goldilocks looked in the window and no one was home.
The door was not locked, because the Three Bears were trusting bears. They did no one any harm, and never thought anyone would harm them. So Goldilocks opened the door and went right in. There was porridge on the table. It smelled very, very good! Goldilocks didn't stop to think whose porridge it was. She went straight to it.	The door was open and Goldilocks went right in. She saw the porridge on the table, and it smelled very, very good.
First she tasted the porridge of the Great Big Bear. But it was too hot. Then she tasted the porridge of the Middle-Sized Bear. But it was too cold. Then she tasted the porridge of the Little Wee Bear.	First she tasted the porridge of the Great Big Bear, but it was too hot. Then she tasted the porridge of the Middle-Sized Bear, but it was too cold. Then she tasted the porridge of the Little Wee Bear.
It was neither too hot nor too cold, but just right. Goldilocks liked it so much that she ate it all up.	And it was just right, so she ate it all up.

Actual text	Re-enactment
Then Goldilocks went into the parlor to see what else she could find.	
There were three chairs. First she sat down in the chair of the Great Big Bear. But it was too hard. Then she sat down in the chair of the Middle-Sized Bear. But it was too soft. Then she sat down in the chair of the Little Wee Bear. It was neither too hard nor too soft, but just right. Goldilocks liked it so much that she rocked and rocked, until . . .	She saw the three chairs. First she tried the chair of the Great Big Bear, but it was too hard, and then she tried the chair of the Middle-Sized Bear, but it was too soft. Then she tried the chair of the Little Wee Bear, and it was just right.
the bottom of the chair fell out! Down she went—plump!—onto the floor. Goldilocks went into the bedroom where the Three Bears slept.	So she rocked and rocked until it broke and she fell down, bump!
First, she lay down upon the bed of the Great Big Bear. But it was too high at the head for her. Then she lay down upon the bed of the Middle-Sized Bear. But it was too high at the foot for her. Then she lay down upon the bed of the Little Wee Bear. It was neither too high at the head, nor too high at the foot, but it was just right. Goldilocks liked it so much that she covered herself up and fell fast asleep.	First she tried the bed of the Great Big Bear, but it was too hard. Then she tried the bed of the Middle-Sized Bear, but it was too soft, so she tried the bed of the Little Wee Bear, and it was just right, so she fell fast asleep.
By this time, the Three Bears thought their porridge would be cool enough. So they came home for breakfast. Goldilocks had left the spoon of the Great Big Bear in his porridge bowl. He noticed it, first thing. "Somebody has been tasting my porridge!" said the Great Big Bear in his great big voice.	Now the porridge was cool, and the Three Bears came home for breakfast. "Somebody has been tasting my porridge!" said the Great Big Bear in his Great Big voice.
Goldilocks had left the spoon of the Middle-Sized Bear in her porridge bowl, too. "Somebody has been tasting my porridge!" said the Middle-Sized Bear in her middle-sized voice.	"Somebody has been tasting my porridge!" said the Middle-Sized Bear.
Then the Little Wee Bear looked at his bowl. "Somebody has been tasting my porridge, and has eaten it all up!"	Then, the Little Bear looked at his bowl, "Somebody has been tasting my porridge, and ate it all up!"

Actual text	Re-enactment
cried the Little Wee Bear in his little wee voice. The Three Bears went into the parlor....	
Goldilocks had pulled the pillow of the Great Big Bear out of place. He noticed it, first thing. "Somebody has been lying in my bed!" said the Great Big Bear in his great big voice.	"Somebody has been lying in my bed," said the Great Big Bear.
Goldilocks had pulled the blanket of the Middle-Sized Bear out of place. "Somebody has been lying in my bed!" said the Middle-Sized Bear in her middle-sized voice.	"Somebody has been lying in my bed!" said the Middle-Sized Bear.
Then, the Little Wee Bear looked at his bed. "Somebody has been lying in my bed—and here she is!" cried the Little Wee Bear in his little wee voice. This woke Goldilocks up at once. There were the Three Bears all staring at her.	"And somebody has been lying in my bed—and there she is!" said the Little Wee Bear. Goldilocks woke up and saw the Three Bears all staring at her.
Goldilocks was so frightened that she tumbled out of bed and ran to the open window. Out she jumped.	Goldilocks was so frightened she jumped out the window!
And she ran away as fast as she could, never looking behind her.	And she ran as fast as she could.
No one knows what happened to Goldilocks after that. As for the Three Bears, they never saw her again.	And the Three Bears never saw her again. The End.

An interesting phenomenon in this kind of story retelling is that, when the child becomes knowledgeable about what reading entails, she may become less willing to retell an unfamiliar story. Once the child understands that reading the story means reading the actual words in the text, if she is not familiar enough with the story to know the words, she may say that she cannot read it. A child who is less sophisticated about the reading process, however, suffers no such constraints with unfamiliar material. She may simply compose her own story or recreate the story by reading the illustrations.[8]

Familiarity with books and spontaneous attempts at independent reading make it much easier for a child to learn how to read. Encourage play with books in readinglike ways. When a child asks what a page says, tell him. Later, when he asks for help with a word, give it and receive his precocious attempts at mastering the written word with warm praise.

We have already seen how the emotionally charged and patterned language of good children's literature helps the child to anticipate words and action. Making predictions of this kind is part of the child's natural inclination toward hypothesis construction and verification, and is used frequently in reading. Teachers can capitalize on the child's natural problem-solving strategies when reading aloud by occasionally leaving out highly meaningful words for him to fill in. The tendency to fill in the gaps is irresistible. With language as strongly rhythmic as this, even on a first reading children can complete:

Hickory, dickory, dock
The mouse ran up the _____.

and they love to do it! With repeated readings, they can anticipate and recall entire phrases or refrains, such as this famous one:

Cats here, cats there.
Cats and kittens everywhere.
Hundreds of cats,
Thousands of cats,
Millions and billions and trillions of cats.
            (Wanda Gág, *Millions of Cats*)

His winning combination of nonsense and rhyme has endeared Dr. Seuss to many children, who eagerly chant along:

Oh, the things they will bump!
Oh, the things they will hit!
Oh, I do not like it!
Not one little bit!
(Dr. Seuss, *The Cat in the Hat*)

A refrain children especially appreciate, like the one from *Millions of Cats*, can be written out on chart paper so that the children can read along when you come to that part of the story. The same kind of thing can be done with favorite and familiar songs culled from song books. The Teacher's Edition for the reading series, *The Sounds of Language* (second ed.; New York: Holt, Rinehart & Winston, 1972), contains excellent suggestions for helping children associate songs and rhymes that are aurally familiar with their written forms. You may even find a favorite chant repeated spontaneously during children's dramatic play. Listen for the children's own chants, too. Some of these should be tape-recorded and played back later for everyone's enjoyment. They can also be transcribed and read back. These activities using meaningful and enjoyable material have several purposes: they stimulate children to use their creative problem-solving abilities on language; they sensitize children to the sounds of language; and they help children to apply their knowledge of speech to writing. One word of caution: *Remember to use a light touch.* First and foremost, literature is to be enjoyed. The teaching that you do with literature should be subtle, occasional, and unpressured. Alphabet and number books, which are an important part of the preschool and kindergarten program, do lend themselves to more direct teaching. But even with these, teachers should avoid being didactic.

An amusing incident from my own experience as a student teacher might help to illustrate the latter point. By way of introducing me to my first placement with a primary grade class, I was observing one morning as the current student teacher read to the children from a Dr. Seuss book. She interrupted her reading frequently to remind them that, "Of course, we wouldn't pronounce a word this way" or "There really is no such word as _____" and similar tidbits. Finally, in a tone of complete exasperation, Jon called out, "Haven't you ever heard of poetic license?"

The Expressive Arts

Before concluding discussion of how to stimulate children's emergent literacy, we should consider the value of the expressive arts in reaching this goal. Art, movement, music, and drama are traditional components of good early-childhood programs. The primary purpose of these activities is to promote the creative expression of the child's personality and thereby foster his emotional and social development. But do they contribute to his growth in literacy as well? The answer is yes. The expressive arts contribute to literacy in obvious and immediate ways by:

- Encouraging children to learn new words associated with an art medium (e.g., paintbrush, tempera, easel).
- Heightening skills in perception (e.g., distinguishing musical sounds by differences in pitch, timbre, stress, duration, and tempo).
- Helping children to predict language patterns and vocabulary through highly rhythmic and repetitive songs, nursery rhymes, and chants.
- Providing media for the use of written language (e.g., labeling pictures, recording songs and chants).
- Encouraging an appreciation of good literature through dramatizing stories.

But more important, the expressive arts aid literacy because the central concern of language teaching is meaning. All the arts—expressive and language—are symbolic representations of meaning. All are outward expressions of inner feelings and thoughts. Exploration of firsthand sensory experience and the enjoyment of literature and the expressive arts deepen and enrich meaning. Sometimes an experience will lead directly to creative expression in an art form. For example, a group of four-year-olds was visibly troubled one morning when they arrived to find that their room had been broken into the night before. After a brief discussion of the incident, some of the children seemed relieved. The teacher felt, however, that dramatizing the scene would help the children better understand and accept the violation of their classroom. She suggested that they act out what might have happened, gave a few ideas, and helped select the first players. The children dramatized the scene spontaneously later that morning and on the following few days. Even though they were not happy about it, the children accepted the break-in and no longer seemed troubled by it. Later, they dictated a story about the experience, which was reread many times.

On other occasions, an experience will be channeled immediately into linguistic form, such as an individually dictated story, which in turn may stimulate artistic, musical, or dramatic expression. Following a kindergarten class' trip to the local zoo, discussion focused on the animals they had seen there. The class dictated a story about the trip, but because the children showed continued interest in the animals, the teacher decided to explore some of the more interesting animals in detail. One of the things she did was to examine how the animals moved—monkeys clambered, bears lumbered, penguins waddled, snakes slithered. The children dramatized each animal's locmotion. Some pantomimed specific animals for others to guess. According to Don Holdaway, symbolic expression in the arts can help to clarify and sharpen linguistic meanings, especially for those children who do not express themselves easily in language.[9] The stories several of the children dictated after the dramatization were richer in descriptive detail and knowledge than the original group story. Here is one:

The Snake

I am a snake.
I am long and squiggly.
I slither along the ground.
My skin is green and black.
I look slippery, but I'm not.
I scare people.

In an environment where children are active in all the arts, they can express and experience meaning symbolically in many different ways and learn how to communicate freely both with and without language.

An Illustration

Some of the many ways young children experience the nature and function of written language are more clearly illustrated in the context of a real classroom situation: a half-day program for four-year-olds staffed by a teacher and an assistant. Parents drop off and pick up their children. The room has a lavatory that the children use on their own, as the need arises. The room is on the first floor of the child-care center and opens onto an enclosed outdoor play area. The amount of time devoted to different activities varies from day to day to accommodate unexpected events and important occasions, but the general plan balances rest and play while allowing large blocks of time for individual and group activities and carrying out routines.

- 8:15–9:15:   Arrival. Exchange of greetings between teacher and parents. Teacher welcomes each child and chats briefly with parent, while making an informal health check. Children proceed into room to their cubbyholes (labeled with their names), where they store clothing and other possessions. They remove their name tags from the attendance chart and check the job chart to see if they are assigned some special responsibility. If they are uncertain about the latter, they ask the assistant teacher, who checks the job chart with them again. They select materials such as puzzles, table games, crayons and paper, and blocks for free play.

- 9:15–9:25: Clean-up. With the teacher and assistant's help, children put materials back into containers and return them to shelves. Each of the storage areas is labeled. Cut-out shapes of the different kinds of blocks are pasted at the back of the shelves to help children remember where to return them.

- 9:25–9:45: Sharing time. Children gather around the teacher, who is seated at the piano. She and the children check the attendance chart to see who is absent. A short discussion ensues on what they did yesterday, today's plans, and other topics of interest to the children. One child shows the class a toy he got for his birthday. Two or three others chime in with their own birthday experiences. (Teacher decides that "birthdays" is a good topic for a chart; she makes a note to herself to plan some time for developing a chart with the group that records children's birthdays by month.) Another child excitedly tells about a baseball game she is going to. Teacher invites children to pretend they are playing ball as she plays simple rhythms at the piano evocative of ball-playing movements, such as jumping, sliding, reaching high, and bouncing.

  Children wash hands in preparation for snack. Three children have the job of assisting with the snack. (They have read their names on the job chart earlier.) One child gets napkins, another a tray of carrots and celery, and a third child retrieves a large can of apple juice. With the assistant teacher, these three help set up for snack time.

- 9:45–10:00: Snack time. Children seated at tables, talking among themselves. Teacher and assistant spend some time at each table and engage the children in conversation. Children clear their own places and move to different activity areas.

- 10:00–10:45: Activity time. Children play in the different activity areas at block building; dramatic play; woodworking; water play; table games and puzzles; art activities (e.g., easel and finger painting, collage, clay, play dough); reading, writing, and listening to tapes; working on experiments in the science and math area (e.g., sorting seeds and then classifying them by such variables as size, color, or shape; seriating a set of Montessori objects by weight).

  The teacher or assistant sets up a special activity table where she assists a small group of children in such projects as cooking or crafts.

Whichever teacher is not already working with a small group sits at the library table for about fifteen minutes, with paper and pencil, for individual dictation. She spends an additional ten to fifteen minutes reading with one to three children. When not directly engaged with children, both teachers circulate around the room, giving assistance where needed and conversing with children.

- 10:45–11:00: Clean-up. Teachers assist children in putting materials away and straightening up the room. To the tune of "This is the Way We Wash Our Clothes," everyone sings, "This is the way we clean our room, clean our room, clean our room," as they do their chores.

  Preparation for going outside: Children put on their outer clothing and then go to the adjacent outdoor play area, where the assistant teacher is waiting for them.

- 11:00–11:30: Outdoor play. Children use outdoor play equipment such as tricycles, monkey bars, large and small balls, and the sandbox. Teachers intervene as necessary and engage children in conversation where appropriate.

- 11:30–12:00: Quiet time and dismissal. Children return to room, put outer clothing back into their cubbyholes. They join the teacher, who reads or tells them a story. They plan for the next day. Teachers say goodbye, as children are picked up to go home.

There are many opportunities for the teacher to stimulate the development of literacy in three- to five-year-old children. Sometimes these opportunities are part of planned experiences, as when the teacher assists the children in reading a list of ingredients or records their account of an entire cooking episode after it is completed. Most of the time, however, teaching for literacy in the nursery school or kindergarten is serendipitous: the teacher takes advantage of an unplanned opportunity such as writing the label a group of children request for their block construction or finding a familiar word in a street sign on a short walk in the vicinity of the school (does that say *Rose* Street?). Encouraging development in literacy goes on in a relaxed atmosphere, where the emphasis is on taking what children already know and applying it to what they need to know in ways that are meaningful and purposeful.

Summary

In this chapter we have seen that the way to ready children for reading and writing is to *let* them read and write. Children will learn about the conventions of print and practice their growing literacy skills when they have positive experiences with enjoyable, purposeful, and meaningful written languages. This strategy involves:

- Incorporating the positive qualities of real-life learning into school through experiences that are functional, emotionally satisfying and important, tolerant of immature performance, and unpressured.

- Using everyday printed matter, such as children's names, signs, labels, and brand names to trigger their natural curiosity about written language.

- Encouraging children's emergent writing in nonconventional as well as conventional forms.

- Encouraging children to dictate their own stories to help them make the connection between the spoken and written forms of language.

- Reading aloud to children and encouraging them to handle books themselves in order to familiarize them with the unique qualities of written language and the properties of books.

- Stimulating symbolic expression in verbal and nonverbal ways through all forms of the language and expressive arts.

Activities

1. Tape-record an informal conversation between you and the mother (or father) of an infant or toddler. The focus of the conversation will be for the parent to tell you about his/her child. Then have the parent tape about fifteen mintues worth of informal interaction with the child when you are not present. (This can be done during the child's play time or after the child's nap, bath, or lunch, for example.) Analyze the tapes to compare how the parent spoke with an adult and with a very young child. What differences do you find in the parent's speech in the two situations in such features as length of sentences; complexity of sentences; variety of vocabulary; variation of pronunciation, stress or emphasis; use of playful nonsense words; and number of well-formed sentences? (If you use videotape, you can also make note of differences in nonverbal communication, such as facial expression, posture, gestures, and distance between speaker and listener.)

2. Ask four children who know you—a three-, four-, five- and six-year-old—to draw a picture about something each finds interesting. Preface this activity with some discussion about the child's interests. When the child is finished, ask him/her to write something on the paper about the picture. If the child objects, what reasons does he/she give? If the child does write, even if it does not look like conventional writing, ask the child what she/he has written and what marks say what words. Ask the child to tell you what writing is and how writing is different from drawing pictures. Compare your interviews with the four children on their willingness to write, the nature of their writing, their statements about what writing is, and their ideas about how writing represents language.[10]

3. Collect two or three packages of highly familiar products such as toothpaste, gelatin dessert, or cereal. Work with a child who is not yet reading conven-

tional print. On three separate occasions, show the child: a) each product box with words and graphics intact; b) each product box with words obscured; and c) each product name written on a separate piece of paper (e.g., *Jell-O*). In each instance, ask the child what each item says. Was the child able to read all three types of symbols? What differences did you find?[11]

4. Read a story you like to a group of preschool children who know you. Select a book with a story line that is familiar to them (e.g., Ezra Jack Keats's *A Snowy Day*). Afterward, elicit a discussion on the children's own experiences with the story's theme. When the children have had sufficient time to explore the topic, invite them to dictate a group story. On another occasion, when one child from this group has had a personal experience that is particularly interesting, invite her or him to dictate a story to you about it. What differences do you note between the story dictated individually and the story dictated by the group?

5. Develop a list of about ten frequently used reading terms, such as *word*, *sound*, *book*, *sentence*. As you say each term aloud, separately ask a preschooler, a child in the primary grades, and another in the intermediate grades what each term means. Then ask each child to show you an example of each term in a book. With the book in hand, say "Show me a _____." Did any child know all the terms? Which terms did the children miss most frequently? Was it easier for them to show you what the terms meant in the book than to tell you in their own words?

Further Reading and Viewing

Printed Materials

Butler, D., and Clay, M. *Reading Begins at Home: Preparing Children for Reading Before They Go to School.* Portsmouth, N.H.: Heinemann, 1982.

Cunningham, P. M., Moore, S. A., Cunningham, J. W., and Moore, D. W. *Reading in Elementary Classrooms: Strategies and Observations.* New York: Longman, 1983. Chapter 10.

Leeper, S. H., Dales, R. J., Skipper, D. S., and Witherspoon, R. L. *Good Schools for Young Children*, 3d ed. New York: Macmillan, 1974.

Schickedanz, J. *More than the ABC's: The Early Stages of Reading and Writing.* Washington, D.C.: National Association for the Education of Young Children, 1986.

Taylor, D. *Family Literacy: Young Children Learning to Read and Write.* Portsmouth, N.H.: Heinemann, 1983.

Film

Foundations of Reading and Writing. 16mm film. New York: Campus Films.

Filmstrip

Literacy Development in the Preschool. Filmstrip with audio cassette. Portsmouth, N.H.: Heinemann.

Chapter 4

Reading
and Writing
More Conventionally

Preview

Most children come to first grade eager to learn. Their nursery school and kindergarten experiences have been, for the most part, positive, and they are ready to apply their native problem-solving abilities more directly and consciously to the task of learning to read and write. They already have at least some familiarity with print and a genuine curiosity to learn more about it. This chapter describes how teachers can build on the children's literacy experiences in nursery school and kindergarten and extend their understanding of written language through functional, meaningful, and integrated language experiences. Here are the chapter's major themes:

1. *Ideas for getting the literacy program started.*
2. *Using self-composed texts with children who have little or no understanding of print, a moderate understanding of print, or a more extensive understanding of print.*
3. *The importance of reading from books and other printed material.*
4. *Three prerequisites for the efficient use of printed material.*
5. *The importance of the individual conference.*
6. *Ways to assist parents in working with their children at home.*
7. *How to introduce the literacy program gradually.*
8. *Ways to encourage independent writing.*
9. *Effective sharing of written work.*
10. *Some of the purposes of an individual writing conference.*
11. *Helping children learn handwriting.*
12. *Dealing with matters of form in beginners' writing.*

A First-Grade Class

It is 10:30 on a crisp December morning in Mrs. Malone's first-grade classroom. The twenty-five children in the class range in age from just six to almost seven years old. When I come to the door of the room, the general impression I receive is one of purposeful activity. Some children are moving about; others are seated at tables working quietly or talking among themselves. At first I do not see Mrs. Malone, but as I look closer I notice that she is seated at a table in the back with two children. Becky, Louise, and Donnell notice me as I enter. I have been there before and they greet me warmly. Once inside the room, I can better observe what is happening.

Here is what I see: The room is organized around several activity or interest areas: math and science, dramatic play, blockbuilding, language arts, expressive arts, and table games. Children sit around tables that can accommodate four to five at a time. Mrs. Malone's desk is on the right side at the back of the room. Two children in smocks are painting at the easels. A rather elaborate construction is underway in the blockbuilding area, where the four children working on it are having an animated discussion about Westway, the proposed replacement for New York City's West Side Highway. One of the children has written a sign saying *Westway* and taped it on the construction. In the math/science area, three children are recording their observations of the growth of several lima beans planted under different conditions. When I inquire about their findings, the children eagerly show me their recorded observations. They have made some tentative hypotheses about the effects of light and water on the beans' growth, but they will wait to draw their final conclusions until the end of the project. Meg shows me a resource book they have used on this project and reads a passage from it that she finds particularly interesting. Several children are reading books they have selected from the language arts area. I note that these books range in difficulty—one or two are wordless picture books, while others are very familiar stories with highly patterned language (e.g., Seuss's *Cat in the Hat*). One child appears to be engrossed in Gene Zion's *Dear Garbage Man*, which is considerably more difficult. Two of the children are using paper markers, narrow rectangular pieces of construction paper, to keep their place while reading. They have placed the markers above the line they are reading rather than below it as is the more usual case. When I ask Mrs. Malone why this is so, she tells me that placing the marker above the line fosters sentence, rather than line, reading. Tricia is using a headset to follow along with a story she is reading from a paperback book. Near the language arts area a table is set up for cooking. A list of ingredients for making tortillas hangs nearby and placed at separate stations around the table are very simple illustrations for each step of the recipe (Figure 4–1).[1] This arrangement nicely accommodates several children as each one proceeds around the table following the single-portion recipe. No one is making tortillas at the moment, since this recipe requires Mrs. Malone's supervision.

The room is graced with several interesting and attractive charts. Isabelle is making her own copy of the *Terrarium* chart hanging in the math/science area. A quick perusal of the dramatic play area reveals several children recreating a familiar

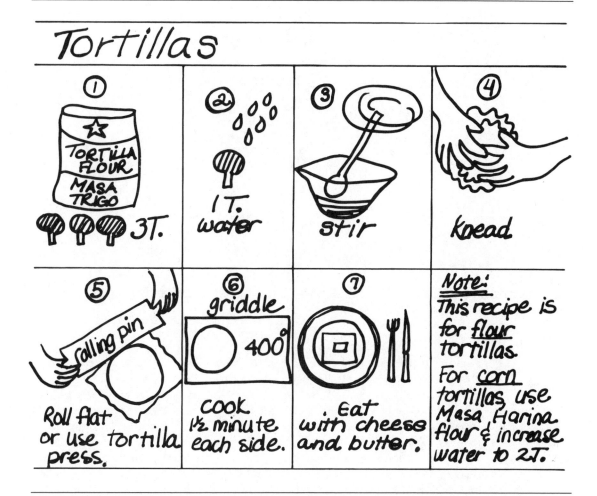

Figure 4–1   A recipe for tortillas (from *A Child's Cookbook*, Orinda Cooperative Nursery School, Orinda, CA, 1974)

domestic scene—washing and drying dishes and then stacking them away in the cabinets. Apparently, before I arrived, these children, or others who had used the area earlier, were involved in dramatizing a shopping episode. They left the shopping list shown in Figure 4–2.

Six or seven children are seated at tables. Some are working on puzzles, picture dominoes, and other commercially produced games, while others are using materials prepared by Mrs. Malone. By the time I reach Mrs. Malone, the two children who were sitting with her when I arrived have left; one of them is illustrating a dictated story, and the other has joined his pals in the dramatic play area. With Mrs. Malone now is Joey. Joey's mother has just had a baby, and she will be coming

Figure 4–2   A shopping list

home from the hospital at the end of the week. Joey has many mixed feelings about his new brother. He has been talking about the baby and is about ready to begin dictating a story for Mrs. Malone to write down. It is now 11:00. In about twenty minutes, Mrs. Malone will ask the children to put their materials away and straighten up the room. Then they will gather around her for a morning story before they go to the lavatory and are dismissed for lunch.

In Mrs. Malone's class the children, of course, are learning many things besides reading and writing. In fact, rather than being explicit subjects themselves, reading and writing are used as tools in learning about other content areas. We emphasize reading and writing because literacy is the focal point of this book.

Compare this first-grade class with the group of four-year-olds described at the end of chapter 3. Are they more alike than different? First, both classes are activity-oriented. What this means, essentially, is that they are organized around the principle, derived from Piaget's theory, that children learn by active involvement with their environment. In both classes, the teacher's role is to structure the environment in ways that will capitalize on the children's potential for learning and to intervene and interact with the children to heighten their learning. Second, in both groups the children's activities are imbued with real purpose and meaning. Children are not involved in tasks that are either arbitrary or meaningless. Instead, what the children are doing is linked to the daily life of their classes—real tasks with real meaning for them. Third, neither class is structured in artificially compartmentalized blocks of time devoted to separate learning tasks, e.g., a reading period. Learning is going on in a much more natural, real-life manner that is both integrated and continuous. Fourth, in neither class is there an artificial boundary imposed between prereading and reading experiences. Because of their greater maturity and experience with print, the six- and seven-year-olds are doing more conventional reading than the four-year-olds, yet, in both classes, the children are learning about the written form of language by active experimentation with real print for real purposes.

Regardless of age, learning to read and write requires active encounters with meaningful and purposeful written language set within natural and holistic contexts. This view contrasts sharply with the *mental age concept* in literacy, which says that learning to read should be postponed until the child has reached a mental age of six-and-a-half years. Supported by a single study conducted on a limited sample of children more than fifty years ago,[2] the mental age concept is associated with programs in which young children engage in reading readiness activities such as matching shapes and discriminating between colors. Recently, however, traditional readiness activities have begun to be replaced by drills such as "chanting," in which children recite a particular sound in unison over and over. Auditory and visual discrimination activities are being supplanted by workbooks for preschool and kindergarten children, which train them to identify and make letter/sound associations. But both the mental age concept and the *reading as skills mastery* approach miss the mark. Neither appreciates the young child's aptitude for creative problem-solving or the necessity for providing children with language experiences rich in meaning and purpose. They also ignore the fact that "simple" does not necessarily mean "easy," especially when the material children are to learn is divorced from any meaningful context.

In comparing a nursery school class and a first-grade class, we see that they can be very much alike in their understanding of how children learn and in their approach to teaching. However, we must also acknowledge important differences. The first grade is a full-day program, although all-day kindergarten programs are becoming more popular. In Mrs. Malone's first-grade class, as in most others, there is just one teacher. The first-grade curriculum is more formalized than the nursery school or kindergarten curriculum; however, a growing concern of many early-childhood specialists is the increasing tendency to formalize the kindergarten curriculum to make it more like that of a first grade. There is more "content" to be covered in first grade, and more guidelines (e.g., state or local curriculum guides) must be considered. Assessment of children's performance via testing and reporting is more prevalent. There are more intrusions into first-grade class time through the use of resource teachers, special programs, and remedial programs. Such practical considerations affect how teachers organize their classes and carry out their teaching plans. Therefore, before proceeding to look more closely at literacy instruction in the first grade, let us consider the very practical matters of classroom design and management.

Class Design and Management

One of the reasons for children's unhappiness in school is *discontinuity*, the disparity or difference between what they experience in school and what they understand. This discontinuity can take various forms: the difference between their speech and the teacher's; between how the teacher expects them to behave and how they are used to behaving; and between the limits set on their freedom in school and those outside it. Certainly, children need to learn to cope with change, and some discontinuity is necessary to create the discomfort that stimulates the search for a problem's solution. Often, however, discontinuity works against a child's learning when the class environment is the antithesis of what he has experienced at home—artificial, arbitrary, remote and dull. We have already seen how the preschool and kindergarten settings build on the child's experiences before school by creating an atmosphere that is lively, natural, and full of meaning. First grade is the time to build on the foundation laid in the preschool or kindergarten class. How can we make it a continuous experience?

Arrangement of Space

The first thing to do is to arrange a first-grade classroom very much along the lines of a preschool or kindergarten setting. The absence of blockbuilding, woodworking, and dramatic play resources in primary-grade classes is regrettable. Primary-grade youngsters delight in working with wood and blocks as well as with other media. In addition, their greater competence adds richness to the imaginative and conceptual level of their play. Such materials and media are also an excellent outlet for developing literacy skills. Unfortunately, the potential of these play materials for learning how to read and write is still not fully understood or accepted. Concerned that these materials will divert children from "real" learning, some educators substitute such things as graded readers and mimeographed worksheets for them, though these may hold little or no interest for the children and have questionable educational value.

Thus, it should *not* be the basic design of a classroom that changes in the primary grades. What distinguishes the first- (or second- or third-) grade classroom from one in the preschool or kindergarten is the sophistication of its resources, which reflect the children's development. Materials for making permanent records of observations, such as graph paper, construction paper, and scissors for bar graphs, would be set out in the math/science area. There would probably also be more books, and these would reflect a wider range of reading difficulty. There might also be a microcomputer in the language arts area in addition to a primer typewriter.

Materials

The primary classroom, like the preschool or kindergarten classroom, should be equipped to stimulate and challenge children's intelligence. This means that there should be appropriate equipment and materials in sufficient amounts and diversity to foster learning: tables and chairs to promote social interaction; easels, brushes, and paints; puzzles and games; blocks; books; writing materials; science and math equipment; balls and jump ropes; a workbench, wood, saws, and hammers; a primer typewriter; and perhaps a microcomputer. Even though this list is incomplete, it gives an idea of the range of material and equipment needed.

Knowing *what* you need and knowing *how* to obtain it are, of course, two different matters. But even with limited resources, it is possible to convert a bare room into a lively and richly engaging environment for learning. First, rearrange your own desk and the children's tables and chairs according to the kind of informal design you have seen in kindergarten classes. If there are individual desks for the children rather than tables, group these together into sets of four to six. Second, determine the room's existing supplies and equipment. Third, draw up a list of the things you consider essential for creating a good environment for learning. Remember to be practical and realistic. More can be added over time. Fourth, subtract from your list what the room already has and divide what remains into categories according to possible sources: materials that must be purchased; materials that can be found, borrowed, or collected; and equipment and supplies that you can make yourself.

Ideally, you should begin collecting good materials long before that moment of cold reckoning in an empty classroom. When you do begin, you might be surprised at how much is available just for the asking. For example, I have seen many small couches and loveseats set out on sidewalks to be carted away, that would make fine additions to classrooms with very minor repairs and cleaning. You can find useful items at flea markets and yard sales. If you know people who are purchasing new cookware, ask them for their old pots and pans, which are superior to the flimsy, doll-size equipment usually found in classrooms. Actually, practically nothing should be discarded before passing under your scrutiny—can I use this now, or perhaps later, in school? If the answer is yes, then save it from the trash heap. Some of your neighborhood stores might contribute items too—carpet squares and remnants, for example, or old wallpaper books (good for artwork such as collage). If your supply of books is meager, check some out of the local public library. If you are fortunate enough to have a school library, arrange to borrow a number of books on a monthly basis. The kindergarten teacher might be able to give you some consumables, such as tempera and construction paper, or lend you other supplies, such as blocks. You may be able to construct some equipment, such as a chart rack, yourself, or arrange for someone else to help. The children's parents can be excellent resources here.

Schedule

There are many hours in the first-grade day, especially for the recent kindergartner. How well I remember the eager faces of some children as lunch time approached. "Can we go home now?" they would ask. By midyear, almost everyone had gotten used to the full-day schedule, but it was difficult for some of them at first. Shaping the day around the familiar preschool pattern—regular routines within large blocks of alternately active and quiet time—will help to make the transition easier.

The six hours between 9:00 AM and 3:00 PM that children spend in your class may be considerably reduced, once you subtract the lunch hour and the varied claims on the five hours that remain, such as working with the remedial reading teacher or the speech teacher, or visiting the science resource room. Nonetheless, there are ways to organize your time. The day divides naturally at the noon break into a morning session of three hours and an afternoon session of two. Assume that your children have a special class (e.g., music, art, gym) three days each week.

Those children in your class who work with a special teacher (e.g., the speech teacher) leave and return to your class at various times during the day. Here is how a typical day might look:

Morning session—9:00 AM to noon

- 8:45–9:00 AM: Teacher greets the children as they arrive; they remove and store outer clothing and other possessions, check attendance and job charts, and work with quiet materials, such as puzzles and paper and pencil; some children start to work on their special projects, such as a bulletin board display.

- 9:15–9:30 AM: Children continue working quietly; teacher chats with individual children, inquiring about their specific work projects.

- 9:30–9:45 AM: Children gather around the teacher, review attendance, discuss the day's plan, and share interesting happenings.

- 9:45–10:15 AM: Class goes to the music teacher.

- 10:15–10:30 AM: Class returns to the room, visits lavatory, and has mid-morning snack.

- 10:30–11:30 AM: Children work individually and in groups in the activity areas on planned, ongoing projects, such as a science bulletin board display; on more spontaneous activities such as writing out an account of a "happening" described earlier that morning in sharing time; and in more open play activities such as block construction or painting with tempera. Teacher moves about the room unobtrusively supervising the activities, intervening when it is necessary (e.g., reminding a child who asks how to spell *skyscraper* to spell it as best he can), and talking with the children about what they are doing.

- 11:30–11:45 AM: Children clean up the room, go to the lavatory, and put their outer clothing on.

- Noon: Class is dismissed for lunch.

Afternoon session–1:00 PM to 3:00 PM

- 1:00–1:15 PM: Children return from noon recess, store outer clothing, and gather around teacher; tired after the vigorous activity on the school playground, they are ready to listen to a story.

- 1:15–2:00 PM: Children return to work in the various activity areas on individual or group projects; teacher uses this time to meet with small groups or individual children for a writing/reading conference or skill teaching (e.g., drawing inferences), or to read aloud to two or three children at a time or write down a child's dictated story.

- 2:00–2:15 PM: Children clean up the room and go to the lavatory.
- 2:15–2:45 PM: Children work on a class project under the teacher's supervision. For example, interest in the various anecdotes shared by the Hispanic children in one class has sparked an investigation of Hispanic customs. The children have already purchased the ingredients and prepared a Spanish dish, and have also learned some traditional Spanish songs. Today, the class has begun to work on a papier maché piñata for the approaching holidays. The language arts area is bright with the colorful results of this group project: recipes; song lyrics; stories; and beautiful tempera paintings depicting aspects of traditional Spanish culture.
- 2:45–2:50 PM: With the teacher's assistance, children put materials away.
- 2:50–3:00 PM: Children get their outer clothing and other possessions and gather around the teacher; they review the day's activities and make plans for tomorrow.
- 3:00 PM: Dismissal.

This is quite a busy schedule for teacher and children alike. Of the teacher it requires stamina, as well as the kind of knowledge of children we have already discussed. It also requires a well-defined teaching plan based on knowledge of how children learn to read and write, which is what this book is designed to provide. A schedule like this one, which can and should be varied in keeping with your own preferences, changing needs, and daily events, has major advantages for the children:

- It uses and directs the physical energy and enthusiasm of young children in a beneficial way.
- It values the child's expression of self, both as an individual and as part of a group, in various ways and through varied media.
- It stimulates the learning that occurs through social interaction.
- It provides a structure that is sufficiently predictable for children to feel secure enough to experiment.
- It provides many opportunities to use whole, meaningful, and integrated language.
- It enables children to use their natural abilities.
- It sets up real problems in learning for which children can devise real solutions.

Getting Started

It may be difficult to get under way with a program that requires as much teacher initiative as this one. If you have been teaching you can draw on your own experience in getting started and let the following discussion serve as a reminder of the things you need to remember to take care of. For beginning teachers, these suggestions may be even more important for getting off to a good start.

The room should be arranged and organized before the children arrive in early September. It is a good idea to model the daily schedule as closely as possible on that in the kindergarten during the first few weeks of the new school year. The children are already familiar with this plan, and it will help to make them feel comfortable in their new class. Children should not be overwhelmed with too many new activities introduced too quickly. The first few weeks are best spent in getting to know each other and in familiarizing the children with new routines. Helping first graders accustom themselves to the routine of eating lunch in school, for example, can be helpful, since even a mundane experience like this can be confusing or frightening to some of them.

The children will most likely have spent their kindergarten year in a room organized around various interest centers, so the arrangement you have designed will be familiar. Nonetheless, it is a good idea to spend time in the first few weeks introducing the children to the interest areas, acquainting them with materials and equipment, and developing guidelines and routines to assist them in knowing how to use these resources. For example, to help children learn how to assign themselves to an interest area, a pegboard chart with name tags, like the one illustrated in Figure 4–3, can be used. The children check in and out of an area with their name tags. The number of hooks in each area limits the number of children who can work there at any given time.

With experience, children become less anxious about having a chance to use all the interest areas. They learn that the materials and equipment are there for them to use and that everyone can have an opportunity to work in all the areas. With time, children will become quite independent in using the activity areas; eventually, they can organize "turns" lists themselves. One of my most cherished memories as a first-grade teacher is of a little boy who, all by himself, had set up the record player and organized a small group. Without disturbing anyone else in the class, he was teaching them a simple folk dance!

The informal reading and writing experiences of kindergarten comprise the foundation of your literacy program in the first few weeks: reading aloud to and with the children; taking down the children's individual and group dictation; and encouraging the children to read and write independently. These activities will continue to be an integral part of the program throughout the year. As you work with the children in these first few weeks of the school year, carefully observe what they are able to do in reading and writing. You will likely find some who have little or no concept of what written language is, who probably do not, as yet, understand the symbolic function of print and might not even be able to recognize or write their first names. Others will probably already display reading- and writing-like behaviors. They might be able to recall enough of the language and plot of a highly familiar story to be able to "read" it without actually identifying any of the words; or they may well be able to read and write their first names and other strongly contextualized words, such as familiar product names and signs. Finally, you may have a few children who can read some words even when the words are out of their familiar context. These children already have an implicit understanding of the link between spoken and written symbols and perhaps a beginning notion of the relationship between some sounds and letters.

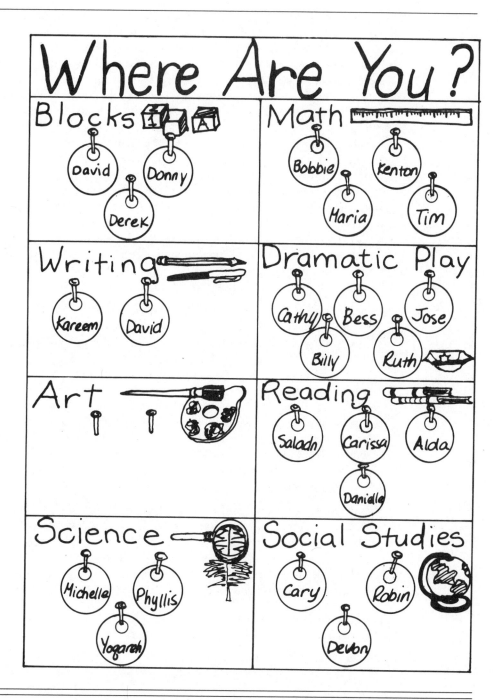

Figure 4–3   Interest area check-in chart (adapted from *Getting Started in the All-Day Kinder-garten*, New York: Board of Education of the City of New York, 1983)

Setting up reading groups now should not be a priority, but neither should you postpone opportunities for the children to read and write real language. The purpose of these first weeks of careful observation is to provide the teacher with an accurate picture of the children's current status in reading and writing so that her expectations about children's performance are appropriate and so that she can plan suitable experiences to extend and refine the children's development.

Most parents will expect their children to be plunged immediately into the typical first-grade fare of reading instruction—readiness activities, reading groups, workbooks, and take-home worksheets. Therefore, it is most important to arrange to speak to them very early about the purpose and sequence of the teaching plan. By opening this channel of communication at the beginning of the year and providing many opportunities throughout the year to continue the dialogue, you can alleviate the parents' concerns and help them understand the process of literacy development. Planning events like a "back-to-school-night" meeting, conducting conferences with individual parents, sending home informative brochures (e.g., "Reading Aloud at Home," "Suggestions for Storybooks"), and arranging informal get-togethers help to give parents the information they need to make informed decisions about their children's school programs.

Expectations.   Some educators worry about "pushing" children, while others are concerned about the effects of standards that are too low. The final answer to the question of what to expect of a particular child must depend on that child's particular needs and abilities. Here we can only suggest a general guideline. We know from research that very young children do not learn well under conditions that are either too novel or too familiar. Learning is best accomplished under what are called "mildly discordant" or novel circumstances. Applying this research to the classroom, we can say that teachers will want to challenge children to use all their abilities, try hard, and take pleasure in their accomplishments. Expectations that are either too low or too high are likely to result in failure. Expectations that are realizable, yet require the children to reach or try just a bit more, are much more apt to bring success.

When to begin reading and writing.   Finally, there ought to be no perceptible starting point for teaching reading and writing, because all the children *will be* reading and writing from the very first day of the school year as part of their everyday activities. Here is a list of some of the literacy activities one first-grade teacher's class was involved in during the first month or two of school. Notice how many activities *all* or *many* of the children were able to participate in:

- Listening to stories (all).
- Dictating group stories (all).
- Dictating individual stories (all).
- Experimenting with paper and pencil (all).
- Writing own first name (many).
- Writing for personal and functional reasons (many).

- Reading self-written texts (many).
- Copying charts (few).
- Simulating reading aloud (few).
- Recognizing words out of context (few).
- Reading a dictated story (few).
- Reading a story from a book (very few).

This teacher reported that most of the children made quite rapid progress in literacy in the first few weeks, which she attributed to two factors: that reading and writing were going on all the time and that the children needed to know how to read and write in order to participate in the normal, day-to-day business of class.

Now we are ready to consider the first-grade literacy program in more detail: reading self-composed texts; reading books and other printed texts; and writing independently.

Reading Self-Composed Material

Independently Written Material

Children's own individually written texts constitute a very important source of reading material. As Graves and Calkins have shown, when children are freed from unnecessary constraints on their writing, such as an overemphasis on mechanical correctness, and are encouraged to choose their own topics, even very young children can and do write on their own.[3] The teacher's understanding of the normal developmental sequence in writing (such as an appreciation for invented spelling), an environment where both children and teacher write all the time, and an atmosphere of warm acceptance for children's efforts, combine to stimulate young children to write. And, what they write, they read.

Once he realizes that he *can* write on his own, and that what he produces will be enthusiastically received, the young child often becomes very excited about independent writing and does it frequently. Writing becomes a tool for everyday transactions. For example, Figure 4–4 shows a note that Kelvin and Vincent passed back and forth, telling each other to "shut up!" They are both five. The words the child uses in composing are personal and meaningful, so that when he meets them again, either in his own texts or elsewhere, he may well remember them.

Writing notes, preparing reports, composing stories and poems, drawing up lists, and writing letters are just a few of the many kinds of independent writing the first grader does. The process of thinking about what he is going to write, actually putting the words down on paper while deciding how to write and spell them, reading what he has written, and possibly revising it and reading it once more, gives the child the kind of *meaningful* repetition of written forms that is so important in learning to read. Later in this chapter, we will discuss writing independently at some length.

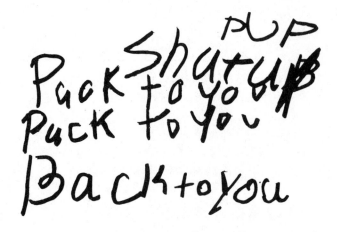

Figure 4–4   Kelvin and Vincent's note

Dictated Material

The children's individually and group-dictated stories or experience charts can also comprise a useful component of the reading program. If dictation is already familiar to the children, it can help to bridge their nursery/kindergarten and first-grade experiences. Moreover, as mentioned before, dictated material has two important qualities: it is highly motivating, since it is so personal and immediate, and it illustrates beautifully the link between the spoken and written aspects of language.

After careful observation of the children's approach to reading and writing, you should have a good idea of their understanding of print. With some children, the task will be to awaken their consciousness of print, as one would with children in kindergarten. When you record their dictation, say each word aloud as you write it. As you read it back in a natural-sounding voice, point to each word as you pronounce it. As the children join you in rereading the story, draw your hand under each line of print as you read it. Count all the words with the children and make note of words that appear more than once. Encourage the children to locate specific words and to reread the story in unison. There are other ways, as well, to heighten children's awareness of print and introduce them to the concept of words. For example, children may trace, copy, type, or stamp (with a rubber letter stamp) letters from a chart or dictated story, or reconstruct words from a chart using individual letters printed on letter cards, rubber letter stamps, a typewriter, or a microcomputer.

Key words and word banks.   A dictated story·is a veritable King Solomon's mine of reading vocabulary. Because the stories have rich associations for their authors, many of the words will be meaningful and interesting to the children who dictated them. Usually, it is the meaning-bearing or content words—nouns, adjectives, and action verbs—that children remember first. But as children recombine these words to encode new sentences, function words—conjunctions and articles—become necessary, and these too become part of the child's growing reading vocabulary.

When Sylvia Ashton-Warner worked with Maori children in New Zealand, she discovered that the children learned certain words quickly and remembered them.[4] These words, which held the most significance for the children, she called *key words*, and they became the basis of the child's reading and writing vocabularies. Key words and *word banks*, which are collections of key words of various kinds, are two important features of a *language experience approach* (LEA) to reading. According to MaryAnne Hall, in the language experience approach, instruction is built upon the use of reading materials created by writing down children's spoken language. The reading material thus represents the child's own experiences and language patterns. In addition, in LEA the communication processes of listening, speaking, reading, and writing are integrated.[5]

Select key words in the course of rereading an individually dictated story. After the child has dictated the story and you have discussed it together, read it aloud. Then invite the child to reread it with you. Based on what you know of this child's competence with print, her interest in this particular story, and her ease in rereading it along with you, determine how strongly to urge that she reread it again alone. If she does read the story alone, ask her to select some special or interesting words that she would like to keep. Underline each of these words. The next time the child reads the story with you, underline each word she still remembers again. Finally, on the third rereading of the story, type or print on a small card each word that the child can still identify. The child adds these words to her word bank, which can be a manila envelope or small box, and they become part of her own growing reading vocabulary.

Among the functions of word banks that Hall notes are these:[6]

- They comprise a record of each child's reading vocabulary.
- They are resources for writing activities.
- They provide reinforcement for learning the reading vocabulary through repeated exposure.
- They are a source of independent activities with letters, words, and sentences.

Group word banks. Interesting class or group projects often yield new vocabulary, which can be collected in *group word banks*. For example, a class study of Hispanic customs could turn up Spanish words for clothing, songs, games, and foods that could be grouped by category with their English translations. You should illustrate and type or print each word in manuscript on a three-by-five inch index card. File the cards by category in an appropriately sized file box or sturdy folder—one for animal words, another for clothing words, and so on. Title and illustrate each box or folder to identify its word category. The advantages of this kind of system are that it makes identification of word categories easy, it is very accessible to the children, and it permits the reclassification of words as needed.

Group books.   Another kind of dictated text that provides a very good source of reading material is the *group book*. Group books are collections of accounts dictated or written by individual children on a common theme. At the beginning, the topics are quite simple, and each child contributes a single sentence or phrase. For example, a prekindergarten class book on "wheels" had the following sentences, each contributed and illustrated by a different child: "Bikes have wheels"; "Cars have wheels"; "Trains have wheels"; "Planes have wheels"; "Wheels are round." After a child illustrated her page, the teacher recorded the comment below the picture and asked the child to write her name. Later, the teacher bound the stories into a very simple book. She punched three holes in the story sheets and in the oaktag front and back covers, pasted reinforcements around the holes to prevent tearing, and placed small metal looseleaf rings through the holes. She wrote *Wheels* on the front cover, and the children illustrated both front and back. (Appendix B presents directions for binding books more elaborately.) You can also purchase bound blank books that consist of twenty-eight pages of good quality white paper with a hard cover and sewn pages. (They are called *Bare Books* and can be obtained from Treetop Publications, 220 Virginia Street, Racine, WI 53405.) Group books should be set out in the language arts area for the children to browse through and read. You may want to duplicate copies of these as well for the children to keep.

More ambitious group books evolve naturally, when children are involved in a unit of study that is of sufficient interest and importance to them that they want to make a permanent record of it. This kind of group book represents truly functional writing because the book is a record of the children's observations and findings in an important investigation.

Repeated exposure to reading words.   You may find that a few children require practice in reading words to be able to remember and identify them when they meet these words outside their original context. You can design a number of activities for these children to give them repeated exposure to reading words. For example, you can use key words to play a variation of the Candyland game. A turn of the spinner or a toss of a die indicates the number of words a child must read from his word bank in order to move that number of spaces around the board. Children can also find and cut out examples of key words in old magazines, workbooks, and newspapers. They can make a dictionary of their key words by alphabetizing them, writing one word on each page of a bound book, and then adding an appropriate illustration for each word.

Duplicated copies of group stories also lend themselves to this kind of reading practice. If a child has two copies of a story, he can cut out the words from one copy and match them with the words in the intact copy. Another idea is to cut a copy of the group story first into sentence strips, next into phrase strips, and then into word strips. The child reconstructs the original story after each cutting, first from the sentences, then from the phrases, and finally from the words. Or, mix up the sentence strips from a story for the child to rearrange in correct sequence.

If they are actively involved in purposeful and interesting language experiences, most children should not require the kinds of additional practice described above.

Even when attractively presented, such practice, if used unnecessarily or inappropriately, can result in the very opposite of its intended effect, boring children and dampening their interest in reading and writing. Remember that such activities should be used sparingly and only with those children who indicate a need. Children should spend the great majority of their time in purposeful reading and writing that grows out of everyday experiences and their active exploration of interesting topics. This kind of literacy activity provides a meaningful exposure to reading words that should be sufficient for most of the children.

Reading Books and Other Printed Texts

If we were to rely solely on the children's own texts for reading material, we would be depriving them of at least two things: the chance to enjoy the pleasures of good literature and the opportunity to become familiar with the conventions of book language. By the time they get to first grade, children have had many experiences with print, if from no other source than the stories that have been read to them and that they have read in their own way in the nursery school and kindergarten. This is the tradition you will continue and expand.

The best way to do so is by reading aloud to the entire class, to small groups, and to individual children as frequently as you can. Remember, very often the book that the children will want to read by themselves is the one read aloud by the teacher.

Prerequisites

There are three prerequisites for children's reading printed texts. First, have a good collection of books and other printed materials ranging widely in reading difficulty. You can draw this pool of reading material from a variety of sources: library or trade books, textbooks in the various content areas, reference books of different kinds, graded readers, magazines, and newspapers. A number of strategies can help you collect this material. If several teachers are participating in this program, you can all pool your complete sets of different graded reading texts and then redistribute among yourselves several copies of each level from each series. You can borrow twenty-five or more different books from the school library each month. You can mount a local or even communitywide drive to collect old but usable and appropriate books. You can urge or even pester children, school personnel, and parents to donate magazines and newspapers on a regular basis. You can even start a fund to purchase some of the reasonably priced paperback editions of trade books, such as those published by Scholastic Books, Inc.

Second, have a reasonably accurate notion of the level of reading difficulty of each item in your classroom reading collection. You need this information in order to guide children in selecting material that is neither too easy nor too difficult. Being familiar with the printed material is also necessary in helping a child locate a particular book and in evaluating his grasp of the material.

You can estimate the level of reading difficulty in a given piece of material either informally or formally. Do not assume a book's difficulty simply on the basis of what *kind* of book it is. Picture books can range in reading level from the first- to the sixth-grade.[7] Even those that are wordless can be quite sophisticated.[8] Read through the book, making note of both the written text and the illustrations. Check these characteristics: length of story, length and complexity of sentences, size and complexity of vocabulary, complexity of plot, size of print, and number and size of illustrations. As you review the materials for these characteristics, you should begin to be able to group them into approximate levels of difficulty—beginning, intermediate, and advanced. Graded readers and some easy-to-read trade books indicate their reading level. The *Children's Catalogue* (New York: H. W. Wilson), summarizes the plots of many books and indicates a grade level range for each.

A more formal way to determine reading difficulty is through the use of a *readability formula*. Calculated statistically on such characteristics as the number of syllables and sentences in a passage, a readability formula can give you a more exact index of the difficulty level of a piece of reading material. The *Fry Readability Scale* (Jamestown Publishers, P.O. Box 6743, Providence, RI 02940) is packaged as a handy slide-rule-like device for easy use. While it is unnecessary to use a read-ability formula on all of your reading material, practice in applying it to some of the books will help to make your informal estimates more precise. A readability formula, however, should be used only with caution when making an individual book selection for a particular child, because the formula does not measure reader variables—interest, experience, and purpose—which are so important to the read-ing process.

Third, have an efficient organizational scheme for grouping the material by level and arranging it for children's easy access. Place books and other materials on child-level shelves in the language arts area. A simple system for organizing material is to color-code it by level of reading difficulty. Assign a color to each level: yellow for beginning, red for intermediate, and blue for advanced. Fix a strip of appropriately colored adhesive tape around the edges of each shelf to identify the level of reading material it holds. Attach a matching self-adhesive circle or other symbol to each item at each level. In this way, both you and the children can identify immediately where any piece of material belongs. Later you can expand this system to include independent activities that go along with the reading ma-terials. The activities are written up on five-by-eight inch index cards, which are stored in file boxes. Both cards and boxes are color-coded to correlate with the levels of difficulty of the reading materials. A simple and efficient system like this one facilitates easy retrieval and storage of materials and helps the children to work independently.

Books and other printed materials do *not* replace the children's self-composed texts; they simply expand what is available for children to read. By using printed matter, you merge the features of a language experience approach to literacy with the major characteristics of an *individualized reading program*: self-selection, self-pacing, and individual conferences. Children select what to read and determine how fast they read. The teacher arranges individual conferences with each child one or more times a week to assess the child's progress and to determine whether any changes in materials, experiences, or teaching strategies are needed. Some-times, based on what she learns of children's performance through individual conferences, the teacher decides to call a group together for instruction. For ex-ample, if she finds that several of the children are having difficulty in drawing inferences, she may find it more efficient to work on this with them as a group, rather than individually.

Folk Literature

The books that children read do not always have to be self-selected. *You* can introduce books that provide excellent and enjoyable reading experiences to the class. Once you have introduced a book, the children will be eager to read it on their own. Books with accompanying recordings, such as those of Bill Martin or those published by Scholastic Books, are especially useful for this purpose, since children can follow along in the text as the record or tape plays.

Folk literature provides an ideal transition from listening to reading, because its highly patterned language increases predictability. The repetitive pattern can involve words or syntax, as in "The Farmer in the Dell," or linking words, in which the ending phrase of one sentence becomes the beginning phrase of the next. Another pattern occurs in cumulative stories like "The House that Jack Built," which opens with one episode that is repeated together with the second one, then both episodes are repeated with the third one, and so on. Some folk tales combine several patterns; "The Turnip" includes repeated and linked words and cumulative structure.

In addition to its highly patterned language, folk literature is an excellent medium for reading for several other reasons: it is designed for repeated tellings (or readings); it is usually quite brief and dramatic; and its highly rhythmic character aids fluency and naturalness in reading aloud. Moreover, repeated exposure to the repetitive patterns of folk literature can encourage children to use the patterns in their own writing, substituting their own words for those in the story or poem.[9]

For all of these reasons, folk stories, poems, songs, and chants are prime candidates for conversion into Big Books, oversized versions that you rewrite and illustrate yourself or with the children.[10] First, read the story (poem, song, or chant) to the children, holding the book so that everyone can see it. As you read aloud, draw your hand under the lines from left to right. Then invite the children to read or sing along with you. Next, encourage the children to read the text alone. Perhaps two or three will want to read it in unison.

You can develop many good activities with Big Books, which the children can work on by themselves or with you: Write the story's key words on cards and illustrate major sequences in the story on other cards. Make sentence strips of important sentences from the text. Put all of these into a sturdy manila envelope and fasten it inside the back cover of the book. Some of the things the children can do with these materials are: matching word cards to words in the book; alpha-betizing word cards; tracing or copying word cards; recreating the story sequence with picture cards; matching sentence strips to sentences in the story; and, when pairs of sentence strips are provided, cutting up and then reconstructing sentences.

Graded Readers

A basal reading program is a sequential reading approach based on the assumption that learning to read consists of mastering a hierarchy of skills. It is the kind of program that is used most frequently in teaching reading.[11] It consists of a series of graded reading textbooks, generally from the readiness through the sixth-grade level. An important component is the teacher's manual that accompanies each level. The teacher's manual describes in precise detail how and when to introduce new material, what skills to teach and how to teach them, and what to do to review and reinforce these skills. Supplementary materials include workbooks, duplicating masters, charts, films, records and filmstrips, and tests.

Because the directions for the teacher are so carefully programmed in a basal reading series, an inexperienced or insecure teacher may find this kind of program useful for a time. As she gains more experience and confidence, however, the teacher can begin to introduce more individualized and novel approaches to the basal design. A typical pattern might be to begin with the traditional three reading groups that meet with the teacher every day. As the children indicate a need for diversity of experience and the teacher feels comfortable enough to begin to experiment, the pattern might change to permit the children within the groups to work on independent activities and group projects in some of the time periods originally devoted to round-robin reading. She might start, for example, by adding a special book club in which the children read trade and other kinds of books in addition to the basal readers. The children might be encouraged to report on their books in interesting ways, such as dramatizing a favorite scene, or writing an advertisement for the book. A social studies unit might lead to wider reading as well as opportunities for oral and written reporting. Gradually, the teacher may find that the basals have become a subordinate feature of her literacy program as she provides more and more language experiences that are tailored to the needs of individual children, integrate reading and writing with the entire curriculum, incorporate daily events and real experiences, contain useful and interesting information, and use the children's own language.

Sustained Silent Reading

One of the best ways to help children appreciate reading as a valuable experience is to incorporate a *sustained silent reading* (SSR) period into the daily plan. This is a period of five to twenty-five minutes when all—children, teacher, and other adults (such as student teacher or aide)—silently read a piece of material of their own choice. The children do not have to be reading in a conventional sense to participate. What *is* important is that there are no interruptions, that no reports or other records are required, that each participant selects just one piece of material for the entire session, and that the teacher participates enthusiastically along with the children.[12] In reading just as in writing, the teacher is a model the children will want to emulate.

SSR can be started at the kindergarten or nursery school level and continued through the elementary grades and beyond. The amount of time devoted to it will vary according to the children's level of development, as will the range of reading material. At all levels, however, SSR requires a large and varied collection of reading material from which to select. In addition to the classroom collection, children and teacher may want to bring in something from home to read during this period. SSR helps children to understand that reading is important enough to be savored by and for itself. It helps to counteract the effect produced by a hurried reading of short or fragmented texts, which often characterizes reading in school.

The Individual Conference

The individual conference is crucial in your teaching plans for several reasons: it is a time for you to determine how well a child is progressing; it is an opportunity for you to give individual attention to the child; it is a chance to interact with the child in a friendly and supportive way; and it provides an opportunity to decide on whether to alter your teaching strategies and materials, based on what you have learned from meeting with the child. Because the individual conference is relatively short (generally five to fifteen minutes) and infrequent (one to three times a week), you must use the available time carefully.

There are several teaching strategies you can use to structure a conference in order to make it as useful as possible. *Scaffolding* is a concept that developed out of research on the interaction of parents with very young children who were learning to speak. The adult reduces the child's difficulties in carrying out some task by limiting the number of alternatives available. In looking at a book with a toddler, for example, the adult might say, "Uh-oh. Who's waiting for Angus on the other side of the hedge? See the geese. What's going to happen to Angus when they see him?" Some object to the concept of scaffolding because they find it too asymmetrical. It assumes a dominant role for the adult and a passive one for the child. Instead, they use Halliday and Hasan's notion of *tracking*, in which both participants interact more equally.[13] In conversation, the partners track each other, each making note of what the other says and adjusting to it. Both participants actively structure the conversation. Using tracking in the individual conference, you would try to elicit the child's comments and reactions and use them as the basis for your own reactions and interpretations. You would regard the child as a significant participant.

The conference gives you a chance to sample, in a general way, the child's reading comprehension, word identification, interest, and fluency. However, your records may also remind you to check on some specific behaviors as well—how the child blends sounds or recalls a sequence of facts, for example.

At some point during the morning or afternoon work period, ask a child to join you at the table in the language arts area. It is important that this be a relaxed and comfortable meeting. The child joins you with her folder and book. Have a pencil and the form you use to keep track of the child's performance. In the following example, it is March in the first-grade year. Melissa's performance is about average in her class (M = Melissa, T = Mrs. Kaufman):

T: Hi, Melissa! How you doin' today?

M: Fine.

T: Have you finished reading *The Three Billy Goats Gruff*?

M: Uh huh.

T: Did you like it?

M: Yes! Remember, you read it to us. Now *I* can read it too!

T: What part did you like the best?

M: Oh, when the Big Billy Goat Gruff beat up the mean old Troll.

T: Can you read that part to me?

[M reads aloud with some hesitation, but finishes the passage.]

T: That's great, Melissa. Some of these words are very hard, aren't they?

M: Yeah.

T: This one *[points to* crushed*]*, for example. Remember?

M: *Cr* . . . Oh, I know. "Crushed him to bits, body and bones."

T: Right. Do you think the billy goats were right to beat up the troll?

M: Yes!

T: How come?

M: 'Cause he wouldn't let them cross the bridge to get grass.

T: I see. I think the troll was a bully. Are you going to use this story for a project?

M: Well, maybe we could do a play. I could be the big billy goat, so then I need two more billy goats and the troll. *[Giggles.]* I think Bobby should be the troll.

T: Do you want to make a play of *The Three Billy Goats Gruff* ?

M   *[Excitedly]*: Yes!

T: Okay. Let's write this down.
      [On a three-by-five-inch card, T *writes:]*

Melissa	*March 15, 1982*
<u>Project</u>: A Play of	
"The Three Billy Goats Gruff"	
<u>Need</u>: 3 billy goats	
1 troll	

T: You can decide later if you want costumes. Okay? Let's read this together. *[M and T read project card.]* At our next conference, will you be ready to tell me when you're going to do the play?

M: Uh huh.

T: Fine, Melissa. Are you set on this? *[Gives card to M.]*

M: Uh huh. Oh, Mrs. Kaufman, how can we make the bridge and things?

T: Can you use some furniture?

M: Oh, I know. We can use a table and put a chair on both sides to climb up on it.

T: That's a great idea! Now, have you found another book to read?

M: Remember the book about cats that you read to us?

T: You mean *Millions of Cats*?

M: Yes, that one. Can I read that one?

T: Sure, Melissa. I think you'll find it on the red shelf. Go get it now.

[M finds the book.]

T: Okay, Melissa. You read *Millions of Cats* and we'll get together again on Thursday to talk about it. Okay?

M: Okay.

After the conference, Mrs. Kaufman makes some brief notes about Melissa's reading of *The Three Billy Goats Gruff*, the anticipated dramatization, and her new selection.

With careful preparation and support from you, most of the children will be able to operate as independently as Melissa after the first six to eight weeks of the school year. You may find that a few of them are capable of initiating and carrying out very worthwhile learning experiences with even less intervention on your part. While your basic role is to monitor, guide, and assist all the children where necessary, how much guidance they need from you will vary.

You are likely to find a few children who are capable of much independent work, but the majority will probably require a good deal of guidance on your part. Remember, they are just six years old. The least mature children will need your supervision the most: meeting frequently with them in individual conferences; keeping very close tabs on progress; monitoring carefully their carrying through of tasks; and supervising directly their work on assignments. Your goal should be to help every child become an independent, active, and creative learner. Always praise the children for initiative. Show them you value self-determination and autonomy.

Parents

Children should be encouraged to take both books and self-composed texts home to read with parents and others. The additional practice will be beneficial, and their sense of accomplishment and pride in being able to read to loved ones will be highly motivating. A good way to facilitate reading at home is to start a lending library of books in the classroom. If the system is simple and efficient even the youngest children can participate in the checking in and out of books. For example, the titles of books to be loaned can be printed on tongue depressors. When a child borrows a book he places its sign in a can clearly labeled "Out," and then when he returns the book he moves the book sign to another can labeled "In." You can keep your own record of when and by whom a book was borrowed. For children more proficient in writing, you can use a file box of three-by-five-inch index cards on which a child would write the name of the book and the date it was borrowed, and then either note the return date or cross out the title when he brings the book back.

Parents must be informed participants, however, for children's literacy experiences at home to be successful. As we observed in the first chapter, parents and other concerned persons should understand the goals and practices of your literacy program. You can use both informal and planned meetings, letters, and brochures to accomplish this. Parents also need to know *how* to use the material their children bring home effectively: for example, to read a book or story aloud first to the child and then together with the child, and finally to encourage the child to read it alone. Some parents may have unreasonable expectations for their children, such as perfection in oral reading or recognition of every new word after a single exposure. Parents should be helped to see the parallels between children's development in spoken language and their development in written language. They should be encouraged to adopt the same kind of positive and accepting attitude to their children as they learn to read and write that they showed when their children were learning to speak.

Ongoing and informative contacts between you and the children's immediate family are the best antidote to unreasonable expectations. Occasionally, a single graphic experience can go a long way toward helping parents better understand what is involved in reading and writing. I found the use of Squiggle Primers with parents on Open School Night to be both amusing and informative. These were little books that simulated the sentence patterns and vocabulary of real primers (e.g., *See Spot run.*). The only difference was that I created a new alphabetic symbol for each letter:

$$! = s \qquad '' = e \qquad \# = p \qquad \$ = o$$
$$\% = r \qquad \& = u \qquad ' = t \qquad @ = n$$

Thus, *See Spot run* read *!'''' !#$' %&@*. The parents had to deduce the new letters in order to read the primers, and in the process they learned something about beginning reading.

Writing Independently

Just as the first grader will demonstrate increasing mastery in reading conventional print, he will also be able to do more encoding himself in conventional written symbols. What is needed for this to occur, however, are three essential qualities of language experience that are too often missing in school: *functionality, interactivity*, and *self-generation*.[14] Children need to use language to get things done; they must be able to communicate freely with each other; and they must have the freedom to select the topic of their communication. A successful writing program is one that has these qualities built in. Donald Graves' ongoing observations of the composing processes of elementary school children bear this out.[15] Graves has found that when children decide whether or not to write and select what to write about, they write longer and more frequently than when topics are assigned. Moreover, he has found that children do not need contrived motivation for writing in the kind of informal environment we have described. Children want to write when they have something they know will be accepted and valued to communicate, and when they are given sufficient time and encouragement.

One of the inevitable consequences of a program in which writing goes on all of the time is that children begin to write independently. Although the timing will vary from child to child, first efforts at independent writing are usually of a practical, rather than an imaginative, nature. Researchers have even found that children as young as three will "sign in" to the classroom when they arrive each morning.[16] One child will ask to make an entry into a log about a baby hamster's growth, while another may write an invitation to his parents to a PTA tea. Figure 4–5 presents several examples of first-graders' writing efforts.

Halliday identifies seven functions of spoken language:[17]

1. *Instrumental* (I want): to satisfy personal needs.
2. *Regulatory* (Do as I tell you): to control another's behavior, feelings, or attitudes.
3. *Interactional* (Me and you): to get along with, as well as separate oneself from others.
4. *Personal* (Here I come): to express individuality and concepts about self.
5. *Heuristic* (Tell me why): to seek and test knowledge.
6. *Imaginative* (Let's pretend): to create new worlds and fantasies.
7. *Representational* (I've got something to tell you): to communicate information and descriptions, and to express propositions.

When writing is an ongoing part of each day's activities, the seven functions of spoken language find expression in written language as well. Here are some examples of writing activities for each of the functions:

1. *Instrumental:* Signing up for activities; making lists of needed supplies; writing on topics such as "What I Want for Christmas."
2. *Regulatory:* Making signs; writing directions; drawing up rules for activities such as use of the blocks.
3. *Interactional:* Writing notes to classmates and teacher; writing letters; writing invitations.
4. *Personal:* Dictating stories individually; writing stories independently; composing books about self and family.
5. *Heuristic:* Writing up observations of, for example, a science experiment; composing questions; composing a book to summarize findings of an investigation.
6. *Imaginative:* Dictating and writing stories; writing the script for a simple dramatization of a familiar story; drawing a simple comic strip and writing the characters' dialogue.

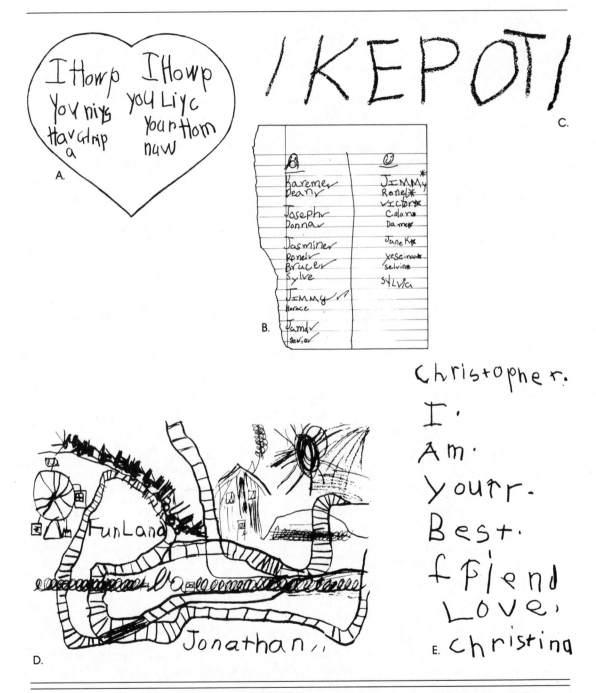

7. *Representational:* Writing messages; preparing a bulletin board display; contributing to a class newspaper.

Encouraging Independent Writing

Teachers can encourage independent writing by providing each child with a book consisting of several blank, unlined pages stapled together inside a cover of heavier paper, such as oaktag. Children begin to use these books by drawing in them. You can write the child's brief description below each picture as a caption. The child can trace over the caption or rewrite it just below your sample. Sometimes children expand these books into journals, in which they record accounts of particularly interesting occurrences.

Most children do not need special encouragement to write when they are in a program where writing goes on all the time as an integral component of each day's events. In such an environment, writing is not a special event, such as each Thursday's "creative writing period." It is, instead, simply another outlet for communication—a way to convey and receive ideas and feelings. When writing is so familiar, and when the attitude toward writing encourages experimentation and choice, most children write freely and frequently.

But even in this kind of setting some children may require more assistance to get going. For such children, one way to start is to gather three or four of them around the table in the language arts area to discuss a recent experience, such as a trip, which would be the story theme. Have the children recall the experience by asking focusing questions: where did we go; do you remember how ———; what did ——— look (sound, smell, etc.) like; what did you learn about ———; did you enjoy ———; etc. In addition to stimulating the children's recollection of the experience, the purpose of the discussion is to generate ideas for writing and to demonstrate acceptance of the children's contributions. Encourage the children by receiving their ideas warmly: "That's a very good idea, Geraldine. I'll be looking for that in your story." You want to encourage the children to express themselves orally, because talking and writing are interdependent.

Once the children start writing their stories, your task is to encourage them. This is definitely not the time to be concerned about neatness and form. As a matter of fact, one of the things you want children to understand about writing is the need for revision. This means accepting erasure, crossing out, and generally messy papers as part of the writing process. Encourage the children to spell words as best they can. "Listen to the word. Spell it the way it sounds to you. You can change it later if you need to." Stories are usually short, and after fifteen to twenty minutes you can invite those who want to, to read their stories aloud to the others. Your own enthusiasm and support and the favorable reaction of their classmates will create interest in this new activity.

Sharing

The opportunity to share their work with others provides children with an excellent motivation for writing, *if* their work is received with respect and enthusiasm. Your own role as a model is very important here. When you read or listen to a child's work, always comment on its positive features first. Be especially alert to personal touches, those features of the writing that mark it as an individual's own, unique work. Direct the other children's attention to what is good about the writing: "*Snowflakes felt like flower petals* is a very nice way to describe snowflakes, Robert. It helps us to remember how soft they are. Rita wrote, *Snowflakes feel like my puppy's nose.* That's very good, too. How are snowflakes and your puppy's nose alike, Rita?" "They're both wet!" This approach not only engenders enthusiasm for writing, it is also an unobtrusive way to teach children how to use language effectively in writing.

It is important to allow children to decide whether or not to share their work. Writing is often a very personal matter, and the child's privacy should be respected. Once they see that their work is treated with kindness and positive interest, however, most children will be eager to share it. When a child asks that a paper not be read aloud, respect her wish, of course, but remember to make a favorable comment about it nonetheless.

In addition to reading aloud, sharing writing can take other forms. Collections of independently written accounts on the same topic or theme can be bound as class books in the same way the dictated stories were. Duplicating copies of these class books for each child provides another excellent source of reading material. Make attractive displays of the children's writing on bulletin boards both inside and outside the classroom, or have stories published in the school newspaper. But if children feel they must compete for the public display of their work it may trigger rivalry and feelings of insecurity. It is possible to recognize and reward excellence without creating a sense of inferiority in some of the children: first, by concentrating on what is positive in each child's work; and second, by reserving your more evaluative comments for the privacy of individual conferences. If you do use some form of public display of writing, therefore, it is essential to have a system in which all of the children will have the opportunity to display their work at one time or another. Rather than displaying only the best work of the best writers, display the best work of *all* the children.

The Individual Writing Conference and Revising

One of the most exciting experiences children can have in first grade is to see their own development in writing over time. Each child should have an individual folder in which he can store his dated writing samples to show a clear chronology. Changes in handwriting, spelling, and content are remarkable, as the sample of one first-grader's work in Figure 4–6 illustrates. Note how the illustrations that accompany the writing start as a predominant feature of the text, and end as an incidental one.

The child's writing folder is the focal point of his conference with you. The folder can also be very useful when conferring with parents, because it contains concrete examples that illustrate and describe their child's progress.

By concentrating on the child's *own* work as represented by the samples in his folder, you shift the standard of comparison from his classmates to himself. How well Johnny is doing is judged by how well Johnny has done. Schools provide

Figure 4–6   Samples of one first grader's work. A: September 1985. B: Mid-October 1985. C: Late November 1985.

Continued

"Do This, Do That"

I have a problem. When I am doing my homework nobody even talks to me. When I want to watch T.V. my mom calls me to the dinner table. I have to go! I go. Please help me! won't you please help me? I don't like it at all.

D.

E.

Jennifer the Gingerbread Girl

The old woman opened the oven to see if I was done. I ran away through her garden down the road and then a bear ate me. I tickled the bear's tummy. He opened his mouth and I ran out. Then I ran through the grass there was a land of gingerbread men. I stayed there. I met all the gingerbread men. We had a party. then after that we played a game. We had fun! Then we all went to sleep. We all got up in the morning. we had breakfast. We play in the garden all morning. Then we had lunch. We went swimming. We had fun! Then we went to bed. We lived happy ever after.
The End

Tell Me a Silly Willy Story

One day I was walking in the air. I saw a bush. I said hello to the bush. The Bush said Hi to me! Then I jumped down from the sky. I saw a desk floating in the sky. Th I saw my mom floating and my dad flying. I flew to school. and wrote a story with my hair. I walked up the wall and the whole class was sitting on the board. The teacher section the side of her desk and landed. Then everybody said This is lots and lots of fun. I I met a cat in school. It was red, purple, green, orange, yellow and blue. The walked on my head. Then a dog come in and played a game with me.

F.

G.
Memorial Day

On Monday May 26th it is Memorial Day. You should put your head down and pray. You should pray for soldiers. The soldiers fought in the war. They fought for freedom. They fought for America. We remember them. We should respect them! May 26 is It is very important date! It is one of the most impatant holidays! We have no school because it is an important holiday and we don't take off just because we want to. Was your Dad in the Army? My Dad was in the Army. The Army is not fun to be in. You have to fight in the Army. Nobody likes to be in the Army! Do you know what the red means on the flag! It means blood. Red is the color of blood. I'm glad America is free!!!!!!

Figure 4–6   Samples of one first grader's work. D: Early December 1985. E: Late January 1986.
Continued   F: Early March 1986. G: May 1986.

many opportunities to measure children against each other through tests, report cards, grade sheets, and the like. *Your* evaluation should be of a more personalized nature. Careful examination of Johnny's performance will reveal specific information on his growth in literacy, which you can use to help set reasonable expectations and goals for him. In addition to the child's folder, your own notes on aspects of his development in writing—originality, spelling, handwriting, and story sense—will be useful in the conference.

When the child's writing is the focus of a conference, begin by inviting her to read her most recent additions to the folder. Make positive comments on her writing and note the growth she has shown since you last met for this purpose.

One of the goals of the literacy program is to teach children that writing requires revision or reshaping. An excellent way to do this is through your own example. When preparing some written communication, such as a letter to parents, allow the children to see you revise it. Show them how you must pay conscious attention to such matters as clarity, organization, and description to make it the best letter that you can. "Will the parents understand what I mean here? Is there another way to say this more clearly? I think I should move this sentence to the end." When children see that revision is a normal part of the writing process, they may be ready to revise their own work. For some children, this may not occur until late in the first-grade year, or even later in the primary grades. Children need time to develop their composing abilities before they can think about refining their work. Often, it is not the idea of revision itself, but rather, the difficulty and tedium of the mechanics of rewriting that postpones revision. One way to help is to solicit revisions from the child and then write down his dictated revised version for him.

To begin, select a written account in which the child is particularly interested. After he has read, and you have praised, the story, pose some questions that are parallel to the ones he has seen you use on your own written work: "Why did Funny Bunny run away from home? [No clear indication in the story.] How do you want to say that Funny Bunny was afraid of the Blue Monster? Where does this new sentence go?" In the very beginning, you might want to write what the child decides he wants to insert or add; this will save time and fortify the young writer. But encourage the child to take as much control of the revision process as he can and as soon as he can. Start very slowly and praise the child's revised version warmly: "Geoff, this is much clearer. Now I can understand why Funny Bunny was afraid. Please read the story. I'd like to hear it again."

Your questions will help to guide the child to attend to significant points. Usually, they will be of three broad kinds:

- *Process questions:* Why do you want to write this story? What are you going to write next? Do you think you could write this a different way?

- *Information questions:* Where did you lose your present? How did you feel about losing your present? Who owned the puppy?

- *Evaluation questions:* What part of the story do you like the best? How do you feel about writing this story? Is there something about the story you would like to change?

As children grow older, they develop a better sense of audience. Their thinking and writing become more decentered, and they no longer omit details necessary for understanding the plot (e.g., the cause of Funny Bunny's fear). It is easier for them to attend to language directly as their metalinguistic awareness grows. At this point, many children are able to work in small groups at proofreading, revising written work, preparing rough drafts, and starting over, if necessary.

Handwriting

Part of being able to write independently is gaining a mastery of the physical act of writing. However, handwriting is often difficult for young children for several reasons. It requires a degree of small-muscle control and near-point visual accommodation some six-year-olds may not yet have achieved. The relatively frictionless contact of pencil on paper makes controlling the pencil difficult. And writing is tiring work.

The best way for children to learn handwriting is naturally and functionally. When a three- to five-year-old's playful experimentation with writing nonconventionally is encouraged in nursery school and kindergarten, she has the chance to explore and learn about the business of encoding meaning in written symbols. Scribbling around, not merely under, drawings, writing strings of letters, numerals, and nonconventional symbols in a letter to Grandma, as well as signing her name to her art work in increasing approximations to standard forms are all activities that help the young child master handwriting.

Children learn handwriting functionally as a natural part of their day-to-day communication. They write notes to the teacher. They sign their names to pictures. They send letters home. Children learn to write because they need to know how to write. What you can do is help them acquire handwriting skills as efficiently as possible. There are several ways to go about it. First, select a particular manuscript alphabet system, learn it, and use it consistently. The choice may not even be yours—the system may have been selected for you by your school—but there are only slight variations among the different systems with no apparent effect on ease of learning. Whichever system you have, you should be sufficiently skilled in it to be able to write on chalkboard and paper easily and quickly. A manuscript chart should be prominently displayed in the room at the children's eye level, and each child should have a personal copy of the manuscript alphabet as well. The terminology you use to describe handwriting should be accurate and consistent: e.g., uppercase letter, lowercase letter, alphabet.

Second, choose suitable paper. Unlined paper may be best for children who do not project print in lines across the paper, and it is less likely to distract children from the composing process before they are really ready to be concerned with matters of form, such as penmanship. At some point, however, most children will want to use lined manuscript paper to write on, especially when they see you using it yourself. I have found that the best paper has ruled one-inch spaces divided in half with dotted lines. The one-inch spaces are separated by half-inch spaces to accommodate lowercase letters that fall below the line (Figure 4–7). The dotted midline provides a helpful guideline for sizing the letters. Children can negotiate

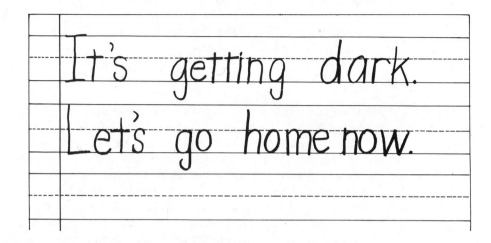

Figure 4–7   Ruled paper with guidelines for manuscript letters

the one-inch overall space of each line without too much difficulty. When children use paper with wider spaces, they often have trouble maintaining control of the pencil on the paper and find it difficult to make full circles and straight lines when the distance the pencil must travel is too great.

Children are routinely offered jumbo or oversized pencils in kindergarten and first grade because it is believed that they lack sufficient small-muscle control to handle regular pencils. However, most young children write at home with regular-size pencils and are used to them. They could probably continue to use them in school without harm. Fine-line felt-tip markers are also familiar writing implements to many children. In addition to their attractive colors, felt-tip markers provide more friction on the writing paper and are, therefore, easier to control than pencils. Of course, they are more expensive than pencils and dry out quickly if left un-capped.

Third, show children how to hold a pencil and position their paper correctly for writing. The pencil should be held firmly about one inch above the point, between the thumb and the index finger, and the remaining fingers used as support under the pencil's shaft. Encourage the child to use whichever hand she is com-fortable with. This will be the hand that she usually uses to pick something up or extends when she is offered something to hold. Manuscript paper should be placed directly in front of the child on the table and should slant about thirty degrees to the right for the left-handed child and somewhat less to the left for the right-handed child. The child should place whichever hand she is not using in writing at the top of the paper to prevent it from slipping.

With encouragement and many opportunities to write for real purposes, the first grader will learn to write all the letters. This is definitely *not* the time to be concerned about perfection of form. Such fussiness will do little more than instill in children an intense and long-lived distate for writing. The older child's greater familiarity with the forms, combined with his increasing sense of audience and his growing understanding of the importance of communicating comprehensibly, will help to sharpen his skill in handwriting.

Matters of Form

Most people are much more tolerant of variations in speech than they are of those in writing. We enjoy hearing the differences in pronunciation and vocabulary among people from various parts of the country as long as their dialects do not vary too greatly from what is considered standard or accepted usage. Parents do not correct their young children's speech. They seem to understand intuitively that such things as overgeneralization are indications of growth and not simply errors. But writing receives a very different reaction, perhaps because it is more formal than speaking. A beginner's spelling errors, for example, are rarely appreciated as signs of his developing grasp of written language. While we may enjoy listening to different dialects, writing, for the most part, is supposed to be *adialectal* (without dialect). Thus, even very beginning writers who are at the stage in writing independently that is equivalent to the toddler in speaking are often held accountable for matters of form.

Teachers who correct a beginner's writing for spelling, punctuation, and gram-mar totally forget that it represents the child's first efforts. Such an approach ignores the facts of development. We know that a skill must first be well established before it can become part of the child's regular repertoire of behavior. The child must practice and refine the skill until he can use it efficiently and easily. At this point, the skill often becomes a tool for accomplishing other goals. This is what happens in learning to sit up, walk, read, and write. If we were teaching someone to swim, would we insist that his timing be perfect or that he be able to do the butterfly stroke? Certainly not! In the beginning, we would concentrate on simply keeping him afloat, and his clumsy, uncoordinated movements would be perfectly acceptable. As the swimmer became more skilled, we would begin to attend more closely to matters of form. Likewise, in working with the beginning writer, teachers should concentrate on appreciating the child's first efforts, putting concern with matters of form aside for the time being and focusing on *what* the child writes rather than on *how* he writes it.

Concern with matters of form at an inappropriate time can have a very det-rimental effect on a child's writing. Writing is difficult enough to begin with. If the child is burdened additionally with criticism on matters of form, she may simply decide it is easier *not* to write at all. Surely some of the moans I hear in response to a teacher's announcement of a writing activity are from children who have learned to dislike writing for this very reason. Most writers in the field of beginning literacy agree that children are encouraged to write when teachers ignore mis-spellings and other mechanical errors and reward expression and creativity instead. Donald Graves reminds us that we should allow children the same freedom to make mistakes in their writing that they have in the equivalent stage in their oral language development.[18] When children are just beginning to write, they need to feel confident enough to take risks, but it is difficult to take risks when your every move is being evaluated.[19]

When children have many opportunities to write in an atmosphere that encourages writing, they are able to acquire writing skills without duress. Quite often, by the time the child has developed a degree of writing proficiency, her sense of audience is developed too, so that she understands the *need* for correct spelling, punctuation, and grammar. Later in the primary grades, the child appreciates that in order for *others* to be able to understand what she has written, she must write (or rewrite) it correctly. Writing conferences with the teacher and with classmates offer excellent opportunities to learn the mechanics of writing functionally and meaningfully. Research indicates that children do become proficient in the mechanics of writing when they are in the kind of literacy program I have described. Children in language experience programs, for example, have significantly higher achievement in spelling than children in other kinds of reading programs.[20] And Burrows, Jackson, and Saunders, who studied the writing development of elementary school children over several years, found that the mechanical skills children first mastered in writing they meant to share with others eventually transferred to strictly personal writing.[21]

Summary

This chapter has concentrated on how to foster reading and writing at the beginning of the primary grades. Incorporating some of the positive features of the preschool or kindergarten class helps children to make the transition from preschool to primary grades and allows them to build on their earlier literacy experiences. In first grade, children have more sustained and formal contact with written language in these ways:

- Reading self-composed texts.
- Building word banks of key words.
- Composing group books.
- Reading books and other printed texts.
- Writing independently.

Activities

1. Use several group-dictated stories from a first-grade class to develop a series of matching and discrimination activities that will give children practice with the vocabulary in the stories. The activities should be appropriate for the children's level of achievement and interests and allow children to work independently once the activities have been explained to them.

2. Arrange to visit a kindergarten and a typical first-grade class. Contrast the arrangement of space, the schedule, and the materials available in both

rooms. Describe how you would modify the first-grade class in order to create an environment that fosters literacy learning.

3. Select a folktale with a short, simple plot and repetitive language. Read it with a first grader who knows you. Reread it and invite the child to read along with you. How many rereadings are necessary before the child can recall the words of a repetitive pattern all by himself? Describe some activities you can create with this folktale to help the child learn to read it.

4. Ask a first-grade teacher if you can see one child's writing samples collected over several months, or, preferably, over an entire year. Analyze the writing samples for changes in handwriting, spelling, sentence structure, plot, detail, and expressiveness. Describe how these characteristics develop in the child's writing. Cite specific examples to illustrate indications of growth.

5. Compare a set of first-grade level basal readers, several stories individually composed by first-grade children, and several trade or library books suitable for reading by first graders. Describe how these three sets of reading materials differ in vocabulary, sentence structure, topic, plot, and imagination.

Further Reading and Viewing

Printed Material

Ashton-Warner, S. *Teacher*. New York: Simon and Schuster, 1965.

Flood, J., and Lapp, D. *Language/Reading Instruction for the Young Child*. New York: Macmillan, 1981.

Hall, M. A. *Teaching Reading as a Language Experience*. 3d ed. Columbus, Ohio: Merrill, 1981.

Holdaway, D. *The Foundations of Literacy*. Sydney, Australia: Ashton Scholastic, 1979.

Temple, C. A., Nathan, R. G., and Burris, N. A. *The Beginnings of Writing*. Boston: Allyn and Bacon, 1982.

Filmstrip

Reading—A Way to Begin (includes record). New York: Bank Street College of Education.

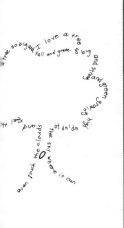

Chapter 5

Becoming Proficient in Reading and Writing

Preview

By the time they reach the upper primary grades (grades two to three), children have several years of experience with written language behind them. Yet some will still be struggling to decipher the written code, while others will already have sufficient control of it to be able to use their literacy skills as tools for learning. Regardless of their level of achievement, however, children are ready to begin to use their abilities in expanded ways to learn more about their world. This chapter discusses how the teacher can help children do this with confidence, extend their reading and writing to a range of purposes, and continue to develop confidence in their literacy skills in the later primary grades. The themes explored in this chapter include:

1. *Useful strategies for working successfully with children of widely varying abilities.*
2. *Organizing the classroom in order to encourage children's self-sufficiency.*
3. *Helping children learn to read expository material.*
4. *Techniques that children can use to gather and organize material for reports.*
5. *Helping children learn to write in their own words.*
6. *Emphasizing silent reading.*
7. *Ways to stimulate poetry and story writing.*
8. *Using creative dramatics.*
9. *Criteria to use in selecting poetry to read aloud to the children.*
10. *Using choral reading.*
11. *Poetic forms that would be appropriate for primary-grade children to experiment with.*
12. *Some good strategies for teaching second- and third-grade children: cursive handwriting, punctuation, and spelling.*
13. *The revising process.*

A Third-Grade Class

Mrs. Trapasso could hardly believe that this evening would be her eighth Back-to-School Night meeting. Eight years of teaching, mostly third-grade classes, seemed to have flown by. As she looked around her room, checking on the bulletin board displays and the materials carefully arranged for the parents to peruse, her face brightened in a smile. Remembering how she dreaded that first Back-to-School Night and the nervousness and uncertainty of her first year or so of teaching, she felt a sense of accomplishment in her growth as a teacher. She had learned from the courses she took at the university, from her contact with other professionals through conferences, books, and journals, and from her colleagues and supervisors. But Mrs. Trapasso was convinced that the children in her classes had been her best teachers. And now, a month and a half into the new school year, she was still learning.

Satisfied that everything was just right, Mrs. Trapasso walked over to the door of the classroom to greet the parents as they arrived. Outside, a table had been set up with some light refreshments. She had learned that this helped to set a congenial mood for the evening and eased the sometimes awkward first moments of the parents' arrival. After the parents had helped themselves to the refreshments, Mrs. Trapasso invited them to look around the room and then seat themselves at the tables.

When it appeared that everyone who was coming had arrived, Mrs. Trapasso sat down in one of the children's chairs and began to speak. "I'm so pleased that all of you were able to come this evening. Even though we will have many opportunities to communicate this year at conferences, during Open School Week, and so forth, Back-to-School Night is an especially fine chance to talk about the goals I have for your children this year and the plans I am making to achieve those goals.

"You know, before you arrived tonight I found myself almost chuckling at my own inexperience when I first began to teach. As a matter of fact, some of *you* know about that inexperience too, when some of your older children were in my classes. Right? Ah hah, is that what those looks of fear and trepidation were all about when I greeted you tonight? [All laugh.] Well, you can relax. Thanks to your patience and all that I have learned about children from the many I have worked with over the years, I have been able to develop a teaching plan that is suited to how children learn.

"Think of your own kids now in this class. How would you describe them?" The parents had little difficulty in responding: "Rambunctious." "Curious." "Independent." "Mischievous." "A dynamo." "Exactly," said Mrs. Trapasso. "Yet, most school programs seem to be designed for the very opposite kinds of traits—passivity and dependence. Most classes today are not very different from those you and I knew as children: a lockstep approach to teaching with lots of drills and busywork to take up the slack. Hardly a plan to foster imagination and a desire to learn.

"Let me tell you about what we do in this room. Children know a lot. They come to school with many interesting experiences. And they want to learn more *if* we listen to them, *if* we acknowledge that what they tell us is important, and *if* we use their interests and energy in teaching them. In the first couple of weeks of school, I direct most of my energy at finding out about the children in my class. What are their interests? What do they know? What do they want to know more about? I want to learn as much about them as individuals as I can. I want to know what makes them tick. [Many of the parents were smiling now.] Because, you see, when I do, then I can develop a unit of study that captivates their interest and challenges them to learn. Ideally, these units of study develop around the interests of a group of three to five children. You know, sometimes it's hard for us teachers to acknowledge, but children learn more from each other than they do from "traditional" sources such as schools; even the research bears this out. But I do not discourage a child who wants to pursue her study alone. Think of Edison and Galileo. And for those who still need the security of more structure and teacher guidance, I develop a *class* unit of study.

"Now, let me show you some examples of the work produced by children in some of my other classes." At this point, Mrs. Trapasso held up or pointed out in the room: an elaborate report on the topic of pollution in the school's immediate vicinity; an exquisite map constructed by a group of children after a thorough study of a local conservation area; and a collection of samples of advertising bias, including an audiotape. "But as captivating as these *products* of learning are, I want to stress the significance of the *learning process*. That is what the children will take with them when they leave this class: a spirit of inquiry and a knowledge of how to find out.

"Now, time's awastin', as they say, and I know you have important questions you want to ask. Mr. Turner?"

Mr. Turner: I wish my third-grade teacher had been more like you, rather than . . . Well, anyway . . . [*parents laugh*]. What do you do about the skills? As everybody is happily pursuing their studies, when do you teach them reading, writing, and 'rithmetic?

Mrs. Trapasso: Good question, Mr. Turner. As the children pursue their studies, I confer with them individually. In the course of doing this, I assess how they are progressing in their literacy skills. When necessary, I spend time during individual conferences or arrange to work with children in small groups to instruct them in some skill they have demonstrated a need for. The essential point is that I teach according to their needs. Sometimes, I teach whole-class lessons, too, for example in teaching the cursive alphabet. And there is much valuable learning of a *purposeful* nature that goes on in the course of intensively studying some topic. You would not believe the amount of mathematical work that was involved in the pollution study I showed you earlier. Mrs. Wright, did I see your hand up before?

Mrs. Wright: How in the world do you keep track of what everybody's doing?

Mrs. Trapasso: By building the recordkeeping into the children's work as much as possible. The best example of this I can show you is here in this box. [*Mrs. Trapasso pointed to a gaily painted corrugated box next to her.*] Here is where we keep the children's writing folders. [*Looks of acknowledgment on several parents' faces.*] Yes, I was certain that the children had told you about their writing folders. In addition to holding their writing samples, the folders provide an easily accessible place to record information. Let me show you. [*Mrs. Trapasso held up a folder and displayed how both the front and back covers were used to record information.*] A system such as this has another advantage. It involves the child in his own evaluation, and this is essential. Several times a year, I summarize the individual data to give me some idea of how the class is progressing as a whole. Keeping records is never easy, but I am dedicated to the idea of making it as simple and efficient a process as possible. Mrs. Wilson?

Mrs. Wilson: When I taught, we had curriculum guides and the like to follow. Doesn't this school have curriculum guidelines that the teachers must follow?

Mrs. Trapasso: Our state education department has general guidelines on the amount of instructional time that should be devoted to the various curriculum areas. The state also publishes curriculum guides in the various areas, but there is no mandate to follow them. They are provided, more or less, as resources. I think the concern that you are expressing, Mrs. Wilson, is a valid one: if there is no set plan of instruction, how can we ensure that all the children will learn the content they need to pass tests and go on to higher grades? First, be assured that the achievement tests children take in the elementary grades are designed to be general enough in content so that any child in the United States can take and do well on them. If a child learns to love to read, it's pretty certain that she *will* read well; likewise with writing. That's what we're concerned with here. By the time such a child leaves secondary school, it is far more likely than not that she will have sampled a wide enough array of learning through her own pursuits and her school's requirements to prepare her quite well for college and for life.

I wish we had more time for questions, but as always seems to be the case, these evenings pass too quickly. But I'll be happy to stay and chat with you individually if you like. Again, thank you for coming tonight.

As Mrs. Trapasso's parent meeting shows, children in the upper primary grades have acquired sufficient mastery of the tools of learning to enable them to become self-sufficient, independent learners. They have also had a longer association with school, and depending on the quality of their experiences, they may be more or less eager to learn in school. By the second or third grade, most children are very "schoolwise." They know what teachers like and what school requires. Whether they will play by the rules of the "school game" is another question entirely. Thus, in primary-grade classes, most of the children are more sophisticated and competent than younger ones, but some children are less eager and open about what lies ahead in the school year. But teachers who plan experiences that build on children's strengths and interests also build their confidence and motivation to learn. Children are extremely flexible. Given the sensitivity of a good teacher and the excitement of a good program, most seven- and eight-year-olds will respond positively.

As children's abilities increase, many of the earlier constraints on learning are lifted. There is more freedom now, and more power, too. The teacher's task is similar in many ways to what it was in the earlier grades: to provide support and guidance, to challenge, and to foster independence. But now it also involves helping the children extend the depth and breadth of their learning. The rest of this chapter discusses how the literacy program expands in the later primary grades as children learn to use their abilities with confidence, write and read for different purposes, and develop competence in skills.

Using Abilities with Confidence

In this section, we will discuss ways to help the child in the later primary grades use his growing abilities with confidence. One of the most important considerations is accommodating teaching strategies and materials to the widely varying levels in achievement among second- and third-graders. A very significant strategy is organizing the classroom to capitalize on the child's growing self-sufficiency and thus build his sense of autonomy and independence.

Working with Diversity

An old educational maxim says that school increases, rather than decreases, the differences among children. In one sense it is true—the spread in achievement grows larger the longer the children are in school. In a third-grade class, you may well have children reading anywhere from the primer through the sixth-grade level. Children's writing performance may range all the way from being able to copy dictated material to writing independently with little or no teacher assistance. Diversity is typical. Even in the case of "homogeneous" classes, in which children are grouped according to their rank on achievement tests, you may find as wide a spread as two or three grade levels in reading. Perhaps the concept of homogeneity is outmoded. Can any group really be homogeneous? Probably not when you consider that even the competencies in a single individual are heterogeneous: I may be terrific in reading, but poor in math except geometry, where I excel. When children are lumped indiscriminately into groups created around some mythical norm such as "average," it is virtually impossible for one teaching strategy to provide the learning experiences best suited to their needs. Brighter children may get bored and slower ones may become frustrated, while the rest limp along. But literacy programs designed around the individual child can meet diverse needs.

The range of literacy experiences we have already described should continue into the later primary grades. Many more children will be able to function independently now in both reading and writing, but there must still be structure and assistance for those who need it. The range of materials, however, must broaden to accommodate the wider interests of all the children, and the stronger skills of many or most of them. For example, you will need more books, not only children's literature, but also content books and reference materials. The range of educational experiences you provide should expand to match the interests of the children, which are widening in space and time. The study of events and places farther removed from the here and now becomes appropriate. While preschool children may focus on the subway ride and cafeteria rather than on the museum exhibits on a class trip, second and third graders are ready and eager to go beyond the limits of their everyday lives. They are beginning to be able to appreciate both actual and fanciful interpretations of similar experiences, such as a real and a science-fiction account of space travel.

Teachers' expectations must change too. Beyond being attuned to the abilities and needs of the *individual child*, teachers need to expect children to study a topic of interest and to record experience more intensively than younger children.

Teachers will help children refine their skills so that they can polish their work and be proud of it. While younger children are enthralled with process, with *doing* something, older children become more self-conscious about their work. They are concerned about how the painting looks, whether the words are spelled correctly, or whether the characters' dialogue is accurate. Too much external concern or pressure about matters of form at this point can turn this normal self-consciousness into an unhealthy mistrust or denial of their own abilities. Children may protest that they "can't draw" or "don't know how to write" when they are asked to do so. But if teachers provide the necessary help with form while always emphasizing the primary importance of meaning and content, they can encourage children to continue to grow in skill without sacrificing their self-confidence.

A Period of Transition

It is important to remember that by the second or third grade, some or even most of the children may have had one or two years of schooling that were very different from the integrated and individualized approach you are planning. Perhaps the only reading they have done in school has been from basal readers. If they have never had the opportunity to pursue the study of a topic independently, it is unlikely that they will know how to do so. If the only writing they have ever done was on topics selected by the teacher, who red-penciled their errors and emphasized form over content, they may very well not want to write in your class. Dissimilar experience does not necessarily mean contradictory experience, but since it is different, it requires a period of transition.

Regardless of prior experience, it is a good idea to provide a transition period for all the children at the beginning of the school year, during which you ease them into the routines and requirements of their new class. Children need to reacquaint themselves with school after the break in continuity of the summer recess. They also need time to get to know their classmates and you, their new teacher. For those children whose earlier school experience *was* different, the transition is essential. During the first few weeks of school, you should get to know the children; help the children get to know you and each other; and gradually introduce the children to their new program. We have discussed the first two points in earlier chapters. Here let us consider how to introduce the children to the program.

Much of the answer to this question depends on what you find out about the children themselves. Usually, the more dissimilar their prior experience, the slower and more careful the transition will need to be. Also, the personality traits and learning styles of individual children will have a strong effect on how quickly they will adapt to your program. Children who are quite shy or those who have little self-discipline usually need more time working with the teacher before they are ready to become more independent learners. A very good way to begin the year is with a *class unit of study*. Since this initial investigation will be under your direction, it will provide the necessary structure and guidance for those who need it, and at the same time enable you to demonstrate functionally the procedures and routines used in your class. It is essential that you be very alert to signs from the children indicating that they are ready and able to branch out and spin off their own independent investigations from the common one. There may even be some who are ready to proceed with their own original investigations from the start. Of course, this is the sort of thing you want to stimulate, so you must be ready to provide assistance and encouragement when it happens.

A Class Unit of Study

During the get-acquainted period of the initial weeks of school, you should discover what interests the children individually and collectively. Seven- and eight-year-olds are often fascinated by the natural world, space exploration, prehistoric animals and monsters, pets and other kinds of animals, and television. In selecting a unit of study, you should consider these questions:

- Is this topic of interest to most of the children?
- Would this topic permit sufficient depth and breadth of study to make it worthwhile?
- Is this a suitable topic to study according to the children's needs and values?
- Does this topic contain enough of both firsthand and vicarious experience?
- Is this a topic that lends itself easily to various ways of recording in different media and styles?

Perhaps your class is very interested in pets and other kinds of animals. You might want to begin by having the children think about pets, real and imagined, and start up a bulletin board display under this title. Each child would be invited to bring in a photograph, drawing, or some other visual representation of their real or imagined pet. Patti may bring in a lock from her Irish setter's glorious red coat, and Rico a photo of his box turtle winning second prize at the local pet show. As you and the children look at the display, you find it interesting and attractive, but somewhat chaotic; it is difficult to find any patterns in the children's responses. This is the moment to ask the class how they could rearrange the information or data on the bulletin board so that it is easier to understand. From this discussion, the children will begin to think of different ways to organize their data: by kinds of pets, by real *vs.* imagined pets, by pets of boys *vs.* pets of girls, and so on. Your task will be to introduce them to different ways of charting data, such as bar graphs, and to encourage their own innovation. Look at the reorganized data with the children and discuss the new information that is revealed. Because of the intense personal attachment between many children and their pets, this is a topic that usually finds an easy outlet in writing. You might want to rearrange the bulletin board again so that written descriptions accompany visual ones.

In addition to preparing a bulletin board, you can encourage the children to observe their pets closely and to bring in interesting anecdotes about them. This can lead to many subsequent activities. For example, as the children exchange their information, new interests and leads will arise. You may find out that several children want to become veterinarians. You might arrange for a local vet to visit your class. This would probably generate much enthusiasm, and you might discover that a few of the children are ready to start on a study of their own. Most of the children have begun to do some reading on the pet of their choice; you can read aloud to them from the literature on pets, everything from *Angus* to *Black Beauty*. As the children's knowledge of pets increases, advise them to look for more ways to organize their growing body of information—kinds of pets, feeding pets, care of sick pets, pets having babies, grooming pets. Point out that it is important not only to organize their information but also to display it so that it can be easily understood. They think of charts and graphs and you add these to the bulletin board display. About this time, most of the children have grouped themselves into smaller units for more intensive investigation of subtopics. There are now separate groups investigating different kinds of pets (dogs, birds, cats, fish, amphibians and reptiles), pet feeding, and pet shelter, as well as the earlier group involved in the study of veterinary medicine. One or two children have struck out on their own. Jon, for example, who is very bright and quite independent, saw a documentary on TV about the evolution of animals and is immersed in trying to trace the history of the dog back to its origin.

Work with each of the groups, helping them to locate needed information and then summarize and organize it. Help tie their findings together in whole-class discussions. Encourage individuals and small groups to report orally on their findings. When they have gone far enough to need a way to integrate and report all of their findings, initiate a discussion about a report. What is most important is that the children *understand* why they need a way to summarize their findings coherently and attractively in a permanent form. The children are often very excited about the opportunity to put together their own report, which will be placed proudly alongside all the rest of the books in the language arts area. Give them the help they need in mechanics, assist them in revising, and, where necessary, in rewriting, and provide suggestions on illustrating and binding. The children may be so delighted with the final product they will be overjoyed at your suggestion that you duplicate copies of it for each of them to take home.

Even this brief description indicates that by the conclusion of the first class unit of study, the children will have gained experience in several important skills: using books of different kinds to gather information; summarizing data in various ways; organizing information into logical categories; working by themselves and with others in investigating a topic; and reporting orally and in writing. In addition, they will have learned that *their own* ideas and interests are important and that it is interesting and highly enjoyable to study a topic intensively. What is more, as an integral part of their study they will have learned what the guidelines are that underlie the organization and management of their new class. Rules for using and storing materials, working independently, and carrying out class jobs make sense when they are set in the context of a meaningful task. Most of the children will be eager to go on to a study another topic at this point, perhaps some offshoot of the original one or something entirely new. Some will require more guidance; you may need to explore their interests with them to come up with a topic and provide more assistance and support than the others require. A few children, who have caught on to the approach early on, will have already forged ahead to topics of more personal interest.

Organizing for Self-Sufficiency

In addition to adapting teaching strategies to children's needs to encourage them to use their abilities with confidence, the teacher can also help children by organizing the classroom so that it capitalizes on their independence. For example, arranging books and other materials through a system such as color-coding (see chapter 4) greatly simplifies their use and thereby contributes to children's sense of self-sufficiency.

In classrooms that foster independence and maturity there are sufficient guidelines and structure to create a predictable, secure environment; free will and decision-making are valued and children are encouraged to make rational choices. Dependence and immaturity, on the other hand, seem to flourish under two conditions: chaotic situations in which guidelines are few or inconsistent, making predictability impossible (children do not know what to expect); and highly controlled situations that permit little or no choice (children must take their cues from the teacher on everything they do). As a teacher, you can do several things to build independence.

Storing materials.   Storing materials in a way that makes their return and retrieval easy is very important if children are to be independent. Let us take the example of writing folders to illustrate how material can be stored for easy use. Recall, for instance, that Mrs. Trapasso kept all of her children's writing folders in an attractively decorated carton. This was placed in a fixed location in the room, so that the children knew where to get their folders at the beginning of the day and where to return them. Likewise, by using the folders' front and back covers to record information about the children's writing, Mrs. Trapasso provided a simple and convenient way for both herself and the children to follow their progress.

The information on writing folders might include what the child has written (titles and dates), new ideas to write about, skills the child knows and can use, and topics the child knows about.[1] Additional information might include: "Skills I need to learn," "Things I want to find out about," and "Books and other reading material I have used." It is easy to attach a sheet of paper once the space on a cover has been used up.

When children record their progress in this way, it gives them a sense of the momentum of their own growth. If you study four or five of the folders each day, it will keep you very much in touch with the children's progress. In addition, parents and school administrators can gain important insights about the children's writing development as well as a better understanding of the literacy program from the writing folders.

Regularity in scheduling.   Regularity in scheduling also helps to build self-sufficiency. It is a good idea for each child to have a regularly scheduled weekly reading/writing conference time. This helps the child to plan her work for the week. If she is to meet with you on Thursday, for example, then she knows she has three days to work on researching her topic, preparing her draft, revising, etc. After she meets with you on Thursday, she has another day of the current week to act on whatever ideas you have discussed. This also helps to build some consistency into your own schedule and enables you to prepare for these conferences. Of course, you must also expect several unplanned conferences daily. A child might need to discuss a problem or question that comes up suddenly. Typically, such conferences are quite specific and short. A child may be uncertain about which reference book he should consult or which of two introductions to use for a story. In addition to consulting with the teacher, children should be encouraged to use their classmates as resources for assistance and information.

Work folders and assignment logs.   When they have guidelines on how and when to use materials and undertake activities, children can operate with independence. Suppose that every week you want each child to meet with you once for a reading/writing conference, read intensively three separate times, and audiotape oral reading once. The children can indicate which days they have selected for these activities by writing their names on posted sign-up sheets. A separate *work folder* for each child also simplifies keeping track of daily and weekly plans. The work folder can be any sturdily constructed folder with pockets, measuring about nine-by-twelve inches, which the children can decorate to suit their individual tastes. Inside they can keep their weekly assignment logs. Here is what Cal's assignments are like for a typical week in March. Cal is in Mrs. Trapasso's class.

Name Cal Berg   *Week* March 11–15
Activities for This Week

Listening Center—card 7
Math Center—cards 5 and 6
Science Center—electricity experiment
Read *Green Eggs and Ham* to kindergartner
Play Syllabication game
Meet with Satellites Report Committee—audiotape editing session
Make a list of words misspelled at least 3 times (see writing folder)
Microcomputer—card 4

Cal indicates that he has completed each assignment by putting a check next to it and encloses the papers and tapes he has worked on in the folder. After Mrs. Trapasso checks his work, she staples completed assignments to the weekly logs. Audiotapes are returned to be used in other assignments.

Sometimes a child receives feedback very quickly—when the teacher observes a particular problem that should be handled as soon as possible, for example. Because the work folders are stored in a permanent location, the teacher has ready access to them at all times. If she finds that a child has not been carrying out assignments or has been completing them only selectively, she will want to meet with the child at once to determine what the problem is. Otherwise, feedback on assignments is incorporated into the ongoing dialogue between child and teacher in reading/writing conferences and in the many informal interactions that occur every day.

Activity cards.   It took Mrs. Trapasso eight years to develop the many individualized learning activities that Cal's weekly assignment log illustrates. It would be unrealistic to expect to start teaching with a full complement of activity cards, but you can begin to collect ideas right now. When you have about ten, you might want to begin writing them up on individual five-by-eight-inch index cards. Because these are to be used by children, you will want to keep the directions simple, write legibly, and illustrate wherever possible. You can make the cards more durable by covering them with a clear adhesive material.

Moffett and Wagner find that activity cards are especially useful as reading material.[2] Because they are a kind of expository writing, activity cards provide experience in comprehending this kind of discourse; when used in partnership, they allow children to check each other's reading and pool knowledge and deductive powers; the directions reinforce children's familiarity with various words by repeating them frequently; and the activities themselves offer children clues to help them deduce the meanings of the words in the directions.

You can find ideas for activities in workbooks, the teacher's manuals that accompany basal readers, language arts reference books, and curriculum bulletins—and don't overlook your own imagination. This last source is the most valuable, because it never dries up. Once you have caught on to the idea of activity cards, you will be able to create many of your own. Remember always to evaluate the ideas you find from the perspective of your own philosophy of teaching and your understanding of children. Figure 5–1 illustrates a sample activity card that would be suitable for children in the later primary grades.

You can find many other interesting language arts activities in these resource books:

- Allen, R. V., and Allen, C. *Language Experience Activities.* Boston: Houghton Mifflin, 1976.
- Greater San Diego Reading Association. *Reading Games Unlimited.* San Diego, Calif.: The Association, 1972.

Area: Language Arts   **Subject:** Writing
Topic: If I Could Talk to the Animals

Directions
1. Cut out pictures of at least 5 different animals from our magazine collection.
2. Pretend you can talk to these animals. What would they say about the world and how people treat them?
3. Paste the pictures of the animals on a strip of paper.
4. Make a comic strip of the animals. Write what each one says in a bubble over its head.

Figure 5–1   An activity card for the later primary grades

- Heilman, A. W., and Holmes, E. C. *Smuggling Language into the Teaching of Reading.* Columbus, Ohio: Merrill, 1972.
- Spache, E. B. *Reading Activities for Child Involvement*, 2d ed. Boston: Allyn and Bacon, 1976.

In addition to cultivating children's self-sufficiency, a teaching plan designed around independent activities frees the teacher to use her time efficiently. While children are doing their individualized assignments, working on preparing a report with others, writing or reading by themselves, or using the resources in the different classroom interest areas, the teacher is able to meet with some children in reading/writing conferences, conduct small group teaching sessions with others, and interact informally with individual children. This is a *productive* use of the teacher's time, since it is geared to the actual needs of the children. Children can learn more in this kind of class than in a traditional program because it focuses on the *quality* of teacher/children interactions rather than just the quantity. Teaching to the *real* needs of the children in your class rather than those *presumed* by a reading text or curriculum guide allows a more satisfying and effective use of your time and the children's.

Creating a good emotional tone.   Probably the single most important element in creating a good emotional tone in the classroom is the teacher. A teacher who is enthusiastic, confident, supportive, kind, and fair, yet firm, is apt to have students who are responsive, interested, and involved. These teacher attributes find expression in how the classroom is organized, in the management routines and guidelines that are established, and in the ongoing transactions between teacher and children.

The way the teacher participates in a reading/writing conference illustrates how her positive attitude can influence an everyday interaction with a child. First, she selects a comfortable setting for the conference, away from the distractions and activities of the rest of the class. Seated for good eye contact and at a height as close as possible to that of the child, the teacher greets him with a question designed to open the dialogue: "Hi, Kareem. How's it going today?" Kareem holds his paper but may offer it to the teacher. He feels secure about the conference, because he knows when and where it will take place, what the teacher expects of him, and how she will react. He knows, for example, that the teacher will probably ask him a few questions about his writing. Some questions will help him to focus on the writing process ("Where do you want to begin?"). Others will simply reflect what he tells her ("Is this the next episode in Mr. T's space travel adventure?"). Sometimes the teacher just wants to find out if Kareem's facts are straight ("Which of the planets is the hottest?"). Actually, the teacher uses questions sparingly; she asks only those that have a real purpose and that the child should be able to answer. Another thing Kareem appreciates about his teacher's questioning strategies is that she *waits* for him to answer. She gives him time to think (at least fifteen seconds), rather than rushing in with an answer of her own. Because we are attuned to the rapidly patterned back-and-forth of dialogue in normal conversation, it is very difficult to stop and wait in a teaching situation to allow the child enough time to respond. Yet this has been found to have a significant effect on children's learning.[3] (It might be helpful to role-play conferencing with another teacher in order to develop these important skills. Obviously, videotaping such practice sessions would make them even more valuable.)

Although Kareem probably could not label precisely the other behaviors his teacher displays in conferences, he does know that what she does helps him to feel secure and interested. First, the teacher conveys positive recognition. By using Kareem's own words in commenting on his work, she provides specific confirmation of his accomplishments. Second, the teacher emphasizes the importance and worth of Kareem's contributions in the conference dialogue by following his lead, encouraging him to ask questions and make suggestions. Third, the teacher keeps the conferences useful, so that Kareem sees their purpose: they are focused; they demonstrate rather than merely note solutions; they emphasize meaning first, form later; they provide realistic, constructive feedback; and they set reasonable expectations. Leaving the conference, Kareem has a clear understanding of how to proceed. He knows that help is available if he needs it, but he is comfortable with the knowledge that his progress is primarily his own responsibility.

Children are helped to use their abilities with confidence when the atmosphere of the class is emotionally supportive. They will take risks and experiment *if* they know that their efforts will be appreciated. Children need to know how to handle problems when they arise. Your own example of calm composure is very important here. Some of the proudest moments I have had in teaching involve incidents in which young children were able to handle embarrassing or even potentially dangerous situations calmly and competently. Children also need to know how to cope with more ordinary problems, such as what to do when they do not know how to spell a word. Try to anticipate these day-to-day problems and discuss possible solutions with the class. For those situations that are apt to come up regularly, it may be a good idea to post an attractive chart illustrating the steps to follow in handling each problem.

Writing and Reading for Various Purposes

In this section, we will look at how children use their developing abilities in reading and writing. We will consider the preparation of reports, silent versus oral reading, and the writing of stories and poems.

Preparing Reports

One of the corollaries of children's intensive and extended investigations in the later primary grades is the preparation of both oral and written reports. As she accumulates more and more information, the child sees the need for an efficient and coherent way of organizing it. In addition, the child's increased sense of audience coincides with her natural inclination to share what she has learned with classmates and others and thus reinforces the need for a report that is both attractive and intelligible. In the following discussion, we will review the various steps involved in preparing reports.

Time to reflect.   One of the things teachers often overlook in the composing process is the need for a period of reflection before the actual writing begins. The child may have a good idea, but unless he has time to play with it, perhaps to try it out with his peers or maybe even forget it for a while and then come back to it, it will scarcely have a chance to germinate and flourish. But in many classrooms, time for reflection is omitted. The children have an experience, perhaps a trip to the zoo. Immediately after the class returns to school, the teacher initiates a discussion about the trip, distributes paper, and waits as the children write their reports. In addition to denying children the freedom to choose whether or not to write on this topic, such a hurried practice hardly gives them the chance to recall, much less ruminate, about their experience. Perhaps one child observed a zoo attendant handling the animals roughly. This disturbed him. He wonders what it is like for the animals to be penned in, perhaps at the mercy of a cruel "caretaker." With enough time to explore his own feelings about this issue, to discuss it with others, and perhaps even to do some reading on the topic, this child may well be able to compose a story that is far more alive and meaningful than the rather dull and repetitive reports children usually turn out in these circumstances.

Reporting orally.   Although some children are comfortable working from notes or even from a fully written report in preparation for a talk, there are several reasons why, generally, it is a good idea to have oral reporting precede written reporting. Children need to have many firsthand experiences with a topic before they are ready to gather new material from books. If children are familiar with a topic before they read more about it, they will be less prone to copy masses of information verbatim. In addition, sharing findings with classmates requires that the children synthesize the material so they can report it in their own words. If the oral report is a group project, the children's interactions with each other provide an excellent opportunity for them to learn about meeting an audience's needs. When you confer with either an individual child or a small group, you can help them to work out strategies for handling the sequence of a report. You might suggest that they create a simple prop—a set of pictures arranged in the order of the report—as a sequential guide. Or they can write the major points of the report on strips of chart paper. The strips can be pinned up as each point is raised in the report.

Rehearsal for writing.   Once a child has made a conscious decision to write, she will usually do a number of things to get ready for the actual writing itself. In this pre-writing, or rehearsal, stage of the composing process, she may doodle, make long lists of words, draw up an outline, daydream, or read or talk about her topic.[4] Sometimes children find it easier to write if they express their ideas and feelings physically by dramatizing or pantomiming an experience first. Talking about ideas before writing stimulates interest and new ideas. Before discussion has exhausted the topic, and when excitement is at its peak, children are ready to begin writing.

Interviewing.   Interviewing is an important technique for gathering information, and one you can help children learn. Probably the simplest way to instruct them in this skill is through role-playing. Wait until they are far enough into their investigation to feel the need to interview someone on their topic. In the example of the class study unit on pets used earlier, when children's curiosity about the veterinarian's role was high, you might have suggested inviting a local veterinarian to class. The children, undoubtedly very excited at the prospect of being able to interview the veterinarian, would be ready to learn the techniques of interviewing.

Start by playing the interviewee's role yourself. Bring some interesting object to class—an old handmade quilt, for example—on which the children can focus. Tell them that their job in the interview is to ask you the questions that will give them the information they want to know, in this case, about the quilt. Suggest that it is a good idea to come to an interview with a set of questions already formulated. You might remind the children here of the press interviews with the president they have seen on TV. Give them time to brainstorm and develop a set of questions about the quilt. When they are ready, they can ask you the questions, which you can write on the chalkboard. Afterward, they can evaluate their questions based upon what they learned about the quilt from your answers. Repeat this procedure several times with a child as the interviewee.

From these role-playing experiences, you and the children can develop guidelines for good interviewing: welcoming the guest and making him feel comfortable; preparing questions in advance; composing questions that are clear and to the point; constructing questions that are designed to elicit facts as well as the interviewee's interpretations and opinions; and organizing questions so that they build on already elicited information. As the teacher, remember that an important component in demonstrating successful interviewing is helping the interviewee prepare by telling him the purpose of the interview, suggesting areas of particular interest to the children, and advising that he bring concrete objects related to the topic (e.g., the veterinarian would have various relevant instruments, such as a stethoscope).

Reading expository material.   Preparing reports usually entails reading in the content areas (e.g., science), either in textbooks or reference books. But children may find this material difficult because the concepts may be too technical or complex; the level of reading difficulty of many content area textbooks is higher than their grade level designation (e.g., a third-grade social studies textbook may actually be written at a fifth- or sixth-grade reading level); or the format of such expository material is quite different from the style and structure of stories, with which children are more familiar.

There are several things you can do to assist children who are reading in this new mode. First, you should scrutinize the content-area textbooks and other informational books available to your class in order to calculate a more accurate index of their reading levels. The informal and formal techniques for this purpose described in chapter 4 will be useful here. Second, if you find that a child's difficulty with a book is at the conceptual level, then in your conference with him you can help by simplifying and clarifying the material. Of course, providing the child with concrete background experience prior to reading would be a great help to his understanding of the concepts. Another way to approach this problem is to pair children off in their content-area reading in a tutor-tutee arrangement. This way both children learn, and the child who is apt to have difficulty has a ready source of assistance available to him. Third, to assist the child in reading the material you can tape-record selected passages, which the child can listen to as she reads along in the text, or you or an aide can read the text aloud to those who are unable to read it by themselves. Fourth, you can teach children about the structure of expository material.

One way children can learn about the expository style of writing is by comparing the structure of story and expository modes. Read aloud two different passages on the same topic, one written as a story and the other as exposition. Discuss and illustrate the style and structure of stories (written subjectively and containing characters, plot, and setting) and contrast this with the expository mode (written objectively and in such organizational patterns as listing, cause-and-effect, and comparison and contrast). Have the children scrutinize the records and logs they keep as part of their independent and group study projects for the characteristics of exposition. As they become more aware of the characteristics of expository writing, they should continue to write in this style to learn how this kind of text works. You might ask the children to record what occurred on a recent trip. Some might want to do this as an objective sequence of events or a straightforward guide, such as "Facts and Features of the Hayden Planetarium," while others might want to write about their perception of this trip as a story. Here is an ideal opportunity to contrast the two modes.

Before we leave this discussion of expository material, I want to emphasize that textbooks and reference books do not exhaust the sources of information children can tap in preparing reports. In addition to its aesthetic value, good children's literature is often highly informative. For example, Robert McCloskey's *One Morning in Maine* reveals much interesting detail about island life, such as the alignment of seagulls in preparation for a coming storm, through a rich and beautifully written story. Encourage children to delve into books of all kinds, both primary and secondary sources, in gathering information. Encourage them as well to seek out other resources—interviewing an eyewitness to a recent devastating storm, for example, or collecting an authentic Cajun recipe from a relative.

Silent versus oral reading.   Reading for information means reading quickly and efficiently. These are characteristics of *silent* reading, yet children often spend much of their time in school reading orally. Beginning readers profit from oral reading because it helps them see the connection between speaking and writing and because it is an overt confirmation of their reading ability.[5] Reading aloud also has useful and enjoyable purposes, as we will discuss below. But beginning in the second grade, children should devote more time to reading silently.

The common practice of "round-robin reading," in which one child reads aloud as the others in her group supposedly read along silently, may actually deter rather than encourage proficient reading. Eye movements during oral reading show more fixations, longer fixations, and more regressions than eye movements in silent reading. If the teacher emphasizes reading expressively, this slows down the process still more. My own experience in conducting and observing round-robin reading indicates that many children are quite restless in these groups and do almost anything *except* read along silently. The few who do read along silently must slow down to match their pace to that of the child reading aloud, and they may pronounce each word subvocally or even aloud as it is being read. Thus, emphasizing oral over silent reading may sabotage children's ability to read quickly and efficiently. Moreover, children may equate reading with the performancelike characteristics of an oral reading presentation. Finally, because oral reading is so much slower than silent reading, it may impede comprehension as children focus on how they sound and forget what they have read earlier.

Rejecting the round-robin option does not have to mean that children never read in groups. The teacher should encourage opportunities for children to group themselves for reading in order to meet a real need, perhaps to research a report topic. I know of a third-grade class in which a "sci-fi" craze resulted in one group of children reading, discussing, and carrying out all kinds of interesting activities. This kind of arrangement has important advantages over groups organized by the teacher around some external criterion, such as reading level. When children group themselves for reading, it is because *they* see the need for it. They want to work together, and their motivation level is high. Moreover, such groups are usually composed of children with abilities different in both kind and degree. There will be strong and weak readers represented, and the tutor-tutee interactions will be useful for all. Some children may participate because of a particular talent, such as drawing, which the group needs for its project. This kind of group offers children the chance to value and express a whole range of abilities and talents rather than the narrow spectrum of typical school achievements. Instead of responding to the predigested questions and activities offered by a basal reading manual, children in this kind of group raise their own questions about what they have read, share opinions, and make purposeful decisions on what to do next, based on need.

Emphasizing silent reading does not mean, however, that children in the later primary grades should not have the chance to read orally. They should, as long as it is for appropriate purposes: to interpret material designed to be heard, such as poetry; to share reports, stories, and poems with others; and to help identify their reading strengths and weaknesses. Practice in reading to an audience can begin by reading to just one other person at first, perhaps the teacher or someone at home. Later the child can read to a small group, maybe in the kindergarten. Simple role-playing from books of rhymes, jokes, riddles, and limericks may appeal to some children, and because of their brevity and obvious humor, provide a good forerunner to *choral reading*.

Study techniques.   Children also need to know how to select important or major points, and how to organize the information they find and connect it with what they already know. You can help them develop good study techniques by guiding them through the process of reading and retrieving information from selected passages in a given content area. One technique you may want to use for this purpose is called a *directed reading/thinking activity*, or *DR-TA*.[6] There are several steps in a DR-TA. First, the students survey the selected passage and skim all of its special features, which give clues to the content—title, headings and subheadings, words or phrases printed in a special typeface, illustrations, diagrams or photographs, maps, tables and charts, and questions within and at the end of the text. Second, based on what they have learned from their survey of the passage, the children make predictions about its content. The passages you use for this should be relatively short and simple, so that the children will be able to anticipate the content with some accuracy. Try to select these passages from material the children want to read for some real purpose. List the children's predictions on the chalkboard. Third, the children read the appropriate section of the text to confirm whether or not each of their predictions is correct. Erase those that are disconfirmed. In this step of the procedure, the children have to read very carefully as they gather evidence from the passage to test their predictions and discuss their findings. Once they understand the question, predict, read, and evaluate procedure, the children can work on a passage individually. They can number their own predictions on a piece of paper, then read aloud the portion of the passage that tests each and write either a *yes* or *no* next to each prediction, depending on their evaluation.

A variation of the DR-TA procedure is called an *expectation outline*.[7] From their initial survey of a passage, the children give you questions they think will be answered by the text, and you organize the questions into a rough outline form on the chalkboard. Next, the children read the passage to determine which of their questions it actually does answer. Finally, they read aloud the section of the passage that answers each question. Procedures such as these help to teach children important strategies in reading for information: first, set your purposes for reading; second, skim the text for clues to its content; third, make predictions about the content; and fourth, test your predictions by reading selectively and carefully.

Organizing information.   Seven- and eight-year-olds are usually not ready for elaborate schemes for outlining what they have read, but they can profit from simple ideas that help them to organize the information they are collecting. Organization facilitates both recall and the linking of new learning to old. It also helps in arranging the sequence of a report. Building a *web* (*webbing*) is a good way to begin because of its relatively loose structure.[8]

When the information the children are collecting as part of their class unit of study begins to mount, they will see the need for a simple and efficient way to organize it. This is the time to introduce webbing. Write the title of the unit of study in a box in the center of the chalkboard: Pet Animals. Then, each of the committees formed to study subtopics will give you the name of its subtopic: kinds of pets, pet feeding, pet shelter, care of sick pets. These main divisions are written in boxes around the center with lines running to the center box. Finally, the children on each committee give you the main points under their subdivision. Figure 5–2 shows what this web might look like.

One of the advantages of this kind of pictorial representation is that it ties the work of the several committees together and illustrates the cohesion of the entire project. Because it shows how the findings of some committees are parallel, it may suggest further modifications in organization. For instance, in this example both the pet feeding and pet shelter committees have discovered that adaptation to the

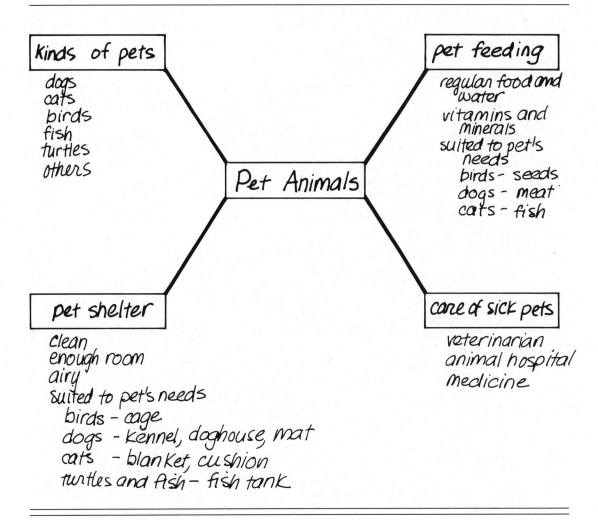

kinds of pets
dogs
cats
birds
fish
turtles
others

pet feeding
regular food and water
vitamins and minerals
suited to pet's needs
birds - seeds
dogs - meat
cats - fish

Pet Animals

pet shelter
clean
enough room
airy
suited to pet's needs
birds - cage
dogs - kennel, doghouse, mat
cats - blanket, cushion
turtles and fish - fish tank

care of sick pets
veterinarian
animal hospital
medicine

Figure 5–2   A sample web

pet's needs is an important consideration. Perhaps as a result of creating this web, these two committees might want to collaborate on further investigation of this point. Webs should be drawn at strategic moments in the course of an investigation. If you transfer each web to paper and date it, the children will have an interesting way of tracking their progress. Webs can also be useful in preparing for an interview. One way to help the children organize their questions is to form a "job web," an idea suggested by Melanie Bigman, a former student. The title of the job is written in a central box, and that box is connected by lines to other boxes, each of which contains a question about the job and space for an answer.

Hennings describes a number of other strategies designed to help children gather data systematically, organize it, and then integrate it into their own writing.[9]

The process begins by providing children with experiences that build their informational background on the topic chosen—doing and observing, talking, reading, taking trips, interviewing, viewing films, and the like. Then they *factstorm*, calling out their information on the topic while you record it on the chalkboard. Next, they organize the facts into appropriate categories. One way to help them do this is to ask the children to examine the ideas or facts on the chalkboard and find those that are similar to each other. Begin by selecting one item yourself, and then ask the children to locate similar ones. If the study has been on pollution, for example, you might point to the item *car exhaust*. The children would then find other examples of air pollution, such as *smoke from incinerators*. Circle examples from each category with the same color chalk. The children then proceed to identify items from other categories, such as noise and water pollution. When all the items are grouped by category, you can rearrange the information into a chart titled "Pollution," which lists various kinds of pollution as subheadings and under each, specific examples.

Drafting paragraphs.   With your guidance, the children can take their organized information and draft paragraphs around it. Focus their attention on the information you have recorded in chart form. Ask them to tell you a sentence for each of the ideas on the chart, and record their sentences on the chalkboard precisely. Read the sentences back to the children and elicit their suggestions for revision on such matters as sequence and a general summarizing statement. When the children are satisfied with the paragraph, have them title it; then you can rewrite it on chart paper. If the children compose several paragraphs in this manner for a unit of study, you should duplicate them so that each child has a complete set. Then you can work with the children on arranging the paragraphs into a logical order for a composite report. Once the paragraphs are rearranged, the parts that are still needed—summarizing and transitional sentences, and introductory and concluding paragraphs—will become obvious. You can again work with the entire class on these parts or with smaller groups who have been assigned to tackle each one. It is a good idea to keep a record of each step of this entire procedure from factstorming to final report. Arranged as a kind of flowchart on a bulletin board, it will serve as a useful reminder to the children of the steps involved in organizing information.

Writing in their *own* words.   As noted earlier, when children do not have sufficient knowledge of a report topic, they are more likely to include information copied verbatim from various sources. The best way to combat plagiarism is to emphasize from the beginning that what is important is the student's *own unique synthesis* of ideas, and to ensure that the student has the necessary experience and skill to be able to reformulate what he has found into his own thoughts and words.

You can discourage mass copying by having children sketch or diagram an important idea. Suggest that they record only those specific facts, such as size or distance, that are really necessary for their report.[10] Ask them to note facts on three-by-five-inch index cards, on which they should also include information on the reference source—name of the book (or other source), author, and page number. It is important to teach children responsibility for accurate citation very early. By the later primary grades, as they are able to produce more writing of their own and thus increasingly know the pleasure of authorship, they can understand the fairness of giving an author due credit.

Another way to help children avoid simply copying what they have read is to provide some guided experience in paraphrasing written material. Work with the children in small groups, divided roughly according to their reading proficiency. Distribute short content-area passages. If the children are unable to read them alone, have them read along as you or an aide reads aloud, or as you play back tape-recorded versions. After a passage has been read, the children convert it into their *own* words, which you record on the chalkboard. Write each sentence on a separate line, so that each idea can be checked when the passage is reread. As they read and/or listen to the appropriate section of the passage again, the children can evaluate the accuracy of their own versions. Then they can modify their own sentences, if necessary, and add others if they find that important information is missing.

When children are ready. When are children ready to compose extensive and detailed written reports? Some educators believe that most are not ready until they are nine or ten, but the most accurate answer must come from your own assessment of the particular children in your own class. Regardless of how sophisticated they are capable of making their reports, all the children in your class should participate in written reporting in a way that is individually appropriate and rewarding. For a few, this might mean reports consisting mostly of illustrative material with much of the writing confined to labels and captions. Even without extensive writing, these reports can reveal intensive investigation and careful analysis. I have seen a third-grade table and bulletin board display of this kind that would have been the pride of many a sixth-grade class.

You can encourage those children who are ready to report more extensively in writing to get their ideas down on paper by having them write everything they can think of on one aspect of their investigation on a single sheet of paper labelled with that subtopic.[11] When they have written all they can think of on this one subtopic, they move on to a different aspect and another sheet of paper. Keep writing sessions short and end them while children's enthusiasm is still high, so that they will be eager to get back to their writing. The separate sheets are also handy for making revisions and can be rearranged easily when the children are working on the sequence of their report.

Regardless of their writing proficiency, what is important is that children have the chance to work on a topic of their own choice, to pursue the investigation over weeks or even months, and to draw the findings together in a careful and polished report that is the rightful object of their sense of *personal* accomplishment.

Writing Stories and Poems

By second grade, children have had lots of experience with stories; and because most of what has been read to them and what they have read themselves has been written in a story format, they have an implicit understanding of story structure. Thus, in contrast to expository writing, you do not have to familiarize children with this kind of discourse. Rather, your task in story-writing is to provide experiences designed to stimulate the children's imaginations and opportunities for them to write without pressure.

Developmental changes in story writing.   By the time children reach the later primary grades, you will be able to observe changes in many of their stories. Two developmental trends will be obvious: the stories become more complex in structure and language and more specific in content. For example, Figure 5–3 presents two samples of writing done by Amy, a child both teachers and parents describe as average. She wrote the first when she was in first grade; the second in third grade. Amy's third-grade writing displays many of the characteristics of the two developmental trends: increased sentence length; increased use of complex sen-

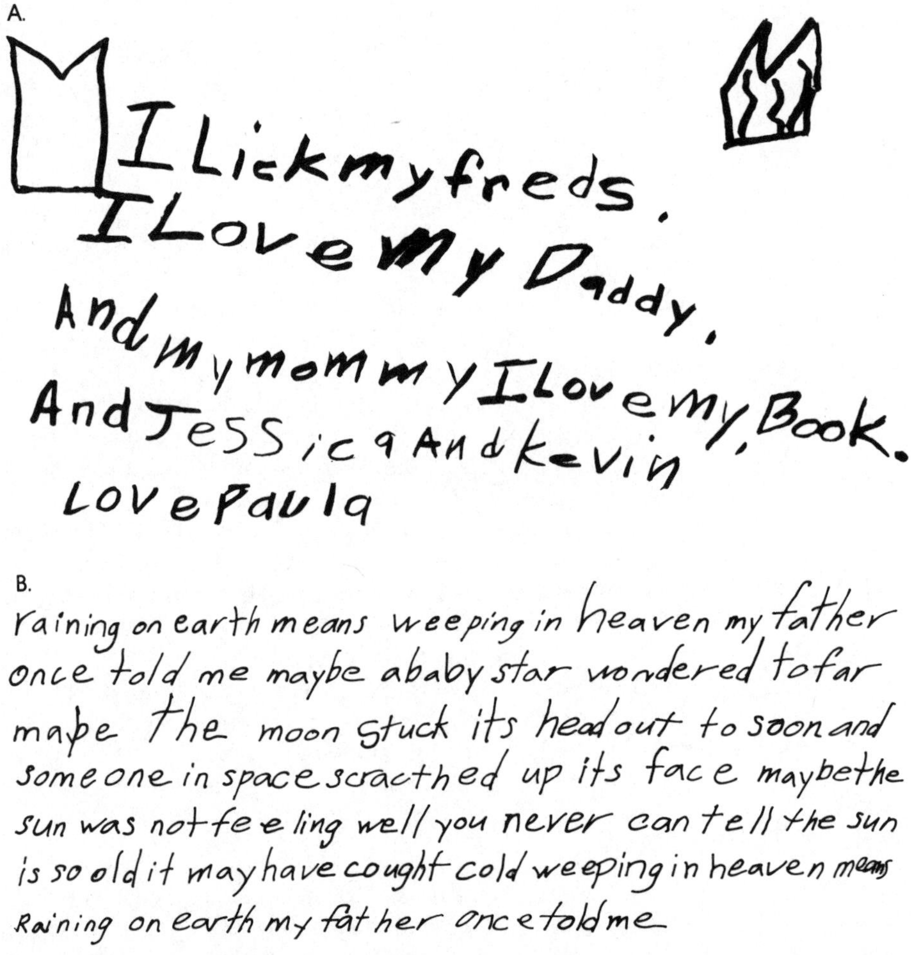

A.

I Lickmyfreds.
ILove My Daddy,
And my momm y I Love my Book.
And Jess ica And kevin
Love Paula

B.

raining on earth means weeping in heaven my father
once told me maybe ababy star wondered to far
maybe the moon stuck its head out to soon and
some one in space scracthed up its face maybethe
sun was not fee ling well you never can tell the sun
is so old it may have cought cold weeping in heaven means
Raining on earth my father once told me

Figure 5–3   Samples of Amy's writing. A: First grade. B: Third grade.

tence structure with more coordination and embedding; increased use of different pronouns and synonyms; increased precision in word use; greater fluency; and increased overall length. In content, the stories children write in the later primary grades tend to change from basic description to the development of events; become less egocentric; describe several rather than just a single event; use more dialogue; and add details, minor events, and explanations.[12]

Variability in writing performance.   Of course, these are *general* trends, and you must anticipate wide variation in the actual writing performance of the children in your class. There is another characteristic of writing that you must also anticipate: the wide variability in the writing performance of the *individual* child. As a matter of fact, irregularity may be the norm for creative writing. Sometimes a child will write nothing for days or even weeks, and then, when his imagination and interest are sparked, go at it almost nonstop for days and days. A child's writing varies not only in frequency but also in quality. Usually, the more personal his involvement in the writing topic is, the longer and stronger his commitment, and ultimately, the better his piece of writing. But there are other factors that contribute to writing variability also, such as how well the child is feeling both emotionally and physically, what his prior writing experience has been, how competently he manages the mechanics of writing, and his relations with teacher and classmates.

Heightening sensory awareness.   Children's story writing is apt to be interesting and expressive when it develops out of firsthand experiences that actively engage their senses. As we noted in chapter 1, the thinking of second- and third-graders is not yet fully abstract; they still need to experience the world on a direct, firsthand basis to comprehend it fully. Thus, what they can see, touch, taste, smell, and hear *directly* they can more easily represent with written symbols than what they experience indirectly. What is necessary is to provide children with experiences that are richly sensory and to help them heighten their sensory awareness.

Make a point from the very beginning of the year to awaken them to the sights, sounds, smells, textures, and tastes of the world. Encourage them to take the time to see, not just look at, but really *see*, what is happening around them. On a fine September morning, take the class outside. Walk to the nearest patch of grass, perhaps to the trees planted outside the school building. Now, together with the children, stare at a tree for two minutes. What did you see? In the beginning, most children will not see much—leaves turning gold and red, a sparrow hopping around the branches, some dog droppings lying near the roots. Try it again, but this time, concentrate as hard as you can. Now one child discovers an insect, marvelously camouflaged, crawling up the trunk; another wonders about the burls and swellings on the branches; someone else remarks on how the sunlight creates patterns of light and shade through the leaves. How wonderful it is to be really able to see.

Do the same kind of thing to awaken the other senses, too. Create interesting sensory illusions in the classroom. For example, get an old umbrella and cut slits in the fabric between the spokes. Darken the room. If you twirl the umbrella round and round as someone flashes a light through it, you can create fascinating light patterns on the wall.

And, of course, talk about what you discover, as did Burrows and her colleagues: "We tell what we see in cloud or fog, what we hear in wind or rain."[13] If you keep a pad of paper handy, you can quickly jot down the children's unique descriptions of an experience.

Creative dramatics.   Creative dramatics, which is characterized by improvisation and children's unique interpretations, offers an excellent channel for oral expression as well as providing opportunities to solve problems, read, and write. Perhaps the most typical vehicle for creative dramatics is a favorite story that one or more of the children have read or heard. With younger children, the reenactment is usually very spontaneous. In the dramatic play area, several kindergartners may dramatize their own interpretation of Goldilocks found sleeping in Baby Bear's bed. Older children will often spend more time planning their presentation. They may meet to discuss such matters as which part of the story to reenact, which characters to involve, and what props to use. Such planning sessions often involve good opportunities to write: sketching out the plot, writing dialogue for the characters, and drawing up a list of props.

With encouragement, the spontaneous dramatic play of younger children can be expanded into more fully developed stories and other kinds of episodes, which can provide material for creative dramatics. The teacher can help to initiate such play by adopting the manner of "let's pretend" in dramatizing very simple episodes, such as tiptoeing across a creaky floor, lifting a very, very heavy box, and balancing a tall stack of lightweight cartons. Children learn that they can convey a message through body movement alone without the use of language. As the children develop a repertoire of movements, they can pantomime stories they have read or written themselves. Ambiguous props and simple materials such as large squares of fabric, which can be used in various imaginative ways, can stimulate this kind of creativity.

Puppets are also very useful in creative dramatics. The simplest stick puppet, made by fastening a picture of a character to a tongue depressor or a popsicle stick, provides a handy medium for dramatizing a story. Standing behind a makeshift curtain or a sturdy carton on a table, even a shy child can feel comfortable talking through the puppet or manipulating it while another child reads or tells the story.

Role-playing is another common feature of dramatic play that lends itself to the older child's expanding interests. Sometimes, as we have seen in the discussion on preparing for an interview, role-playing serves a utilitarian purpose. It can be useful in preparing children for an important experience, such as a trip. As the children enact their own and others' roles on the trip, they may become aware of potential problems and their solutions, and see opportunities that they might otherwise have missed. In addition, role-playing can help bring to life a particularly significant episode the children have uncovered in the course of an investigation, such as the Wright brothers successful launching of their airplane at Kitty Hawk, North Carolina, or clarify the issues in a controversy, such as the community's differing proposals for waste disposal.

Sharing children's literature.   Sharing good literature is another excellent way to spark imagination and at the same time provide a stimulus for writing. Seven- and eight-year-olds enjoy stories about children or animals involved in adventures that are realizable and conflicts that are resolvable. They also appreciate humor, incongruity, and irreverence. And do not forget the ridiculous, à la Dr. Seuss and others. Fine old folktales such as *Stone Soup* and *The Turnip* add the essential ingredient of fantasy.

Sometimes a work of literature can serve as a direct stimulus for writing. Read Tworkov's *The Camel Who Took a Walk* just up to the point in the story where the tiger is quietly waiting to pounce on the unsuspecting camel and let the children compose their own endings. Or, if the children enjoy Maurice Sendak's *Chicken Soup with Rice*, have them create a different recipe substituting their own favorite foods for the months of the year or the days of the week.

Children should also be encouraged to react to books they have read in imaginative ways. Rather than writing a book report, they might opt to design a book jacket and compose a blurb about the book for the front and back flaps. They could compose a letter to the author of the book describing what they liked about it and why. Or, they might try to create a commercial advertising the book.

Literary style and genre.   The study of literature can also awaken children to literary style and genre. Perhaps Dr. Seuss is a favorite. After you read a number of his books with the children, you can ask them what it is they like about the Seuss books. No doubt they will mention the element of the ridiculous that is so strong a feature of Seuss as well as the funny look of his characters and the fanciful words. Someone may note that the stories rhyme. You can add that all of these characteristics are features of Dr. Seuss's style of writing. The next couple of times you read a new Seuss book to the children, have them try to identify who wrote it and indicate why they think so. As they become more skilled at this, choose a title that is not quite as obvious (e.g., *And to Think That I Saw It on Mulberry Street*), so that the children have to discern subtler clues.

In the same way, you can help children become aware of the distinctive artistic features of familiar illustrators like Maurice Sendak and Marjorie Flack. Eventually some of the children may want to try their hands at composing a book of their own like Dr. Seuss's (or another author you have studied).

Moreover, reading aloud good examples of different literary types or genres, such as folktales, myths, and realistic fiction, is an excellent inspiration for children to create their own versions. With many opportunities to listen to good literature, children begin to comprehend the linguistic and literary conventions of different literary genres, the basis for controlling these features in their own writing.

A Curriculum for English, developed by the Nebraska Curriculum Development Center, is a spiral and integrated program of study for grades one through six designed around nine literary genres.[14] Its purpose is to help children understand the structure of different literary models as a basis for organizing their own writing. In the second-grade unit on fable, the teacher reads "The Hare and the Tortoise" and "The Ant and the Grasshopper" to the children. Afterward, she asks questions to illuminate the fables' themes and help the children understand their meaning. She does not outline the characteristics of fable, but rather helps the children to induce them through experience with the literature itself. Among the possible composition activities that could grow out of this study of fables are finishing the story of "The Ant and the Grasshopper" by describing what happened to the grasshopper that cold, hard winter and writing their own stories paralleling the two fables by substituting other animals. "Crow Boy," by Taro Yashima, the illustrative story in the second-grade unit on other lands and people, tells the sensitive story of a shy child's isolation because he appears different from his peers. When they read and discuss the story, the teacher assists the children in recognizing the plot and the distinctive traits of the characters and their feelings. Later, the children might compose stories about how Crow Boy felt when he was staring out the window or at the ceiling in school. If they know children who come from other countries, they might want to write about how these children are alike, yet different, from native-born American children.

You do not have to have a prepared curriculum to help children learn and use the structure of different literary models, but you do need to read aloud to them regularly from different literary genres. Each new listening experience should be linked to prior ones, so that the children can accumulate a bank of knowledge on various styles. Your questions should be geared to helping them induce the nature of literary models. Finally, in follow-up composition activities, they should have the chance to apply what they have learned.

Structured ideas for writing.   Sometimes teachers use structured ideas to try to stimulate children's writing. "Story starters" is an example of this kind of technique, in which the child must write the ending to a story that begins in a typically suspenseful way:

Once upon a time, there was an old broken down house on Juniper Street. No one lived there anymore, but all the kids in the neighborhood could swear that they saw a pair of eerie green eyes peering at them from an upstairs window. . . .

Such structured techniques are very popular, and a number of resource books have been published which consist solely of these kinds of ideas; Ruth K. Carlson's *Sparkling Words* (Geneva, Ill.: Paladin House, 1973) is a longtime favorite.

Structured ideas for writing do have a place in the curriculum; many can be easily converted into language arts activity cards. However, their use should be infrequent and their rank subordinate in the hierarchy of techniques that you use to stimulate writing. For one thing, such ideas often have no real purpose as far as literacy or the appreciation of language is concerned; they are there because someone finds their gimmickry appealing. One of these ideas employs a deck of index cards divided into three equal parts: one-third are character cards, one-third are situation cards, and one-third are place cards. Each card is color-coded to identify its category. The child selects a card from each of the categories and composes a story around the three elements she has selected. The novelty of this kind of activity is apt to wear off quickly because of its mechanical and superficial nature. This raises still another problem with structured techniques. Regardless of how adorable one of these ideas is, it is, nonetheless, contrived. The child can see no real purpose for doing it except that it is one more task to complete. Finally, structured ideas may produce dependence on the child's part if she becomes used to the idea of writing only in response to externally imposed stimuli. Such an approach is not likely to engender power or pleasure in writing.

Structured formats for writing.   However, structured formats can be quite useful in building the confidence of children whose progress in literacy is slow. When two or three children collaborate on writing a book, it alleviates the pressure on the single child to be responsible for all phases of the project and enables all to share in each other's strengths. Likewise, a cumulative book on a given theme, which can be left out in the language arts area with blank pages for individual children's contributions, allows a child to participate in a large project even before her own skills might permit her to complete it alone. Remember, however, that the more control the child has over the writing process, the more independent she is apt to become. And of course, this is to be encouraged.

Helping those who are slow to start composing.   Children will show eagerness to jump right in or various degrees of reticence about starting to compose, depending on their prior history in writing. There are a number of things you can do to help the slow starters.

Begin by reading aloud stories and books composed by other children in the class. As we emphasized in the last chatper, it is essential to build an attitude of *appreciative listening* in the children. There is nothing more apt to kill the timid first attempts of a novice than the cold criticism of an audience. Children learn to take chances and experiment in an atmosphere of support and appreciation. Spend some time every day sharing stories written by the children. Soon, most of the children will indicate their own desire to write.

You should provide at least twenty minutes each day during which the children can write if they choose. This time should be entirely unpressured; the children should be able to select other options as well, such as reading quietly, working on a project, or visiting the school library to do some independent research on a report. As they become immersed in their own investigations, opportunities to write will develop naturally. Because this writing is purposeful, it is rarely mundane and never contrived.

With the children's agreement, you or the writers themselves can read the newly written stories aloud. Again, encourage an atmosphere of attentive and appreciative listening and direct comments to the unique and positive qualities of each piece. A few children will need more assistance, which you can provide through individual conferences. Having a chance to read their stories aloud will, no doubt, add incentive to their writing. Of course, proudly displaying children's written compositions as individual stories or books, alongside other children's literature, will go a long way to underscoring the importance and value of the children's own work.

Sharing poetry.   The same ingredients that make up a successful program for story writing are required for success in writing poems: an appreciative, unpressured atmosphere; an environment rich in sensory experience; and the sharing of good poetry for children.

The poetry preferences of seven- and eight-year-old children parallel their preferences in prose forms. They enjoy humor, rhythm, pleasurable familiar experiences, poems about children and animals and about the ridiculous:

A thousand hairy savages
Sitting down to lunch,
Gobble, gobble, glup, glup,
Munch, munch, munch.
(S. Milligan, "A Thousand Hairy Savages")

Many of the favorite poems of children in this age range come from oral folk tradition and are frequently chanted in street games:

I won't go to Macy's
Any more, more, more.
There's a big fat policeman
At the door, door, door.
He'll catch you by the collar,
And make you pay a dollar.
So I won't go to Macy's
Any more, more, more.

Imagery in the poems should make an obvious appeal to the senses such as the slishes and sloshes of Susie's galoshes in the poem by Rhoda Bacmeister.

You should also make a point of reading poetry that does *not* rhyme. If you always read rhyming poetry, children may come to equate poetry *with* rhyme, and when they compose poems of their own, sacrifice meaning for rhyme. If you look for it, you can find much good nonrhyming poetry suitable for children. Carl Sandburg's "Fog" is a fine example:

The fog comes
on little cat feet.
It sits looking
over harbor and city
on silent haunches
and then moves on.

and "Mountains," by Ann Nolan Clark:

Mountains are the high places,
They reach up and up
To the blue-blue above.
They stand around us,
Looking down at the people.
I like to know
That mountains are there,
Around me
So quiet,
So big
And so high.

You will need to have good sources of poetry available for reading aloud. Three fine anthologies are:

- *Poems Children Will Sit Still For*, compiled by B. S. deRegniers, E. Moore, and M. M. White. New York: Citation Press, 1969.
- *Sung Under the Silver Umbrella*, compiled by the Association for Childhood Education International. New York: Macmillan, 1962.
- *Time for Poetry*, 3d ed., edited by M. H. Arbuthnot and S. L. Root. Glenview, Ill.: Scott, Foresman, 1968.
- *Treasure Chest*, compiled by B. Martin, Jr., J. Archambault, and P. Brogan. Allen, Texas: PLM Resources, 1986.

No doubt you will also want to have collections of the poetry of individual poets, such as Myra Cohn Livingston, David McCord, and Shel Silverstein.

The most efficient way to keep the poems is in your own card catalog. If you write each poem on an index card and label and alphabetize it according to subject, then you can quickly and easily find just the poem you want when the need arises. Suppose it is a wet April morning when the children arrive. The showers have stopped and you want the children to sense as fully as they can the ripeness of early spring. As part of this experience, you read aloud an appropriate poem. You might select this one, classified under the topic "Spring," in your file:

The rains of spring
  Which hang to the branches
Of the green willow
  Look like pearls upon a string.
(Lady Ise, "The Rains of Spring," arranged by O. B. Miller.
From *Little Pictures of Japan*)

Presenting poetry effectively.   It is always necessary to practice reading aloud materials that you are going to present to children. In the case of poetry, this is even more essential because unless you are quite familiar with the poem, the tendency is for the rhythm to predominate over the meaning, which can result in a monotonous, sing-song effect. Practice reading the poem silently at first and then orally. Try to read for meaning and keep the rhythmic pattern subordinate. Read the poem slowly and naturally. If possible, tape-record yourself and make adjustments in your reading where necessary.

There is more to a good presentation of a poem than just reading it well aloud. If hearing a poem is to be a creative experience for the children, the poem must be set against an appropriate background and the proper mood established. Do not overwhelm the children by reading too much poetry at any one time and read to them when they are feeling relaxed and comfortable. For the poem, "The Rains of Spring" cited above, the children's explorations of their *own* perceptions came first. After seeing, feeling, and smelling the effects of the shower themselves, the children were ready to appreciate how an artist's words described a similar event.

Children's poetic sense can be developed through countless experiences of this kind with poetic forms. Such experiences help them to understand the poet's delight in words and provide models for their own free, yet precise, poetic expression. After reading a poem, ask the children what they liked about it—what was especially beautiful or strong, or conveyed a particularly clear picture. For "The Rains of Spring," the children will undoubtedly mention the droplets of rain arranged like pearls. Ask them if they can think of interesting ways of their own to describe the rain droplets. You might want to read another poem about spring rain so that the chilren can compare the imagery of a different poet. The children may want to respond to the poem through the graphic arts—paint, clay, or collage—or through pantomime.

Choral reading.   Choral reading is another way to help encourage children's appreciation of poetry. In *choral reading*, the children say a piece of verse or prose together. The lines are written on the chalkboard or displayed on an overhead projector. You may also want to make an individual copy of the piece for each child. Read the lines aloud together with the children. When the children are sufficiently familiar with the piece, they can recite it by themselves. This kind of social activity, in which the children read in unison, makes it easy for a child to participate, since he is surrounded by the security of the total group. Pieces for reading should have strong rhythm and meter and, in the primary grades, be quite brief. The familiar nursery rhyme, "One, two," illustrates the kind of material to start with. The children should read it first together, and then the class can be divided in two, each half reading alternating couplets:

One, two,
Buckle my shoe,
Three, four,
Shut the door,
Five, six,
Pick up sticks,
Seven, eight,
Close the gate,
Nine, ten,
A good, fat hen,
Eleven, twelve,
Let us delve,
Thirteen, fourteen,
Maids a-courting,
Fifteen, sixteen,
Maids in the kitchen,
Seventeen, eighteen,
Maids a-waiting,
Nineteen, twenty,
My stomach's empty,
Please, Mother,
Give me something to eat.

Choral reading helps children to appreciate the musical flow of words, just as it makes them more conscious of vocal intonations and the rhythm of language. As they become familiar with the procedures, the children will be ready to try more difficult pieces. "There Was an Old Woman" is still simple, yet ridiculous enough to amuse most seven- and eight-year-olds:

There was an old woman who swallowed a fly;
I wonder why
She swallowed a fly.
Poor old woman, she's sure to die.

There was an old woman who swallowed a spider;
That wriggled and jiggled and wriggled inside her;
She swallowed the spider to catch the fly,
I wonder why
She swallowed a fly.
Poor old woman, she's sure to die.

There was an old woman who swallowed a bird;
How absurd
To swallow a bird.
She swallowed the bird to catch the spider,
That wriggled and jiggled and wriggled inside her.
She swallowed the spider to catch the fly,
I wonder why
She swallowed a fly.
Poor old woman, she's sure to die.

There was an old woman who swallowed a cat;
Fancy that!
She swallowed a cat;
She swallowed the cat to catch the bird,
She swallowed the bird to catch the spider,
That wriggled and jiggled and wriggled inside her.
She swallowed the spider to catch the fly,
I wonder why
She swallowed a fly.
Poor old woman, she's sure to die.

There was an old woman who swallowed a dog;
She went the whole hog
And swallowed a dog;
She swallowed the dog to catch the cat,
She swallowed the cat to catch the bird,
She swallowed the bird to catch the spider,
That wriggled and jiggled and wriggled inside her.
She swallowed the spider to catch the fly,
I wonder why
She swallowed a fly.
Poor old woman, she's sure to die . . .

In selecting poetry for choral reading, Stewig suggests these guidelines: begin with poems that contain a lot of repetition of sound, such as Ets's "Jay Bird"; then move on to poetry with repeated refrains, such as the Mother Goose rhyme, "To Market, To Market"; next, try cumulative refrains, such as Rogers's version of "The House that Jack Built."[15]

Songs are another good source of choral reading material. In *Jazz Chants for Children* (New York: Oxford University Press, 1978), Carolyn Graham provides rhythmic interpretations of simple poems, songs, and chants that allow children both to speak and to move rhythmically. A cassette tape accompanies the guide.

In the beginning, concentrate on unison reading. Then, using very simple material (e.g., "One, two"), have different groups be responsible for reading different parts of the poem. This style of choral reading is called *antiphonal*. When individual children indicate a desire to do so, they can be responsible for reading a line alone.

Once the children are satisfied with their rendition of a reading, tape-record it for them to play back and enjoy at other times. Include a transcript of the taped material for the children to read as they listen to the tape.

Writing poetry.   The prerequisites for writing poetry are a wide background of experience; many opportunities to hear good poetry of all kinds; close examination of sensory experiences; and the chance to think and to talk about observations.

Children's first attempts at poetry writing should be very free and unstructured. For those children who indicate a need for assistance, group and individual dictation are good ways to begin because their thoughts are fleeting and may be easily lost as they concentrate on the mechanics of writing. Burrows and her colleagues suggest that many experiences, such as the anticipation of a holiday or an outdoor adventure, are appropriate for group dictation.[16] The children sit around the scribe and offer their unique impression of the experience. The teacher or aide records each child's words, exactly as they are given, on the chalkboard or chart. After everyone who wants to make a contribution has done so, the teacher works with the children in rearranging lines and deleting repetitious phrases, so that the final piece demonstrates individuality and color. Then the teacher rewrites the poem on chart paper and posts it in the room.

Children can also write in small groups of two or three, when at least one of the members writes well enough to serve as scribe. In this case, the children operate without the teacher's direct supervision. In the course of deciding which words to use, rearranging phrases, and choosing the best form to fit their ideas, the children have an excellent opportunity to learn about writing poetry. As they become used to expressing themselves poetically, encourage the children to keep a pad handy on which to jot brief notes or ideas as they think of them, as many professional writers do.

Experimenting with different poetic forms.   Once the children become used to writing poetry, some of them may want to experiment with various poetic forms. This is fine as long as they remember that the meaning of a poem is more important than the form. Otherwise, the children's struggle to find words that fit the formula may result in poems that are little more than doggerel.

The *cinquain* is a form of unrhymed poetry that is easy enough for second- or third-graders to try their hands at. A cinquain consists of five lines: line one is the name of something or someone; line two consists of two words that describe the thing in line one; line three consists of three words ending in *-ing* that describe an action of the poem's topic; line four consists of a four-word comment or feeling about the topic; and line five consists of one word that either repeats line one or is a synonym for it. Here is an example of a cinquain:

Tortoise
Slow, brown.
Eating, sleeping, moving.
Hides his head away
Afraid.

The *diamante* is a somewhat more difficult form. It is called diamante because the words of the poem create the outline of a diamond. The first three lines follow the cinquain pattern: line one consists of a single word that names the poem's topic; line two consists of two words that describe it; and line three is composed of three words ending in *-ing* that describe actions of the topic. Line four of the diamante, however, is composed of four words that describe something that is the *opposite* of the topic in line one. Line five has three *-ing* words that describe actions of the new and opposite topic. Line six has two words to describe the new topic, and line seven names the new topic in a single word. Gary, an eight-year-old, composed this diamante:

Old
Sad, afraid
Wrinkling, failing, dying.
Life, strong, alive, new
Beginning, learning, living
Happy, brave
Young.

Many children enjoy writing *concrete poetry*, probably because it has so little predetermined structure and because of the fun of picture writing. In concrete poetry, the words either outline or form a solid, visual representation of the poem's central idea. Figure 5–4, for example, presents Bernadette's concrete poem about a tree.

Finally, another form that may appeal to children, especially if they are not quite ready to compose by themselves, is called *found poetry*. In found poetry, a piece of prose writing is rearranged into a poetic form. Any prose writing will do, but I have found that advertisements offer rich and often very amusing possibilities. If the prose is very descriptive to begin with, it can easily be converted, as in the case of the following from an ad for *Science* magazine. It was a simple matter to rearrange:

Suddenly, as if out of nowhere, an eerie dagger of light appeared to stab at the topmost rung of the spiral. It next began to plunge downwards—shimmering, laserlike.

into

Suddenly
As if out of nowhere
An eerie dagger of light
Appeared to stab
At the topmost rung of the spiral.
It next began to plunge
Downwards
Shimmering, laserlike.

Found poetry can help to make children aware of the phrasing and rhythmic cadences of poetry.

Far more important than the ability to reproduce a poetic form is the child's enjoyment of writing poems. What you want to emphasize with the children is the

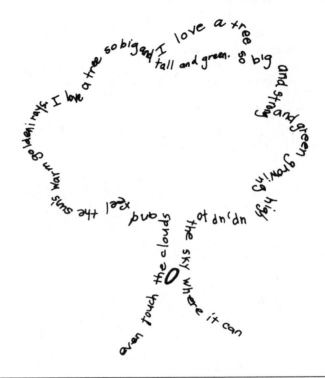

Figure 5–4   Bernadette's poem about a tree

writing of poetry that is genuine and sincere and the use of language in poetic form that is natural, yet original and distinctive.

Developing Competence in Skills

With increasing mastery of the mechanics of writing, children gain both power and precision in written composition. As they get older, they not only *need*, they *want* to have the skills that are necessary to translate their ideas and feelings into written form. Seven- and eight-year-olds are conscious of their audience when they write, and they enjoy working on a project until it satisfies their own standards and those of their audience.

To be most effective in teaching skills, teachers should remember the following points: first, to teach skills as an integral part of the composing process, rather than in isolation, so that children can see their purpose; second, to subordinate the mechanical aspects of writing to the meaning expressed in written form; third, to allow children to write while they master mechanical skills; fourth, to emphasize quality of content in first drafts, while concentrating on skills in later drafts; fifth, to tailor the teaching of skills to the needs of individual children as they arise; and, sixth, to help children learn the skills that are within their grasp. In this section we will consider the teaching of cursive handwriting, punctuation and spelling, and the revising process.

Cursive Handwriting

Cursive writing is neither faster, easier, nor more legible than manuscript. However, because it is the socially accepted form of handwriting for adults, nearly seventy percent of the elementary schools in the United States introduce cursive writing sometime between the first half of second grade and the first half of fourth grade.[17] The most significant difference between cursive and manuscript writing is the need in cursive to slide laterally to join letters, but there are other differences as well: the letters *i* and *j* are dotted and the letter *t* is crossed after the entire word has been written in cursive but immediately after the letter has been written in manuscript; the uppercase cursive letters differ considerably from their lowercase forms, whereas much of the manuscript alphabet is quite similar in both upper- and lowercase forms; and cursive writing differs from book print more than manuscript does. The basic shapes used in cursive writing are slant strokes, connecting strokes, and ovals.[18]

The legibility of cursive writing is dependent upon four factors: proper letter formation; regularity of slant; uniformity of letter size; and regularity of spacing within and between words. Actually, only five lowercase cursive letters differ substantially from their manuscript counterparts—*s, r, f, e,* and *z*—and therefore may need special attention. However, many years ago, a study by Quant found that, in addition to *r* and *e*, six other letters, which are frequently written illegibly, often account for apparent spelling errors in cursive writing: *a, d, o, t, n,* and *I*.[19] A child's preference about *direction* of slant should be honored since it is *consistency* of slant that is the important factor in legibility.

An intermediate step between manuscript and cursive writing, which you may observe as early as the latter part of first grade, is *slant writing*. Spontaneously, a child starts to slant his print consistently in one direction because it is a more natural way to write and improves his vision, hand and body position, and arm leverage in writing. This development makes for an easy transition into cursive writing. Thus, postponing the introduction of cursive writing until some predetermined time in the later primary grades seems rather arbitrary. A better idea might be to permit children to move into cursive writing whenever they indicate an interest in doing so. When a group of children indicate a readiness to move into cursive writing, you can provide them with the help they need, and in the process, engage other children's interest in cursive writing.

In addition, children should have the opportunity to read and become familiar with cursive handwriting; you can post signs and messages around the room written in both manuscript and cursive styles that record the day's date and activities. Display a sample of the cursive alphabet and make individual copies available to the children. You can also duplicate copies of simple messages in both styles for the children to read.

Punctuation

If you listen to native English-speaking children of seven or eight, you will find that they are quite adept at handling the intonation patterns of English. They can skillfully manipulate pitch, stress, and juncture in their flow of speech to indicate their meaning. What children need to learn is that punctuation is the equivalent *graphic* means for signaling intonation in writing. Punctuation in writing is not as effective for conveying meaning as pitch, stress, and juncture are in speaking; but children need to understand that punctuation helps the writer get his meaning across to the reader without the benefit of intonation patterns, facial expressions, gestures, posture, and all kinds of clues from the social context.

Children first become aware of the conventions of punctuation as they are being read to and read along themselves, and when they dictate their own stories and write their own pieces. Listening and watching as a skilled reader expresses the intonation patterns of a story, the child begins to associate punctuation marks with the different kinds of sentences and with the stopping and starting of sentences. As a child dictates to you, she observes you adding commas, periods, question marks, and capital letters to her words. She may ask you about their meaning and start to use some of the punctuation marks herself, following your example. Thus, native speakers have a strong intuitive grasp of the purpose of intonation, and native speaker or not, children's experiences in reading and dictating help to make them more aware of the relationship between intonation and punctuation. What is necessary is to raise their metalingual awareness of this feature of written language.

The best way to teach the rules of punctuation is inductively and individually. When children have many opportunities to write purposefully, they will see the need for punctuation and they will learn to use the forms of punctuation they need. In this way, children can really understand how punctuation works and will be able to induce the rules for its use by themselves. Moreover, you should reserve instruction in the skills of punctuation for those children who need it. Gather together a small group of children who have demonstrated a need to learn more about the use of commas, for example. Working in this more individualized way allows you to direct help where it is most necessary, rather than forcing all the children to participate regardless of need.

Spelling

The most significant part of the composing process is getting ideas down on paper. After that, a writer can give attention to such things as logical sequence and stylistic matters letting concern with mechanical details wait for the final editing stage. If a teacher places too much emphasis on correct spelling, the result may be that the child will limit his writing to only those words he knows how to spell, to the great detriment of meaning and imagination.

Children learn to spell the words that they need when they write for genuine purposes. They learn to spell words functionally. Individual and group word banks, picture and other kinds of dictionaries, and charts of words grouped by category provide ready spelling sources. However, overdependence on such sources can discourage children from taking risks in spelling and ultimately becoming more independent spellers.

Children learn how to handle the spelling of words they are unsure of as they write by spelling a word the way it sounds, for example, or leaving a blank space for the unknown word, or just writing the initial letter. Such techniques allow the child to come back to the word after he is finished composing and do not interfere with his flow of thought. The child usually has little difficulty remembering the word to be spelled because of the personal significance of the piece of writing and the rich contextual clues surrounding the word in question.

Traditional spelling programs. In traditional spelling programs, two to five thousand of the words most commonly found in the writing of children and adults are arranged in a series of instructional units from the second through the eighth grades. The number of spelling lessons ranges from thirty-two to thirty-six per year, and the number of spelling words per weekly lesson from fifteen to twenty.[20] A typical pattern of instruction is organized around the weekly spelling lesson: new words are introduced on Monday; children study the new words on Tuesday; on Wednesday, the children take a trial, or pretest, of the words; on Thursday, they study the words missed on the pretest; and on Friday, they take a final test of the week's spelling words.

Another feature of traditional spelling programs is the teaching of *spelling generalizations*. These are rules about common English spelling patterns, which children are meant to memorize to help them spell. One such generalization states that when two vowel letters appear together, the long sound of the first vowel is heard while the second one is silent (as in *meat*), or as it is often taught for mnemonic purposes, "As two vowels go walking, the first does the talking." However, spelling generalizations often do not hold true. In a study carried out by Davis of the 1,893 words in which two vowel letters appeared alongside each other, only 612 conformed to the rule, while 1,281 were exceptions. Davis was able to find only ten spelling generalizations that applied seventy-five percent or more of the time.[21]

An individualized approach. The problem with teaching spelling in this manner is that it is so arbitrary and does not relate to the children's actual writing needs. If children see no real purpose in learning the words, the task of rote memorization of a weekly spelling list is apt to have very little appeal. A much more sensible approach is to develop an individualized spelling program in which each child learns the words he needs, when he needs them. Each child can compile a list of the words he needs in writing, whose spelling he is uncertain of. An individual spelling notebook provides a useful way to organize the words alphabetically, one page for each of the twenty-six letters. Once the child is able to write a word correctly without consulting his spelling notebook, he can cross it off his list of words.

Another difficulty with traditional spelling programs is that their shotgun approach rarely zeroes in on the particular spelling difficulties of an individual child. Individualized diagnosis is a much more efficient plan. If you occasionally record a child's misspellings and study the words, you may well pick up a pattern in the errors to which you can respond directly. Most children do not misspell a large number of words, but rather, repeatedly misspell the same ones. Group the child's misspelled words by pattern of error and work on two or three words each week. Write the troublesome words on brightly colored, self-adhesive cards and stick them to the child's desk or place at a table. During the week, he can practice copying the words from the cards and then spelling them without looking at the cards. When he feels comfortable writing the words, but still needs to check them, you can cover the cards. When he is sure of his ability to spell the words correctly by himself, you can remove the colored cards.

Spelling and reading.   Some of children's spelling difficulties may be attributable to the less than perfectly regular phoneme/grapheme correspondence in English. However, English is not nearly as irregular as some may believe, and spelling forms continue to become more regular (e.g., *fantasy* for *phantasy*). An extensive computer study found that English contains very consistent patterns and that highly irregular spellings are few.[22] Probably more significant is whether or not the child reads extensively. As you will recall from chapter 1, children start to relinquish their pattern of invented spellings, which is based on how words *sound*, as they become more familiar with the way words *look* through reading.

My own experience with college-level students who spell incorrectly confirms the relationship between reading and spelling. Usually, these students tell me that they read very little when they were in elementary school, and the words they misspell now are often the very common ones found in elementary-level material. Reading a great deal gives children the necessary amount of written material from which to generalize spelling patterns and the frequent repetition of irregular forms required for visual memory.

Spelling games.   One of the enjoyable aspects of teaching spelling is that it lends itself so nicely to word games of all kinds. "Hangman" is probably one of the more familiar ones. Draw a scaffold on the chalkboard with several blank lines next to it (Figure 5–5). The children must find out what word you or one of their classmates has selected by guessing what letters it contains. Each space next to the scaffold represents a letter in the word. Every wrong guess allows you to add another part to the person hanging from the noose. The children must guess the word before you draw the entire figure.

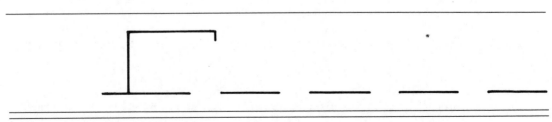

Figure 5–5   The game of Hangman

You can vary the familiar "Tic-Tac-Toe" game by substituting letters for the Xs and Os. The players take turns adding a new letter to the ones already played with the object of creating a word first.

In "I Sentence You," partners take turns giving each other a word. The other person must produce a sentence, in which the initial letters of the words are the same as the letters in the original word: e.g., for the word *dog*, an acceptable sentence would be "Do only good."

Anagrams involve making new words by rearranging the letters of a given word. To begin, use short, simple words such as *rat → tar, art*. A variation on this is "Beheadings," in which the children find new words by removing the beginning letters of the original words, as in *start → art*, and *Max → ax*. In "Kangaroo," they try to find little words in bigger ones, such as *under* and *stand* in *understand*. A more advanced version of the same general idea occurs in "Dizzy Words," in which letters are written in the boxes in a square. The object of the game is to find and circle as many words, written forward, backward, or diagonally, as you can.

These ideas represent only a very small sample of the many possibilities available. As the children's interests and abilities indicate, you can create many variations on familiar games, such as Bingo, Scrabble™, and crossword puzzles. Whether these activities are carried out under your supervision or by the children independently, they can help to enrich the teaching of spelling.

The Revising Process

When it comes to polishing their writing, first graders are usually preoccupied with aesthetic matters, such as legibility and neatness. As Graves observed in studying young writers, children's understanding of what is important in the writing process changes with experience.[23]

Beginners are concerned at first with aesthetic matters such as handwriting and then the conventions of spelling and punctuation. Their primary attention next shifts to the content (topic and information) of what they have written. Making major revisions that involve adding, deleting, or reorganizing content comes last. Graves found that children are able to make changes in all or most of the areas from the outset of writing; it is just that different aspects of the writing process predominate at various stages in their development. By the second or third grade many if not most children will have had sufficient experience in writing to be comfortable focusing on what is central: *meaning*. This will especially be the case if their writing history has emphasized content in first drafts and left mechanical details until the final draft.

Children who have been taught that form supersedes function, however, need special help. They must learn that a sloppy paper is a perfectly acceptable part of the revising process. Encouraged to leave wide margins and write on alternating lines, these children will gradually be able to "mess up" their papers in order to add, delete, or make various adjustments in what they have written.

Steps in the revising process.   Learning to revise their writing will allow children to experience a sense of pride in doing a job well. Seeing a task they have worked on long and hard finally completed brings a wonderful feeling of accomplishment, which is compounded by the enthusiastic response of classmates and teacher.

The first thing children must learn about the editing process is to decide whether a particular piece of writing is important enough to devote the time and energy needed to make it as good as they can. Since revising is hard work, there is no point in their spending time revising something that has no real meaning for them.

The sequence of the revising process includes reviewing the piece of writing for clarity, looking for alternatives in sequencing, and adding and deleting ideas; next checking on spelling and punctuation; and finally, rewriting a last copy giving special attention to handwriting and neatness.

An important part of the revising process is reading over what a child has written. First, the child should read the piece over herself. Reading aloud is often very helpful for actually "hearing" what you have written. Tape-recording the reading and then playing it back permits more careful listening. Does the piece say what she really meant it to? If not, this is the point where the child will want to make some revision. She may do this alone, in consultation with you, or with some of her classmates.

Next, she may ask you or a classmate to read her paper and make suggestions. If this were a collective writing project with one or two other children, this small group would constitute an excellent revising panel. At the beginning, you may want to sit in on the children's discussions to model raising the kinds of questions that are useful for clarifying and sharpening writing. You should not contribute to the composition yourself, but rather, suggest alternatives if the children get stuck.

Another possibility is to use editors, children whose job it is to assist others with their writing by raising questions and pointing out difficulties after the first draft is completed. These children are not necessarily the "best" writers in the class but those who enjoy and are competent in helping others see what needs polishing in their writing. Editors do not make contributions to the composition; the writers themselves provide their own solutions to the points raised by the editors.

Using a microcomputer for word processing.   With a microcomputer, a text-editing program, and a printer, students are able to enter, organize, and edit whatever they write. There are obvious advantages in the use of the microcomputer for word processing. It can reduce the tedium and frustration associated with handwritten composition and thus, may motivate children to write. The ease of editing on a word processor may foster a willingness to revise, and its ability to produce multiple copies simply makes the sharing of children's work easy to accomplish. Some research indicates that children were more successful in written composition in schools where word processing programs were used than in schools where they were not.[24] However, such programs are quite new, and they are not unequivocally successful.

The use of a microcomputer can certainly ease the drudgery of rewriting, but whether it can help to improve the quality of writing is another question. Children must see the *need* for revision before they will want to use the microcomputer to accomplish it. Another important consideration is the quality of the word processing program. Currently, a favorably received program for children is the Scholastic, Inc. version of *Bank Street Writer*, recommended for children in grades four and above.[25] The program commands remain on the screen for children to refer to whenever they need them. Functions include *add*, *delete*, *search*, *print*, and *copy*. Another helpful feature of *Bank Street Writer* is its good mnemonics; that is, the names of its commands are meaningful and therefore easy to remember. For example, the command indicating "move up" is *Up*. Children who are unable to use this program alone can work with the teacher, an aide, or another child. It is even possible to simplify the program further through the use of a special keyboard with keys in alphabetical order and color-coded command keys. *Magic Slate*, published by Sunburst Communications of Pleasantville, N.Y., is a word processing program also suited to younger students. It can expand its text editing features to suit the needs of more sophisticated users, as well.

The increasing presence of the microcomputer in elementary schools may have a significant effect on instruction in literacy. Its applicability to writing programs is obvious. However, it is too early to know whether the microcomputer will become yet another fad in the history of American schools, such as the teaching machines of the 1960s, or whether it will actually make a lasting contribution to education.

The reading/writing conference.　As we have already noted, the reading/writing conference is central to the writing program. It is scheduled to provide a regular, ongoing opportunity for the child to consult with you on his writing progress. In the conference you work with the child at his particular level of development, identifying strengths and weaknesses in his writing and providing strategies for dealing with them.

It is generally a good idea to deal with only one writing skill in each piece of writing. Which skill you select should be determined by how significant it is in conveying the child's meaning. If, for example, the absence or misplacement of commas in a child's composition alters or blurs his intended meaning, then focus on the proper use of commas in this composition. Otherwise, you should select skills according to how frequently the child has difficulty with them. Problems that arise very rarely should not be matters of concern in the conferences.

You can also introduce the child to the vocabulary of editing in the conferences by using terms like *draft*, *revise*, *lead*, and *details* consistently in association with the aspects of writing they describe. Soon children will begin to use the terms themselves. Some may even enjoy using a few of the common professional proofreading marks, such as:

- ʌ , meaning insert a word, punctuation mark, or sentence.
- ≡ , meaning capitalize.
- / , meaning do not capitalize.
- ℬ , meaning delete a word, punctuation mark, or sentence.
- ℙ , meaning start a new paragraph.

You can help each child develop an individualized revising guide, which succinctly lists and illustrates the steps the child should follow in revising his work. This guide can be kept in the child's writing folder or, if there is room, pasted on one of the inside covers.

Another possibility for the writing conference is to draw up a brief list of questions that children can use in evaluating their own work: Is my writing clear? Is my writing suitable? Is my writing complete? Is my writing well organized? Of course, you must work with the children individually and in groups to help them understand what the criteria of clarity, suitability, completeness, and organization actually mean. However, having the children keep the list of questions in their writing folders for ready consultation can be helpful.

Summary

In this chapter, we have seen how children's abilities in literacy grow in the later primary grades. By providing for an increasing range of achievement, organizing the classroom to build independence, and teaching the necessary skills appropriately, you can help the children to expand and refine their abilities in:

- Reading for information.
- Gathering and organizing information.
- Writing and presenting reports.
- Choral reading.
- Composing stories and poems.

Activities

1. Consider your own writing. First, how much writing do you do? What kinds of writing do you do? Is there a relationship between the kind of writing you do and whether it is required or not? What are your own feelings about writing? Try to think about the reasons for your feelings. Second, use a standard manuscript or cursive guide to evaluate your handwriting. How does it deviate from the guide? Practice until your writing would be an adequate model for children. Try to collect several handwritten envelopes and study the writing to determine what factors affect legibility. How does your handwriting compare to that in the handwritten samples?

2. Arrange to observe in a third-grade class when the children are writing. Do any of the children revise their writing before considering it finished and ready to share? What procedures are followed for revision? What role do classmates and teacher play? Try to speak with one or two of the children who do revise. Ask them how they feel about writing and why they are working so carefully. (Adapted from D. M. Lee and J. B. Rubin, *Children and Language: Reading and Writing; Talking and Listening.* Belmont, Calif.: Wadsworth, 1979.)

3. Collect some first-draft compositions written by third graders. List the words that you find misspelled. Are the same words misspelled by more than one child? What are your conclusions about common types of spelling errors? What procedures would you use to help these children improve their spelling?

4. Collect compositions written by several different children in the same second- or third-grade class. Study them to determine the range of achievement in content and mechanics. What procedures would you use to help each of these children develop his or her literacy abilities?

5. Read several unrhymed poems to a group of second- or third-grade children. Afterward, stimulate a discussion about the poems. Did they like these poems? Ask them how these poems were different from most of the poetry they hear. Help the children to realize that poetry means rhythm but not necessarily rhyme. Later, after some interesting experience, lead the children in group dictation of a poem but emphasize that it is to be unrhymed. Concentrate on the freshness of their perceptions and the unique ways they describe the experience.

Further Reading and Viewing

Printed Materials

Burrows, A. T., Jackson, D. C., and Saunders, D. O. *They All Want to Write*, 4th ed. Hamden, Conn.: Shoe String Press, 1984.

Busching, B. A., and Schwartz, J. I., eds. *Integrating the Language Arts in the Elementary School*. Urbana, Ill.: National Council of Teachers of English, 1983.

Calkins, L. McC. *The Art of Teaching Writing*. Portsmouth, N.H.: Heinemann, 1986.

Graves, D. H. *Writing: Teachers and Children at Work*. Portsmouth, N.H.: Heinemann, 1983.

Mearns, H. *Creative Power: The Education of Youth in the Creative Arts*. New York: Dover, 1958.

Filmstrip

The Story of a River (includes record). New York: Bank Street College of Education.

he oven to see if "I was
way through her garden do
food and then a bear ate
ickled the bear's tumm
opened his mouth and

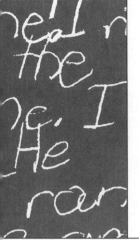

SECTION THREE

Specifics
of
Instruction

In this final section, we will discuss two particularly important areas of instruction, comprehension and assessment, as they were illustrated in the program descriptions in section II. As we have seen in earlier chapters, children construct knowledge of the world and reconstruct meaning in what they read and hear. Thus, comprehension is central to the socio-cognitive view of language learning. Indeed, we may question whether there is any real learning without comprehension! Likewise, good assessment techniques are essential to a successful program in literacy because they provide the teacher with the information she needs to make informed decisions about how, when, and what to teach. She draws most of this information from her informal and ongoing interactions with the children, which is at the heart of the approach described in this book.

Chapter 6

Comprehension

Preview

Comprehension is central to language processing, whether the language is spoken or written. Although conventional wisdom may attribute equal importance to both decoding and understanding words, we know that without understanding, there is no reading. Children comprehend language from infancy on. Indeed, they understand a good deal of language long before they are able to produce any of it. Thus, comprehension instruction should begin at the preschool level with spoken material and proceed into the later grades with spoken and written texts. This chapter investigates what comprehension is and how teachers can help to develop it in their students. To guide your reading, here are some of the major points in the chapter:

1. *Comprehension as process and product.*
2. *Skills mastery programs and comprehension.*
3. *Three levels of comprehension skills.*
4. *General guidelines for comprehension instruction.*
5. *Ways to enrich children's concepts and vocabulary.*
6. *Why direct, firsthand experience is so important in vocabulary and concept development.*
7. *Ways to help children sharpen their prediction strategies.*
8. *Language and text features that aid in prediction.*
9. *Activities you can develop to help children practice reconstructing meaning.*

We will begin the chapter on comprehension with the following passage to help you recall earlier sections on the nature of reading. Before you read it, you may want to skim chapter 2 to refresh your memory.

A solert spadassin in a rudd sark and a silentious sassenach sat down to gleek under a watchet welkin. Blue-eyed Mary sprinkled the tor in the middle of the veld beside them. A claggy spruit ran under the staddle that sheltered them, and tegs played pallall over the steading. The odor of syllabub was warm on the air.

"A man could popple all day on a posset like that," said the spadassin. The sassenach raised his pollex, aiming it at his companion.

"You are a friend. As for myself, I prefer pompion pasty to any gotch of mead."

He toyed with his smallage, but was interrupted by a startling singultus.

"Sirrah!" he shouted. "You spawl like yon stirk. Hast not yet learned to snite? Were I not so swinkled, I would swinge you with my shabble."

Velleity held him as the spadassin rose to say, "A murrain on you who are shaped like a sarplar and setiferous beside. I will be gone as soon as I rid myself of this sparable in my shoon. It, like you, gives me a pedalgia in my hallux."

("English as She is Seldom Spoke," by Edna Kaehele, distributed by Professor J. P. Ives in a graduate reading course at New York University.)

Despite its appearance, the selection is not gibberish. Reread it now and try to answer the following questions:

1. What was the spadassin wearing?

2. What was Mary doing?

3. What were the men drinking?

4. Why did the men get into an argument?

5. Why didn't the two men get into a sword fight?

6. Was the swordsman justified in his feelings toward his companion?

7. What does "murrain" mean?

8. Why didn't the swordsman leave immediately?

9. Is it safe to conclude that this story is a true account of an event?

10. What kind of person was the swordsman?

Did you answer that the spadassin was wearing a "rudd sark"? What do you think a "rudd sark" might be? Perhaps a red shirt? Was Mary sprinkling the tor? How could you tell? Did you know the meaning of "murrain"? If you were unable to define that word, can you tell what "hallux" means? If you are curious, you will find a translation of this passage on page 202.

Your answers to the first several questions are no doubt correct. This is so because you were able to use the syntactic and semantic cues in the passage. For example, to answer the first question, "What was the spadassin wearing?" you located the phrase, "A solert spadassin in a rudd sark. . . ." Without even having to think about it, the words "in a" triggered your implicit knowledge of the fact that the following words would have to make sense as a prepositional phrase containing an adjective and a noun. Graphophonic associations for "rudd," such as *ruddy, rust,* and *red* probably triggered the meaning *red.* If you decided *sark* was more likely to be *shirt* than *trousers,* it may well have been because semantic cues indicated that red is a more likely color for a shirt than for trousers. Of course, the question itself gave an important clue to your answer. That is, you might very well have indicated "red house" if the question asked where the spadassin was rather than what he was wearing.

Questions 6 to 10 were probably more difficult to answer correctly. These questions require an understanding beyond the surface or literal meaning of the passage, which can be triggered by simple syntactic and semantic cues. Your own background of experience, and your prior knowledge, must come into play in order to answer whether the account is real or fictional, or even judge what kind of person the swordsman was. Because so many of the words were probably unknown to you, you could not answer these interpretive and critical questions. Even a question that asked for a literal definition of a word (question 7) was difficult, since the other cues were insufficient to enable you to predict a definition with accuracy.

However, if you were a student of physiology, you might have known that *hallux* refers to the big toe in the human. Also, in the case of *hallux*, the proximity of another word, *shoon* (meaning shoe), and the prepositional phrase *in my* might have helped you predict the correct meaning of *hallux*. Of course, the fact that the function words, those that connect the words with dictionary meaning, are the same in modern English as they were in the English of several hundred years ago is a significant asset in understanding the passage.

Reading involves the reconstruction of the meaning encoded in written symbols by a writer. To understand or comprehend written material is to be able to reconstruct its meaning. The mechanical decoding of words without comprehension is not reading. You observed some of the factors that affect comprehension when you tried to read the passage above: your implicit grasp of the English language, your concepts and vocabulary, and the inherent difficulties of the text. In this chapter, we will investigate what comprehension is and how you can help to develop it in young children.

What Comprehension Is

In older textbooks on reading instruction, comprehension is frequently defined as what occurs when the reader comprehends a passage: He remembers a detail or the sequence of events; he interprets the motive of a story character; or he judges the authenticity of the data presented. Skills such as these are actually the observable effects of the comprehension process itself.

Comprehension is a high-order thinking process, and as such, most of what occurs in comprehending language must be inferred. Current research and theory indicate that comprehension involves the multidimensional cognitive processing of language. Thus, Edward Thorndike's early (1917) equation of reading with thinking still seems quite apropos.[1] Comprehension of meaning incorporates many cognitive processes, such as analyzing, comparing, evaluating, judging, remembering, reflecting, imagining, and seeing relationships. The products of comprehension, recalling the sequence of events or interpreting the motives of story characters, are simply external representations of an inner process. Comprehension is both process and product.

Cues in the graphophonic, syntactic, and semantic features of written language provide the information upon which the comprehension process operates. A number of factors, however, affect how well the reader can use these cues to comprehend a passage. Some of these, as you observed in the example at the beginning of this chapter, have to do with the material itself. How well it is written affects how well it will be comprehended. We have all had frustrating experiences trying to understand material so poorly written that it seems to make little or no sense at all. (Remember the excerpt from a fire insurance policy in chapter 2?) Other characteristics of written material that affect comprehension are the difficulty of the vocabulary, the complexity and density of ideas, and the rate at which new ideas are introduced.[2]

Then, of course, the reader herself has characteristics that affect how well she will comprehend a text: her vocabulary, her background of experiences and concepts, her memory capacity, her ability to decode the words in the text, her level of interest in the material, and her personal opinions and biases.

Skills Mastery Versus Comprehension

Frequent visits to primary-grade classrooms have led me to conclude that certain characteristics seem to dominate much of beginning reading instruction. First, almost every program I see in action contains a highly prescriptive and carefully sequenced plan of skill development designed to allow little or no modification. Instructions to the teacher are explicit, sometimes to the point of a prepared script. Few options are provided for teacher initiative. As a matter of fact, one of the most didactic of these programs, introduced in the 1970s, was touted as being "teacher proof." That is, its directions were so simple, yet so rigid, that any teacher, regardless of competence, could carry the program out successfully.

Another characteristic of virtually every program I have observed is a heavy emphasis on decoding. Increasingly, I come into a room and find a group of children chanting in unison something like, "/buh/buh/buh/buh/." Recently, I found several children in a private school reading the following:

Nat is a cat.
Nat is fat.
Nat is a fat cat.

In some cases, children are not permitted to read any connected discourse until they have mastered a requisite number of phoneme/grapheme correspondences.

Finally, written composition seems to bear little or no relationship to reading instruction. Children frequently learn to write manuscript letters in association with learning letter sounds. But opportunities to exploit the reciprocity of the reading and writing processes are rare.

These programs embody the *reading as skills mastery* approach, in which learning to read is equated with mastering a set of carefully ordered skills. The following interview with a second-grade teacher clearly illustrates this approach (I = Interviewer, T = Teacher):

I: How would you describe the methods you use in teaching reading?

T: This year, it is different from every other because the children did not learn to read last year. What we learn is basic first grade but at a higher level. We use the basal readers, the SRA kits, the basal workbooks, and books in the reading corner. Hopefully, by the beginning of February I could go on.

I: Of the materials you have, which do you think is the most effective and why?

T: The basal reader. The reason is that it's controlled, and the children really enjoy it.

I: How do you use your readers?

T: Exactly as recommended in the teacher's manual. We drill a lot for new words and by a certain time we go on. I believe that there is some validity at least, a lot of validity, to drill and practice. It really helps the children.

I: What do you do for slower readers?

T: I don't believe in grouping, since the children develop a sense of inferiority, but sometimes it becomes necessary to work more with them. When we do SRA, they work more slowly.

I: What's done for enrichment?

T: Well, we have a reading corner. Here, children who have completed all assignments can read on Fridays. This way, I can spend more time with the slower readers.

I: Do you give them [the slower readers] a chance to use the reading area?

T: It doesn't make sense, since they can't read anyway.

I: Do you use the library?

T: No. It takes away from our class time. I feel I get more done in the room.

I: What about reading-related activities?

T: We do some, but not many, because I've divided the readers so that by June we will be finished to level eight or nine.

I: Do you have many writing activities?

T: Mainly what's in the workbooks. Sometimes we do exercises on sentences in a story or poem but not as often as I would like. I have many corrections when we do this, so I figured I'd save this for later in the year.

(Interview courtesy of L. Simon-Corridon)

This represents the Procrustean Bed approach to literacy instruction. According to Greek legend, Procrustes, a fabulous giant, had the rather inhospitable habit of stretching or shortening his captives to fit one of his iron beds. When children are instructed according to a predetermined plan in a series of skills that may have no relationship to their actual needs, they too are being squeezed into a Procrustean Bed of arbitrary curriculum design. Goodman has argued that there is no defensible sequence of instruction in reading skills.[3] Certainly, there is no defensible a priori sequence. Children do need to master certain skills in order to be able to read. However, what skills are taught and when they are taught should be determined by the children's needs. This is functional rather than arbitrary teaching.

Another problem with the skills mastery approach is its decontextualization of reading from meaning. Instead of building on the continuity and integrity of the language processes, it separates and divides language functions into smaller and smaller units practiced in isolation. As Bettleheim and Zelan warn, the longer a child must wait to move from decoding to reading meaningful texts, the more likely it is that his enthusiasm and interest will wane.[4]

Embedding skill instruction in a meaningful context gives the child access to important graphophonic, syntactic, and semantic cues to meaning. Park illustrates how this operates with the easily confused pair of words *me* and *my*.[5] The child's attention may be directed to these words in the book *The Teeny Tiny Woman*, in which the phrase "Give me my bone!" plays a prominent role. Frequent self-motivated rereadings give the child the chance to discriminate between the two words within the powerful context of the story.

Reading material that is enjoyable and meaningful provides many opportunities for repeating and reinforcing the child's reading vocabulary. And meaningful contexts may be especially important for learning function words, since they have virtually no lexical meaning in themselves. For example, Ehri and Wilce found that first graders learned more about the syntactic and semantic features of such words when they were embedded in sentences rather than in randomly organized lists.[6] Reading is comprehending, but comprehending is not just a passive process of decoding sounds and symbols. It is an active, constructive process similar to writing. Both writing and reading are reciprocal processes of meaning construction that mutually reinforce each other.[7]

Moreover, when the text is composed of whole and meaningful language, context, combined with the child's own background experience, can operate in full force. The result is that the child needs far less graphophonic information to reconstruct the meaning of what he has read than if the text were fragmented, artificial, and, in essence, without meaning. Meaningfulness should always be the most important criterion. The child should devote his attention to an unknown word only when not knowing it interferes with his comprehension of a text. When this happens, he should try to make sense of the word first from the context. If this fails, he should scrutinize the unknown word for structural and graphophonic cues to its identification.[8]

Proficient readers respond directly to written symbols. Only when they come across an unfamiliar word for which the context provides insufficient clues do they resort to recoding the written symbols into sounds. The beginner, however, encounters many unfamiliar words in print, and the intermediate process of recoding print into sound symbols before its meaning becomes apparent occurs quite often. Strategies for word identification are important whenever the reader has a sound-to-meaning association for a word but not a print-to-meaning association. With experience, the reader acquires more and more print-to-meaning associations, and strategies for word identification become less important.

In working with beginners, our goal should be to encourage them to develop the print-to-meaning associations for words that characterize proficient reading. To do this, we help them acquire a large battery of words they can identify immediately. These *sight words* give children immediate access to meaning. However, most English words are visually very similar because our twenty-six letter alphabet is used to represent the more than one million words in the English language. Children's ability to identify words on sight is limited. Therefore, we also give them strategies for using the syntactic, semantic, and graphophonic cues of written language to identify the other words they encounter through a process of mediated word identification. By teaching children these strategies when they need them to comprehend meaningful texts, we help to ensure that children use context as a check on word identification. A good source for ideas on instruction in mediated word identification is *How to Increase Reading Ability*, eighth ed., by A. J. Harris and E. R. Sipay (New York: Longman, 1985).

Children learn to read by reading. They learn how to use the graphophonic, syntactic, and semantic cues in written material as they read real language with the guidance of a skilled teacher. Therefore, a child's reading and writing must not be allowed to wait for the mastery of a predetermined set of skills. Instead, observe the child's reading behaviors and then decide whether or not some instructional intervention (such as practice with a given skill) is advised. If you decide to proceed with skill instruction, it should be embedded in a natural context—real language functionally used, such as a group dictated story. In addition, whenever possible use a naturally arising opportunity for instruction, what we have called elsewhere "serendipitous" teaching.

Comprehension Skill Levels

A traditional way of organizing comprehension skills has been to classify them in a hierarchy of levels according to their rank as lower- to higher-order thinking processes. Remembering details would fall below seeing relationships, while evaluating the quality of a text would be highest of all three. These three skills are representative of the three levels of comprehension skills: *literal comprehension; interpretation;* and *critical evaluation*. Neither the length of the unit of language nor the type of question posed affects the level of comprehension. That is, you can be concerned with literal, interpretive, or critical evaluation skills whether the text is a sentence or a book, and regardless of whether you pose questions that are objective or open-ended.

A simple way to visualize the three levels of comprehension skills is in the form of a triangle, with literal comprehension comprising the base; interpretation, the mid-section; and critical evaluation, the highest point (Figure 6–1). This representation of the levels of comprehension skills helps to emphasize their inter-

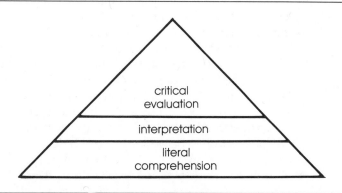

Figure 6–1   Three levels of comprehension skills

relatedness. In order to be able to comprehend interpretively, a person must be able to comprehend literally. And in order to be able to comprehend critically, he must be able to comprehend both interpretively and literally. One more analogy might be helpful before we describe each of the levels in more detail. If you visualize the print on a page, you might describe literal comprehension as reading *on* the lines, interpretation as reading *between* the lines, and critical evaluation as reading *off* the page. The following descriptions should help to make this analogy clear.

Literal comprehension. Literal comprehension in reading involves the understanding of the direct, primary, and literal meaning of written discourse. To comprehend a passage literally means being able to retrieve what has been *explicitly stated* in it, that is, being able to answer the question, "What color was Mary's new dress?" when the color of the dress was given in the text.

Specific kinds of literal meanings include:

1. Stated facts.
2. Stated details.
3. Sequence of facts.
4. Identification of referents.
5. Association of quotations with a speaker.
6. Specific word meanings (denotative) in different contexts.
7. Double negatives.
8. Unusual word order.

Much of literal comprehension has to do with the details in a given piece of material.

Durkin remarks that a very unhelpful procedure teachers frequently employ in comprehension instruction is to require the child to remember *all* the details from a passage.[9] Such a practice is quite unrealistic, because when we actually read for details, as for example in a list of directions, we typically go through the entire list first and then go back to read and remember one direction at a time as we carry it out. In addition to being impractical, insisting that a child remember all the details at once is more a test of memory capacity than of reading ability.

It has been found that teachers pose many more questions dealing with literal comprehension than with interpretation and critical evaluation.[10] Why might this be the case? One reason is probably that literal questions are easier to compose and to answer than higher-level questions. Moreover, since the answer to a literal comprehension question is directly verifiable in the text, there is no room for dispute or discussion, which could be quite valuable in understanding the text. Because literal questions do not require the reader to draw on his own background and experience nearly as much as interpretation and critical evaluation questions do, they may appear to be more suitable to use with beginning readers and with children whose background may be limited in the sense that their reading material may have little or no relevance to their own experiences. We know that the reader imposes meaning on the text. His knowledge and experience are critical factors in comprehension.[11] Thus, if the teacher believes that a reader lacks the relevant background knowledge, she may limit his questions to those that can be answered directly from the text.

Literal comprehension is important in beginning reading and later, too, when children do more reading for information. However, as we noted earlier, literal meanings comprise the lowest level in the hierarchy of comprehension skills. Imagine how dull reading would be without all the rich associations and meanings that come with interpretation and critical evaluation.

If a child's experiential background is "limited," then we can do at least two things. First, we can broaden and deepen his experiences by planning and carrying out interesting activities. Second, we can tap into the wonderful reservoir of ideas and feelings that every child brings with him to school. Although some may not consider what we find there appropriate for school, if it is treated with sensitivity, this material can be an excellent resource for writing.

Questions are the most frequent technique teachers use in comprehension instruction. Some research found elementary school teachers asking as many as 45 to 150 questions per half-hour.[12] But posing too many questions can be threatening to children, and thus hinder their comprehension. The following exercise, which was used in a first-grade class, is a typical literal comprehension activity. Read it and think about why it is or is not effective.

Carmen is a girl. She lives in a big house. Her sister's name is Susan. They go to school in the morning. When they come home they play house with their friends. At night they get washed and go to bed. Susan and Carmen have fun.

Carmen is a _____.
_____dog   _____boy   _____girl

Her sister's name is _____.
_____Susan   _____Joan   _____Ben

When they come home they play_____.
_____races   _____house   _____ball

At night they go to_____.
_____the store   _____school   _____bed.

But there are other kinds of activities besides questioning that help children practice literal comprehension skills. First, children should be alerted to the fact that contextual and structural clues can help them comprehend literal meaning. Recognizing quickly and responding appropriately to such clues as punctuation; the use of definition, comparison, contrast and explanation; various structural changes within words; and the position of words in sentences, can help children in comprehending written texts.

Second, children can be taught to recognize various cue words and phrases that signal specific meanings. One example from this category are words that signal sequence, such as *first, last, finally, then, before, after, later,* and *next.* You can illustrate the function of sequence cue words by highlighting them in describing some familiar daily task such as eating breakfast. Write the description on the chalkboard or a chart, so that the children can see how the cue words operate. Sequence cue words occur frequently in the reading material of primary-grade children. Also make note of other possible sets of cue words and phrases such as: those that signal contrasting ideas (e.g., *yet, but, however, on the other hand*); those that signal relationships (e.g., *because, therefore, since, as a result, for that reason*); and those that signal additional information (e.g., *moreover, in addition, further-more, hence*).

Actually carrying out the directions for some real activity, such as assembling a toy airplane or following a recipe, is a much more enjoyable and effective way to practice literal comprehension skills than completing paper and pencil exercises, and children should have lots of opportunities to try these activities. You might also want to develop some activity cards that list directions for constructing some-thing simple like a pinwheel.

A good way children can practice reading for details is by comparing two different newspaper articles that report on the same event. The children can in-vestigate which article contains more details and whether there are differences or discrepancies in the way the two articles present the details.

If you illustrate through drawings or magazine cutouts the major episodes in a familiar story, children can arrange the illustrations in the proper sequence even before they are reading. This approach is similar to a *flannelboard*, which allows the child to retell the story by arranging the appropriate cutout figures on the board.

You can also prepare cassette tapes with accompanying materials. As the chil-dren listen to the tape, they carry out the directions (which can also be written) with the materials, for example, arranging a set of cards in a particular sequence.

Another idea for encouraging attention to detail is to collect a set of pictures on a single topic, such as cats. Each picture should vary slightly from the next. Write descriptions of the pictures, which the child reads and then matches to the pictures. Or you can reverse the procedure by having the children draw pictures to match the written descriptions you provide.

Interpretation.   If literal comprehension entails understanding what is stated directly in the text, then interpretation means understanding what is implied by the written material. You will recall our analogy of the two levels of comprehension skills to reading on the line (literal) and reading between the lines (interpretation). In order to be able to comprehend interpretively, the reader must be able to reason from explicitly stated ideas to what is only implied. This requires the reader to draw upon his own background of experience and ideas.

Sometimes, an interpretation is very narrow, as when a child must infer that a story character has hurt herself in falling even though this is not explicitly stated in the text. Other interpretations, which are based on more ambiguous clues, require the reader to use more reasoning power. Riddles are a common example of the latter kind of interpretation. To answer even a simple riddle such as "What is black, white, and read all over?" the child must draw on her own knowledge to an even greater extent than in the example of the story character above.

Interpretation includes a wide range of thinking processes:

1. Drawing inferences.
2. Making implications.
3. Drawing conclusions.
4. Making generalizations.
5. Drawing comparisons.
6. Making contrasts.
7. Finding main ideas.
8. Identifying assumptions.
9. Anticipating events.
10. Predicting outcomes.
11. Identifying character traits.
12. Identifying emotional reactions of characters.
13. Identifying motives of characters.
14. Perceiving relationships of various kinds, such as causation and analogy.

Even though instruction in interpretive comprehension is offered less frequently than in literal comprehension, it is, nonetheless, often afflicted by the same skills worksheet approach. Who among us, for example, has not had to "find the best title" for countless paragraphs? Assigning a good title to a piece of writing is a legitimate way to practice locating the main idea. However, such practice is likely to be more useful and meaningful when it is done as a natural part of the composing process, rather than as a workbook exercise. An interesting alternative is to clip off the titles of newspaper articles and then have children classify them by type of story, such as sports, national news, and business.

Finding the main idea is probably the most frequently practiced interpretive skill in the primary grades. Because of this early emphasis, some children may wind up with the mistaken notion that every piece of writing should have a main idea. Not so (e.g., what is the main idea in a shopping list?).

There are many sound alternatives to dull workbook drill on interpretive comprehension. The following one can be used even with children who are not yet reading on their own. After showing the film *The Red Balloon*, by A. Lamorrisse, which describes the adventures of a lonely boy and his enchanted balloon, give the children the opportunity to review the actual events of the film (literal comprehension). Elicit their feelings and questions about what happened to Pascal and his balloon (interpretation). Then, to extend their thinking and feeling about the story, ask questions that continue to probe for deeper meanings: Why didn't Pascal's mother want him to keep the balloon? How did he feel when she threw it away? Why did the boys break the balloon? Why did all the balloons of Paris suddenly fly up into the sky? Afterward, list the story characters (Pascal, red balloon, principal, boys, Pascal's mother) on the chalkboard and ask the children to give you words describing each one.

Likewise, after the children have read on their own you can focus the discussion to help them draw conclusions, make generalizations, anticipate outcomes, reason about cause and effect, make comparisons, and engage in the other kinds of thinking processes that comprise interpretation. Encourage the children to make associations between their personal experience and the reading (or listening) context.

For beginners and those who are progressing slowly, you will want to begin with literal meaning before proceeding to interpretation. More proficient readers are likely to be ready to get to interpretive meaning right away.

Critical evaluation. In critical evaluation, the highest level in the reading-for-meaning hierarchy of skills, the reader evaluates written material by measuring it against some evidence or standard and then making a judgment about its veracity, accuracy, and quality. Critical reading not only requires comprehension of literal meaning and the ability to interpret the author's message, it goes beyond these by involving the reader in an active process of evaluation. The reader assumes an attitude of inquiry and judges the material's quality by comparing it with his own experience or by subjecting it to the test of logical analysis.

When children study a topic in which they are deeply involved, they have many opportunities to read critically as well as interpretively and literally. For example, I knew one third-grade class that became engrossed in studying the upsurge of consumerism in the 1960s and 1970s. These seven- and eight-year-olds investigated exaggerated and possibly fraudulent advertising claims. They scoured popular magazines and newspapers for ads that looked suspicious to them, concentrating on items that could be acquired easily because their investigation was based on the actual product itself. One evaluation involved a comparison of a "deluxe" edition of a classic children's folktale with the regular edition. The children found that the major difference between the two was the simulated leather and gold-lettered binding of the deluxe edition. The children concluded that there was nothing really deluxe about the more expensive edition. The older cloth bound edition was not only cheaper but also more sturdily constructed. Another investigation uncovered the fact that what was advertised as the "super-duper economy size" of a laundry detergent actually turned out to be *more* expensive per ounce of detergent than the smaller size. Rather than passively accepting the advertising claims they had read, these third-graders responded with an active attitude of inquiry—they had examined and evaluated them critically!

According to Zintz, critical evaluation requires competence in five areas: establishing standards of judgment, making comparisons, judging the authority and the background of the source, recognizing relevance and irrelevance, and making inferences and drawing conclusions.[13]

The specific skills a critical reader brings to reading include:

1. Recognition of his or her own biases.
2. Discrimination of fact from opinion.
3. Evaluation of the accuracy, validity, authenticity, authoritativeness, completeness, truthfulness, and currency of written material.

4. Recognition of propaganda, slant, bias, and prejudice.

5. Recognition of different points of view.

6. Recognition of ambiguities and discrepancies.

7. Recognition of words, phrases, and sentences quoted out of context.

8. Recognition of emotionally charged words.

9. Recognition of half-truths.

10. Recognition of exaggerated claims.

11. Identification of author's purpose, mood, tone, and intent.

12. Recognition of techniques used to accomplish the author's purpose.

13. Identification of the audience to whom the writer is directing the message.

14. Identification of the writer's pattern of organization.

15. Evaluation of the quality of writing.

16. Evaluation of the values presented.

17. Evaluation of and reaction to ideas presented in light of the author's purpose.

18. Recognition of material that is glamorized or sensationalized.

19. Evaluation of the pattern of writing.

20. Recognition of which of the reader's needs the appeal is being made.

As with interpretation, the best way to teach children to read and think critically is through normal, everyday activities encountered with a thoughtful, inquiring attitude. This does not mean that children should be encouraged to adopt a cynical point of view toward what they encounter. Critical in this sense does not mean negative; it means discriminating. This is important to remember, particularly in a literacy program in which the children's own writing plays a central role. Applying the skills of critical thinking to reading helps children put things in proper perspective. We do not want children to reject opinion simply because it is opinion. Rather, we want them to be able to discriminate between fact and opinion, look for substantiation, and use opinion when it is appropriate to do so.

Even the youngest children use critical evaluation. A group of prekindergartners wanted to know why the Yangtze River, which is described as being yellow in the book *Ping*, by Marjorie Flack, is illustrated as being blue. Children are forever being asked if they "like the story" they have just been read or told. When a question like this is appropriate, we ought to add, "... and tell us what you liked about it or didn't like about it."

When children discover something they think is improbable or inaccurate in their reading material, we should praise them and encourage them to check out their suspicions, as one third-grader did. He had been reading an information book on the planet Mars and questioned whether its conclusion that the planet could not support life was correct. Following recent exploration of the red planet with much interest, he wondered how the book could be so certain about this conclusion. What evidence, he wondered, was there to support this contention? With the teacher, he checked the book's copyright date and found that it had been published some twenty years earlier. When he read other, more current books about Mars, he found that they were not so certain about the impossibility of life on Mars, either now or at some time in the past. His finding: there was still too little evidence to draw a firm conclusion about life on Mars.

There are many interesting ways to help children practice their critical evaluation skills. Newspapers and advertisements are excellent for this purpose. They allow children to compare how the same event, such as a presidential election, is treated in a regular article, a guest column, and an editorial, and encourage children to learn to distinguish fact and opinion. The children should be alerted to look for cue words that signal opinion, such as *probably, believe, think,* and *possibly*, as they explore which of the articles was most interesting, which was most informative, and why.

We have already noted how a critical approach to consumerism can lead to healthy skepticism about advertising claims and the accuracy of product labels. Recently, I overheard a first-grade child question her teacher about the last sale date on the container of milk she had gotten for a snack. This six-year-old was concerned about whether the milk was still fresh.

Second- and third-grade children are ready to investigate some of the propaganda techniques advertisers employ: *glittering generality*, in which a product is linked with a word that has highly positive associations (e.g., "Use this soap for a *beautiful* you"); *bandwagon*, in which the reader is urged to do what everybody else is doing; and *testimonial*, in which a celebrity personality describes the merits of the product. Children can search for and identify various advertising techniques in magazine and newspaper ads. An excellent way to test the veracity of advertising claims is to send for inexpensive products such as the toy cars or planes that are advertised on television or in newspapers or magazines. When the product arrives, the children have a perfect opportunity to compare the actual item with its advertisement.

The critical evaluation of advertising is not meant to teach children that the use of propaganda and advertising is inherently bad. Organizations that most would consider socially unacceptable (e.g., the Ku Klux Klan) as well as those that are highly valued (e.g., Greenpeace) use propaganda to advance their causes. Remember that one of the functions of language is to influence others. What you want to teach children is how to recognize propaganda and how to decide when it is deliberately used to deceive.

Children should try their own hands at *writing* advertisements, too, perhaps for a favorite book or TV program. As we have said earlier, one of the best ways to learn how a particular kind of discourse works is to practice writing it yourself. This is another example of the interrelatedness of reading and writing.

Ways to Develop Comprehension

Classroom observation of teachers in grades three through six during reading and social studies lessons found almost *no* comprehension instruction going on at all. Rather than teaching for comprehension, teachers devoted most of the time to assessment procedures, such as giving and checking assignments.[14] Apparently, although comprehension or reconstruction of meaning is the *purpose* of reading, it actually receives little attention in schools.

Part of the problem lies in the preponderance of the basal reader approach, which typically emphasizes comprehension assessment over comprehension instruction through the heavy use of literal questions directed at details. Another common feature of basal reader instruction that may also hinder comprehension is the practice of oral rather than silent reading. If too much attention is paid to how he *sounds* when reading, a child's attention may be diverted from the meaning of the passage. Finally, the near fanatical concern many reading programs show for word identification techniques, especially phonics, relegates comprehension to a back seat in reading instruction.

Guidelines for Comprehension Instruction

There are a number of general guidelines you can use in teaching for comprehension. First, and perhaps most important, allow children to read material they find interesting and relevant. More than a set of specific skills or the particular characteristics in a given kind of written discourse, it is children's prior knowledge and their interest in content that affect their comprehension.[15]

Second, choose material that is not too difficult. If a child must devote all of his time and energy to figuring out what the words say, his comprehension will be severely reduced. Whatever comprehension he does achieve under these circumstances will probably be only at the literal level. On the other hand, if he recognizes most of the words in the material, he can concentrate on meaning.

Third, select materials for practicing comprehension skills that are appropriate to the child's needs. If he needs to work on reading for details, use such things as TV program schedules, directions, recipes, and the like. Or if you find that he needs to sharpen his skill in reading critically, give him newspaper editorials, advertisements, and political campaign and special interest group literature.

Fourth, use questions purposefully and sparingly. As noted earlier, question-asking is the predominant strategy used in comprehension instruction. But too often the questions are aimed at retrieving minor facts and details rather than being thought-provoking. The most useful questions are often the open-ended ones framed by the children themselves as they skim through the material they are about to read, searching for clues to the content in headings and pictures and then deciding what to look for. Operating as a kind of mental set, these questions stimulate the children's cognitive schemata and help them make the associations between their own experience and what they will be reading that are necessary for comprehension.

Fifth, encourage children to establish purposes for reading and to use specific comprehension skills appropriate to those selected purposes. Give them many opportunities to practice literal comprehension, interpretation, and critical evaluation skills on suitable material so that they will understand what the different purposes for reading are. They need the chance to carry out tasks appropriate to a given purpose, such as checking the *TV Guide* for a particular program listing, and to receive direct feedback on their performance of the task, such as locating the correct time and station for that program.

Finally, help children learn to vary their *rate* of reading according to their purpose and the level of difficulty of their reading material. We have already discussed how common school practices—emphasizing oral over silent reading or the round robin method—can interfere with the development of proficient silent reading. Habitual use of reading material that is too difficult can also impede the development of a versatile and adaptive rate of reading, since the child may transfer the slow, careful style of reading necessary for difficult material to everything he reads. Encourage children to speed up their rate of reading when they find that the material is unrelated to their purpose for reading, and when the material is easy, familiar, or repetitive. In the same way, children should learn to slow down their rate of reading when the material *is* related to their purpose, is about ideas that are new to them, has many details, is long and complicated, or contains unknown words that may be important to the meaning of the passage as a whole.

Children should become familiar with two types of quick reading: *skimming*, which aims to get the general gist of a passage; and *scanning*, even faster than skimming, which is used to find a particular item of information, such as a word in a dictionary or a telephone number in a directory. Scanning involves several steps: first, having a specific purpose, such as locating the correct time and channel for a TV program in the newspaper television listings; second, proceeding quickly in search of the desired piece of information; and third, once the item is located, rechecking carefully in order to verify that it is the correct item or that it is actually related to the reader's purpose.[16]

The remainder of this section will discuss specific strategies you can use to develop comprehension.

Vocabulary and Concept Development

As we have noted several times, comprehension is directly affected by the reader's own background of experience and ideas. Reading is an interactive process in which what the reader knows affects what he comprehends and what he reads adds to what he knows.[17] It is the words in a passage that enable him to reconstruct the author's meaning from his own experience. But the process cannot occur if the reader does not understand the words, as was the case in the passage at the beginning of this chapter. Vocabulary and concept development are essential for building comprehension.

Ways to enrich concepts and vocabulary.   There are a number of ways to enrich children's storehouse of concepts and vocabulary. The first and most significant way, especially for younger children, is through direct experience. A basic premise of this book is that children need many and varied firsthand experiences—seeing, touching, tasting, smelling, and hearing—and, they need to have language attached to those experiences. In the years from three to eight, children make rapid advances in vocabulary development when their environments are stimulating, as long as they have many opportunities to test and practice these new words against their actual referents. Supplementing direct, firsthand experiences should be those of a vicarious, abstract kind—books, films, tapes, pictures, and models.

Ideally, firsthand and vicarious experiences should complement each other. If they do, young children can receive the direct and concrete feedback they need for their learning to be lasting and real rather than superficial. At the same time, experience with print and nonprint media can extend and refine what they have learned on a more concrete level. Thus, what one class of kindergarten children learned both through visiting a local fire station and being visited in class by one of the firefighters himself was enhanced by pictures and discussions, a filmstrip on fire safety, and two stories about firefighters, which their teacher read to them. That rich experiences yield rich vocabulary was amply demonstrated in the children's dramatic play when they labeled and used various pieces of firefighting equipment appropriately.

The older children get, the more they can rely on vicarious experience to expand their reservoir of concepts and vocabulary. But through the primary grades at least, it is always a good idea to ground their activities in direct experience. Sometimes an unusually effective piece of prose or poetry has the power to convey a particular meaning all by itself. I have seen this happen, for example, with a group of third-grade children who, after listening to Hans Christian Andersen's exquisite tale, *The Emperor's Nightingale*, seemed to understand the meaning of the word *porcelain*. Yet, even in this case, had it been appropriate, a chance to feel the fragility of a real piece of porcelain, to see how light passes through it, and to hear its distinctive sound when gently struck, would have added more to the children's understanding.

Another way to expand children's vocabulary is through direct word study. We have already noted the significance of individual and group word banks for reading and writing development (see chapter 4). These collections of words are also useful for vocabulary development. In addition, you should display sets of words grouped by category in charts around the room. Such charts are very useful as a reference when children write. One chart might contain *When* words and expressions, such as *now, once upon a time, then, later,* and *after*. Other charts would most likely develop from the children's own investigations. From a study of space travel, the children might collect such words as *astronaut, space capsule, docking, satellite, weightlessness,* etc. Further classification into subcategories would evolve as children continued the investigation in greater depth.

Occasionally, a particularly effective display can be useful in direct word study. A student teacher who was working with a second-grade class simulated a tree with a large branch and leaves cut from green construction paper. Hung from the tree were pear-shaped cutouts on which she had written sets of homophones (words that *sound* alike but have different spellings and meanings). She initiated the study of homophones with this display using the three homophones *pear, pair,* and *pare*. Over several weeks' time, the children added new sets to the tree as they came up in the course of their activities. This project not only engaged the children's interest, it was also effective in its goal of teaching about homophones. Be careful, however, about using activities simply because of their visual appeal or "cuteness." Too often, little real learning results; the children may wind up with shallow verbalizations rather than a real understanding of new words and ideas.

The dictionary.   Although no one is likely to accuse the dictionary of being "cute," its use or rather, misuse in vocabulary development typifies such meaningless teaching. Dictionary activities such as looking up words and writing down their definitions, memorizing symbols in the pronunciation key, and adding the diacritical and stress marks to a list of words are likely to produce little more than tedium and a desire to avoid using a dictionary whenever possible.

However, when the information is actually needed to carry out some meaningful task, a child is apt to see the dictionary as a useful tool. What is more, the word in question should be drawn from a meaningful context, such as a sentence, so that the *primary* clues to the word's meaning—the graphophonic, syntactic, and semantic cues that surround the word in the sentence—are available.

The written context surrounding an unknown word can provide clues to its meaning in a variety of ways: through *definition* (The *serape* is a woolen cloak worn by South Americans); *example* (Marty was quite *perceptive*. He seemed to know what you were going to say even before you said it); and *appositive*, in which the clue to the word's meaning is enclosed in commas (The *alien*, a creature from some distant planet, . . .). When the child is unable to figure out the meaning of the word from its primary clues, he should then consult a secondary source such as a dictionary. Seeing the word in a meaningful context can help the child once he consults a dictionary, since meanings are listed by grammatical function. The child will be in a better position to know whether, let us say, it is the word's meaning as a noun rather than as a verb, that he is looking for if he comes across the word in a sentence instead of in a list.

Familiarity with the concept of a dictionary should begin with the inception of literacy instruction. Some five-year-olds are ready to construct their own picture dictionaries by cutting out magazine illustrations of things that begin with a particular letter, pasting them on construction paper labeled with the letter, and arranging them in alphabetical order.

Commercial picture dictionaries should also be available to the children. *The Primary Dictionary Series*, published by Pyramid Publications in New York, is useful because its definitions are appropriate for children in the primary grades.

From preschool on, children should have many opportunities to practice the kinds of location skills they will need in using a dictionary. The name tags used in making job assignments (e.g., helping with snack) can be arranged alphabetically. Later, you might compile a directory of class members' telephone numbers arranged, of course, in alphabetical order by last name. Once children have advanced to using a standard dictionary, you can show them how dividing the alphabet into segments *A–F, G–L, M–S,* and *T–Z* and using the dictionary's guide words can help them locate a desired word quickly.

Of course, practice in using the dictionary can be enlivened with interesting activities. The children may enjoy looking up the origins of their given names, for example. Or they may want to play the "Compliment or Insult Game."[18] In this game, children sort descriptive words into two categories: "Compliment Words" and "Insult Words." Included in the set would be words that quite obviously belong in one group or the other, such as *annoying, friendly, happy,* and *angry*. But there should also be words such as *brazen, devious, diligent*, and *ebullient*, whose meanings are not as apt to be familiar and need to be checked in the dictionary.

Playing the Compliment or Insult game also provides a good opportunity for children to explore the denotative and connotative meanings of words. Although words like *skinny* and *slender* may denote the same meaning, their connotations are quite different. *Skinny* is apt to wind up in the "Insult" pile, while *slender* would likely be considered a compliment. It is a simple matter to extend this activity to other *pro* and *con* categories, such as Foods (Sports, Books, Hobbies, etc.) I Love/Hate.

Sometimes a child who has a particular interest in words will become devoted to the dictionary and enjoy simply leafing through it in the pursuit of new words. I confess to having been one of those myself. To this day, regardless of how rushed or pressured I may be, in scanning for a particular word I always seem to find something else to captivate my eye. I find that this is especially the case with the first dictionary I generally consult, *The American Heritage Dictionary* (New College Edition), which has particularly intriguing illustrations. Of course, you should encourage such exploration in your children, some of whom may even be budding etymologists. These children may also enjoy books like Sam and Beryl Epstein's *The First Book of Words* (New York: Franklin Watts, 1954), whose specific function is to explore word meanings.

Word play.   Other books can also provide excellent stimuli for vocabulary development. Here are some examples. After reading *I Unpacked My Grandmother's Trunk* by Susan Ramsey Hoguet (New York: Dutton, 1983), the children may want to compose their own list of the contents of grandmother's trunk in this familiar cumulative game. Books of limericks and riddles can spur children's own word play. Arnold Lobel's *The Book of Pigerlicks* (New York: Harper, 1983) (limericks about pigs) might lead to dogerlicks, caterlicks, or even snakerlicks. *Unriddling: All Sorts of Riddles to Puzzle Your Guessery* by Alvin Schwartz (New York: Lippincott, 1983) and *Monica Beisner's Book of Riddles* (New York: Farrar Straus Giroux, 1983) are just two of the many books available in which both traditional and new riddles not only serve as brain teasers but might also inspire some "riddling" on the part of the children themselves.

Books of poetry and others that feature figurative language are also good ways to expand vocabulary. For example, in *A Snake Is Totally Tail* by Judi Barrett (New York: Atheneum, 1983) each animal is described with interesting alliterative adverbs and nouns, such as "A kangaroo is partially pocket," and "A giraffe is noticeably neck." The children might go on to describe people, places, or things of their own in a similar way. A collection of poems about the city that pairs them with black and white photographs (*A Song in Stone: City Poems*, collected by Lee Bennett Hopkins [New York: Crowell, 1983]) might lead to a project in which the children compose their own poems using the images of their community they collect via an instant camera. The final product could be compiled as a class book and duplicated so that each child can have a personal copy. In *Word Play and Language*

Learning for Children (Urbana, Ill.: National Council of Teachers of English, 1985), Linda Geller discusses how important this kind of word play can be for language development. She also gives many good suggestions for stimulating language play in children three years old and up.

The media.   Newspapers, TV, radio, and magazines provide excellent material for vocabulary development. For example, advertisers' penchant for creating new product names offers a fine way to study *neologisms*, newly formed words, phrases, or expressions or new meanings given to old words. How many product names can the children come up with that are neologisms? (Egg McMuffin, Chipwich, and Tofutti are the kinds of names you will be looking for.) Next have the children put themselves in the role of advertiser and create their own neologisms to advertise favorite foods or books, or even the school cafeteria's luncheon specialties. The latter might result in some very humorous examples.

Another media source of new words or words used in different ways comes from how sportscasters describe team wins. In the thick of a particular sports season, the sportscaster is confronted with the task of having to report what seems like an endless list of scores. Rather than using the same word over and over again (Michigan State *beat* Ohio State, University of Michigan *beat* Penn State, etc.) to describe game results, the sportscaster searches for a more varied and interesting set of verbs and other words to carry the intended meaning. Some of the words I have heard are: *won, over, trounced, sloshed, zonked, zipped, walloped, murdered, squeaked by,* and *massacred.* You can ask the children to listen for other imaginative ways that radio and TV announcers describe events. They can compile collections of such words, adding new ones as they come across them or exploring different categories altogether. For example, what words do print advertisements use to describe a youthful appearance or the benefits to your pet of eating a particular brand of food?

Word study activities.   Here is a brief sampling of activities you can use for word study. But let me preface it with another reminder to use real, firsthand experience for word study supported by good vicarious experiences whenever possible. If you do not, there is always the danger that children's actual comprehension of a given object or concept will only be superficial. They might acquire the *names* of new ideas but have little real understanding of what they mean.

Now for the activities. Cunningham and colleagues describe a *scavenger hunt* activity that develops out of a group study.[19] Terms associated with the study that can be represented either by the actual object itself or some representation of it, such as a picture, are drawn up in a list and then divided into sets for teams of four or five children each. The teams are given one to two weeks to gather the items on their list, and on a given date, all the participating children assemble and report on the results of their hunt.

Johnson and Pearson have developed an activity they call *feature matrices* from semantic feature theory, which was described in chapter 1.[20] This activity is also part of children's study of a topic. The children select a category from their unit of study. To compose a feature matrix, they choose five or six items from the category and list them vertically along the left side of the matrix; across the top of the matrix they note the features or attributes that the category items may share. Then they fill in the matrix with pluses and minuses to indicate the presence or absence of a particular feature in a given item. To illustrate, here is what a feature matrix from a study of animals might look like:

	Wild	Pet	Farm	Meat-Eating	Grain-Eating
dog	−	+	−	+	−
cat	−	+	−	+	−
lion	+	−	−	+	−
sheep	−	−	+	−	+
giraffe	+	−	−	−	+

Another way to illustrate the commonality of attributes among members of a given category is through a bulletin board display. For example, after a study of animals has progressed to the point where the children have accumulated sufficient information, you could illustrate different kinds of habitats, such as a cave, nest, stream, ocean, jungle, barn, and the like on the bulletin board. Under each illustration you could attach a pocket for pictures of those animals that live in that kind of habitat. The children could then study the animals grouped by habitat to induce their common attributes.

Understanding figurative language.   By the later primary grades, children encounter more figurative language in their reading material; therefore, it might be a good idea to focus some attention on figurative expressions in class. Write sentences containing figurative phrases on the chalkboard: *it was raining cats and dogs; he's as stupid as a bedbug; he moved like greased lightning; she's as thin as a rail; their car was a lemon; they were neck and neck,* etc. After discussing the figurative meaning of each expression, the children could illustrate the literal meaning and describe the relationship between the two.

Or write figurative expressions on cards to be sorted into one of two boxes depending on the meaning of the expression. For example, for expressions of speed like *greased lightning* and *snail's pace*, the boxes would be labeled "Slow" and "Fast." Once they have exhausted all the expressions they know, children might want to compose some of their own. You will find Charles Funk's *A Hog on Ice and Other Curious Expressions* (New York: Harper Colophon, 1985) an excellent resource to use in stimulating the curiosity of those who show an interest in colorful phrases, such as *white elephant* and *pig in a poke.*

There are many different ways for children to practice using synonyms and antonyms. Here are two. In a box, put a set of tongue depressors or popsicle sticks on which you have written words whose meanings the children know. In the same box put other tongue depressors with the synonyms or antonyms of the first set written on them. The children's task is to sort the tongue depressors into sets of words with their synonyms or antonyms.

Another way to do this is to write the words on cards cut to the size and shape of playing cards, which are dealt to the three or four children playing the game.

The rest of the deck consists of synonyms or antonyms of the words that were dealt. The children take turns selecting a card from the deck. If they select one that is a synonym (or antonym) for a word in their hand and they recognize it as such, they discard both cards. If not, they place the selected card at the bottom of the deck. Whoever is out of cards first wins the game.

Prediction Strategies

Reading is an active thinking process. Constructing the meaning in a passage of text involves a dynamic procedure—hypothesizing, testing, and verifying predictions. Likewise with listening; although its symbols are oral rather than written, both involve the active processing of language in order to comprehend meaning. This section looks at ways to help children sharpen their prediction strategies.

Let us consider listening comprehension first. As we noted back in chapter 3, teaching children to predict should begin in preschool. We described how the use of highly patterned language, stories, and songs with repetitive features and the children's emergent reading and writing helped them learn to make predictions about language.

The prediction strategies acquired by preschoolers through listening provide a natural precursor to their experiences in the primary grades with making predictions about written language. However, experience with listening comprehension should not stop at first grade. Children in the primary grades should continue to have many opportunities to listen for meaning. Such experiences are both a natural complement of, and transition to, reading for meaning.

Reading stories aloud provides an ideal medium for children to practice their prediction strategies. Read them a story and stop at some strategic point so they can tell or write their predictions about the conclusion. Or read a story but do not show the illustrations. Afterward, the children can describe or draw what they think the characters look like. Then they can compare their predictions against the story's actual illustrations.

Newspapers and advertisements are also good for sharpening prediction strategies. For example, you can read a headline and ask the children to anticipate what the news story will be about. Or after listening to a list of adjectives culled from advertisements for a particular kind of product, such as pet food, detergent, or soap, the children could predict what kind of product is being touted.

One way to help children move from listening to reading comprehension is to have them carry out transitional activities that involve both listening and reading for meaning. What you want to emphasize is that the essence of both listening and reading is the same—the active processing of language for meaning.

Having the children predict their own endings to stories is a good transitional activity. In the first part of the lesson, read aloud or play a tape of a story up to a strategic moment in the plot. Then ask the children to tell, draw, or write their own predictions about how the story might continue. Once they have done so, listen to the remainder of the story. Afterward, the children *read* another story up to a particular point and then predict, in the same way they did earlier, how this story concludes. Again, they test their predictions, but in this case by reading the remainder of the story.

Prediction is intelligent hypothesizing. The reader selects from among several possible alternatives by systematically evaluating each and then choosing the ones that best match his own expectations of the author's meaning.[21] Webbing and Directing Reading-Thinking activities (DR-TA), both described in chapter 5, are also useful ways to foster prediction strategies.

Word webs.   *Word webs*, a slight variation of webbing and DR-TA, are another good way to help children make accurate predictions about what they read. The basic idea in word webbing is to help the children become aware of their own background knowledge about the content of the reading material. It begins before they start to read as they think of one core word to describe the reading material. Perhaps they are about to read an account of the first space walk. For this they might select *astronaut* (or *cosmonaut*) as the core word. You would write *astronaut* on the chalkboard (or display it on an overhead projector). The children then try to think of as many other words as they can that they associate with astronaut. They might come up with *space travel, gravity, weightlessness, moon, adventure, rocket ship,* and *lift-off,* each of which you write on the board, connecting it to the core word with lines. Once the children seem to have exhausted their store of associations, they are ready to read the material. Afterward, they check their word web to see how many of the words they predicted might be in the material they actually found.

Sometimes a secondary word can trigger many associations of its own. In the example above, a group of space buffs might spin off many other words from *moon—satellite, crater, moonlight, orbit,* and *eclipse.*

Deletion technique/cloze procedure.   Another way to practice prediction strategies by exploiting syntactic and semantic clues in a written context is through a *deletion technique* or *cloze procedure*. Select a short and simple passage. Beginning with the second sentence and proceeding to the sentence before the last, delete every tenth word. In typing up the passage, leave a blank space or type a line of the same length for each deleted word. The children fill in the blanks with words that make sense in the missing spaces; these can be synonyms for the words that were actually deleted. As the children become more adept at making accurate predictions of this kind, you can make the activity more difficult by deleting words at shorter intervals, such as every seventh or fifth word, by deleting entire phrases, and by using longer and more complicated passages. Give the children an opportunity to explain the reasons for their word choices and compare their choices with the actual words from the original text. Deletion techniques offer an excellent way for a child to exploit the syntactic and semantic cues in a written context in order to anticipate meaning.

Unit of study.   A unit of study also provides an excellent opportunity for making predictions. Let us say that a third-grade class has been investigating how animals adapt to their environment. One way to help children anticipate meaning and practice problem solving is to have them work toward the answer to a general question by investigating its implications within a specific context. In the example given, the general question is, "How do animals adapt to their environment?" Perhaps four groups of children tackle this problem by investigating its implications for different kinds of animals: birds, reptiles and amphibians, fish, and insects. Each group studies its own kind of animal to determine how it moves, what it eats, where it lives, and how it protects itself. After a given period of time has elapsed, the four groups come together for a discussion. Under the teacher's direction, they report their findings, respond to questions from other groups, and ask questions of their own. From this discussion and the pool of shared information, each child can see how his own findings tie in with those of his classmates. He is able to make predictions about the answer to the general question, and his understanding of the basic problem, in this case *adaptation*, is greater than it might have been after a solitary investigation.

Cues to prediction in language and text features. Language and text features also operate as aids in the prediction of meaning. We have already mentioned alerting children to the cue words and phrases that signal specific meanings, such as sequence and causality. We acquire much of our understanding of such features inductively as we read and write. But it is a good idea, nonetheless, to heighten children's metalingual awareness of these cues when they come across them in reading. When a child either makes no response or makes an incorrect response to these language signals, it is important for the child to work on them more directly.

There are several different kinds of language and text features. First, there are graphic signals to meaning, such as punctuation marks, typestyle, underlining, and formatting (e.g., headings and subheadings, indentation). Then there are the various sets of signal words mentioned above, such as those that help the reader anticipate a question (*who, what, where, why, when*), an illustration (*for example, for instance*), or a comparison (*like, as*).

Another set of language features that give the reader clues for prediction of meaning are those that the writer manipulates for stylistic reasons. Instead of repeating the same noun over and over, the writer may substitute a pronoun, as in this example: *Bob* (noun) *was hot and tired. He* (pronoun) *decided to stop working right then.* In the same manner, writers use adverbs and other descriptive words, include details, repeat points for emphasis, and compare and define. Once children become aware of these techniques, encourage them to try using them in their own writing. As we have noted several times, children acquire more understanding and control of the features of written discourse when they manipulate them in writing themselves.

Children in the intermediate and upper grades, and some in the later primary grades too, will be ready to study various features of sentences and longer units of text for the clues they yield about meaning. These features include:

1. Kind of sentence (declarative, interrogative, imperative, exclamatory).
2. Kinds of clauses (independent and dependent).

3. How sentences can be related to each other (by joining, excluding, selecting, and implying).

4. The features of a paragraph (topic, details, presence/absence of main idea).

5. Patterns of paragraph organization (enumeration, generalization, sequence, comparison and contrast, question and answer, cause and effect).

6. Kinds of paragraphs (explanatory, introductory, narrative, definitional, descriptive, transitional, concluding).

7. Features of the structure of different kinds of written discourse (narrative and expository writing).

Of course, not all children in the intermediate grades will be ready to apply these abstractions about language to their own writing or even to go very far in identifying them in the writing of others. It is important to remember that children vary widely in their rate of development and to be supportive and understanding of those whose metalingual awareness needs a longer time to grow.

Prediction activities.   We will close this section on prediction strategies with some ideas for activities that can help the children learn to reconstruct the meaning of their reading material.

Dramatization is an excellent way for the children to reconstruct a story actively. One study found that dramatization was more effective than discussion and drawing for developing story comprehension.[22] Acting out the plot helps to bring the characters and setting to life in the children's minds. Simple dramatizations can be carried out even by preschoolers as they reenact some favorite tale, like *The Three Billy Goats Gruff*, with minimal dialogue and the simplest of plots. Dramatizations of full stories are best preceded by having the children act out short, easily visualized scenes, which are read aloud or that they read themselves: walking down some icy stairs, tiptoeing into a bedroom, trying not to awaken a younger brother, shivering on a suddenly cold autumn day, carrying several large but light boxes up the stairs, running across the burning hot sand on a beach in August, and so on. See the section entitled "Creative Dramatics" (chapter 5) for additional suggestions on dramatization.

Another kind of reenactment, a *roller story*, is useful for helping children predict story sequence. A roller story is prepared by illustrating the major episodes in the story along a continuous sheet of paper, such as shelf-lining paper. Each end of the sheet is wrapped around a dowel, which is placed in a hole at the top of a carton. As the child turns one of the dowels, the paper is unwound from left to right, and the story is viewed through the open end of the carton (Figure 6–2). The most suitable stories to recreate in this way are those with a continuous visual element rather than separate scenes. This characteristic adds to the fluidity of the roller story. A good example is Tworkov's *The Camel Who Took a Walk*, in which the background jungle scene could be illustrated on the roller paper, while the story's central character, the camel, could be represented by a stick puppet held in front of the moving background.

Figure 6–2   A roller-story set-up

Other story media are useful for visualizing different text features. For example, a flannelboard is an excellent way to illustrate cumulative plots, like that in the story *Dear Garbage Man* by Gene Zion (New York: Harper, 1957). The children see the elements of the plot grow and then shrink before their eyes.

Another activity designed to help children learn to use details consists of three cards made of heavy cardboard. The cards are constructed with increasingly larger openings cut into their centers (Figure 6–3). On each card write a sentence that describes a detail in a picture. The child places the first card over the picture and tries to predict what the picture is from the clue written on the card. If she is unable to do this with the first card (the one with the smallest opening), she proceeds to the second card and then to the third.[23]

A domino-type game can help children associate words that signal questions with potential answers. Simulating the domino format, write the words and possible answers on cards, as shown in Figure 6–4. The children play the game using the regular rules of dominoes. They may match a word on either end of a card with another word or words that make sense. For example, a card with *who* on one side could be matched on that side with a card with *Jerry* written on it. If *at home*

Figure 6–3   Clue cards

is written on the other side of the *who* card, then a possible match for it would be a card with *where* on it. Figure 6–5 shows what a possible chain of domino cards might look like.

You may also be able to locate some commercially produced materials for practicing prediction strategies. Often these are labeled *thinking*, rather than comprehension activities. One example is called *A New Way to Use Your Bean*, by D. Freeman (New York: Trillium, 1982), which is particularly appealing because its activities all involve cooking.

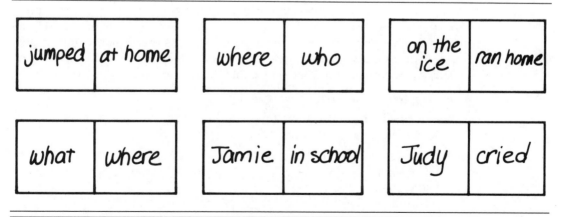

Figure 6–4   Domino cards

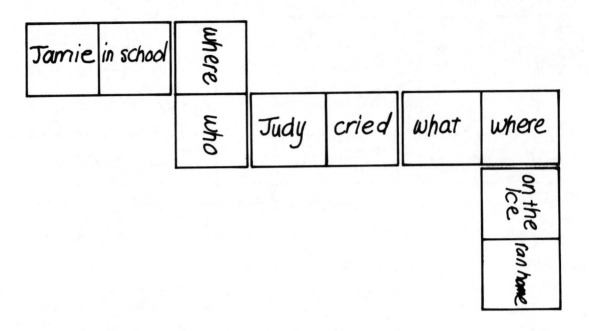

Figure 6–5   A chain of domino cards

Summary

We have discussed how reading is much more than the mere mechanical decoding of words. It is an active process in which making, testing, and verifying predictions about a written text enable the reader to reconstruct the meaning encoded in written symbols by the writer. Reading, therefore, *is* comprehension. In this chapter we have investigated what comprehension is and ways that you can help to encourage and develop it in your classroom. We have seen that:

- Comprehension is both process and product.
- Reading, the reconstruction of meaning encoded in written symbols, involves much more than the mastery of a set of skills.
- There are three levels of comprehension skills:
  literal comprehension
  interpretation
  critical evaluation
- Vocabulary and concept development is an important part of comprehension instruction.
- Making predictions is an integral component of reading for meaning.

Activities

1. Read the following passage and compose one literal comprehension question, one interpretation question, and one critical evaluation question for it.

   Judy was playing in the yard with her friend Billie. It was warm, so they took off their jackets. But, suddenly a cold wind made them both shiver. "Let's go inside and play," said Billie. "No," said Judy, "I want to stay outside." Then, Judy's mother came to the door. "It's time for lunch, children," she called.

2. Select ten words, half of which are content words, the other half function words. Embed the ten words in a randomly ordered list and then in ten meaningful sentences. Select two first or second graders who cannot identify the words in advance. Teach one child the words in the randomized list, the other child the words in the sentences. What differences do you find in the difficulty of learning the words (as indicated by such factors as amount of time required) according to where they were embedded and whether they were content or function words?

3. Arrange to visit a primary-grade classroom while the teacher is conducting a reading or social studies lesson. What percentage of the total instructional time did the teacher spend on comprehension? What specific strategies did the teacher use for teaching comprehension?

4. Design a comprehension activity that does not use questions as a major strategy. Dramatization, a table game, or retelling a story through a different medium such as a flannelboard are some of the ways suggested in this chapter. Arrange to use the activity with a small group of primary-grade children. How did the children respond to the activity? How could you tell whether or not they comprehended the material? If you were to redesign the activity, what changes would you make and why?

5. To compare the ability of young readers in identifying words with their actual comprehension of meaning, prepare a set of ten idiomatic expressions composed of words simple enough to be identified by second or third graders. Your list might include such expressions as: *She's living off the fat of the land; Tony is really going places; He's a wolf in sheep's clothing; Patty laid an egg; Behind the eight ball again.* Ask a second- or third-grade child to read each expression and then tell you what it means.[25]

Further Reading

Durkin, D. "What Classroom Observations Reveal about Comprehension Instruction." *Reading Research Quarterly* 14 (1978–1979): 481–533.

Flood, J., ed. *Promoting Reading Comprehension.* Newark, Del.: International Reading Association, 1984.

Goodman, K. S. "Reading: A Psycholinguistic Guessing Game." *Journal of the Reading Specialist* 4 (1967): 123–35.

Henry, G. H. *Teaching Reading as Concept Development: Emphasis on Affective Thinking.* Newark, Del.: International Reading Association, 1974.

Martin, C. E., Cramond, B., and Safter, T. "Developing Creativity through the Reading Program." *The Reading Teacher* 35 (1982): 568–72.

Translation of "English as She Is Seldom Spoke"

A crafty swordsman in a red shirt and a taciturn Saxon sat down to play cards under a pale blue sky. Blue-eyed Mary skipped over the hill in the middle of the pasture beside them. A muddy stream ran under the small bridge that sheltered them, and deer played hop-scotch over the homestead. The odor of (*syllabub* is the name of a drink of wine and curd, with no equivalent in modern English) was warm on the air.

"A man could toss all day on the (effects of) a drink like that," said the swordsman. The Saxon raised his thumb, aiming it at his companion.

"You are a friend. As for myself, I prefer pumpkin pie to any drink of liquor."

He toyed with his wild celery, but was interrupted by a startling hiccup.

"Sir," he shouted. "You spit like that young bull. Haven't you learned to blow your nose yet? If I were not so tired, I would beat you with my rusty sword."

Indifference overcame him as the swordsman rose to say, "A plague on you who are shaped like a bale of wool and bristly beside. I will be gone as soon as I remove this nail in my shoe. It, like you, gives me a pain in my big toe."

Chapter 7

Assessment

Preview

Assessment is an essential component of the literacy program because it provides the teacher with the important information she needs to make intelligent decisions about her teaching plan. Knowing when to begin a new activity or introduce different material, review something old, or go on to something new depends on what the teacher finds out about a child's progress. The basis of good assessment is careful observation and documentation. And while some assessment procedures are quite formal and occur only occasionally, the most useful assessment procedures are a natural part of every day's activities. This chapter is designed to acquaint you with the fundamentals of assessment in the literacy program. The major points to be discussed include:

1. *The difference between developmental and behavioral assessment.*

2. *Characteristics of a standardized test.*

3. *Why the representativeness of the norming sample in a standardized test is so important.*

4. *How norm-referenced and criterion-referenced tests differ.*

5. *How diagnostic and survey tests are different.*

6. *Problems associated with the use of standardized tests.*

7. *Characteristics of an informal reading inventory, miscue analysis, diagnostic survey, and cloze procedure.*

8. *Some behaviors a teacher should look for in a child's ongoing reading and writing activities to assess development.*

9. *What anecdotal records are.*

10. *Some criteria to apply in the development of a checklist or special record-keeping format.*

11. *Useful guidelines for selecting, administering, and interpreting assessment procedures.*

Approaches to Assessment

Socrates's observation that the unexamined life is not worth living is relevant to teaching. Are we actually teaching if we do not examine what it is we are doing and evaluate its effect upon our students? If we are unresponsive to how and what our students are learning, then we are not really teaching at all. Real teaching involves careful observation of children's learning, evaluation of what we observe based on our teaching goals, and then possible modification of our teaching plan in order to achieve our goals more effectively. Sometimes this kind of teaching is called *diagnostic*, because it is based on the teacher's analysis of children's learning. Children's needs shape the teacher's plan. But too often, one sees the very opposite in schools where the teaching plan is fixed in advance by a curriculum guide or teacher's manual and children's needs are subservient.

Almy and Genishi describe these two different approaches as *developmental assessment* versus *behavioral assessment*.[1] Developmental assessment emphasizes viewing children as unique individuals, each of whom brings his or her own special talents, experiences, and approaches to learning. Behavioral assessment, on the other hand, emphasizes the behaviors that are deemed necessary or appropriate for a given grade level or subject. The focus of its plan is the teaching of these behaviors, often in a prescribed manner. A program based on behavioral assessment is much less open, therefore, than a developmental assessment program, which values diversity and encourages children and teachers both to draw on their personal resources and to develop new ones.

Good assessment should yield information that is useful for instruction. Most of it should come from careful, focused observation of the children in natural situations. This kind of assessment is not a special event; rather, it is a normal part of every day's activities. Of course, some assessment procedures, such as tests, are more formal and are administered occasionally. But these should comprise only a small fraction of an assessment program.

How can a teacher use the information acquired through assessment procedures? Here is a hypothetical but, nonetheless, typical example. Ms. Jones is a first-grade teacher with a class of twenty-eight heterogeneously grouped youngsters. It is the fourth week of September. The data available to Ms. Jones as she maps out her literacy program are of both a formal and an informal nature. First, she has the results of the readiness test the children took at the end of the kindergarten year. Second, she has anecdotal and other kinds of records that are kept on all the children who attended kindergarten in her school. Third, she has the subjective feedback of the children's kindergarten teachers and other involved persons, such as parents. Finally, Ms. Jones has her own impressions of the needs, interests, and competencies of the children as she has observed them during the first weeks of school.

Several alternatives are available to Ms. Jones in how to proceed with the children's instruction. First, she can ignore the data totally or partially by simply distributing her reading readiness materials to the children and beginning, manual in hand, to "teach." We might call this the lockstep approach: everyone doing the same thing at the same time. Or Ms. Jones can use the scores children have achieved on the readiness test to assign each child to one of three reading groups: superior, average, or below average. We could label this the "bluebird" approach, since some such name is usually assigned to groups in which each child is meant to proceed at the same rate and cover the same material as every other child in the same group. However, Ms. Jones rejects each of these alternatives as inappropriate, since they neither diagnose the competencies of individual children nor adapt the curriculum to suit these competencies.

Ms. Jones decides instead to use all the information at hand to design her literacy program. Although she understands that this alternative will probably involve the most work for her, she is convinced that to help children realize their full potential, she needs to use as many different sources of information as she can. Ms. Jones's assessment program is, therefore, continuous and contains inputs of many different kinds. She knows that children are more than the sum of their separate parts, so as she gathers assessment data she is careful to remember that each child is a whole and integrated being and focus on the interrelated aspects of the child's total development. In addition, she keeps her conclusions tentative and open to continual reevaluation because she appreciates the fact that children grow and change continuously.

The remainder of this chapter will consider different kinds of assessment procedures, both formal and informal; then ways to keep records; and finally some fundamental considerations in assessment.

Formal Assessment

Suppose your instructor came to class one morning and announced, without any prior warning, that he was going to give you a test. How would you react? When I have tried this with my students, their reactions invariably fall into one of two categories: fear or anger. Even with advance warning, many of us become anxious, sometimes almost to the point of debilitation, when we must take a test. Why? What is so bad about tests? My students, whose feelings in this regard are probably typical, say that it is the "do or die," "win or lose," "now or never" quality of tests that is so threatening. If you flunk the exam, you may not pass the course or go to the graduate school of your choice or get promoted. We fear tests because often, too much of what is important to us is invested in their results. Tests make us uncomfortable too, because they make overt a comparison, perhaps unfavorable, of our performance with that of our peers. Finally, we do not like tests because sometimes we find them unfair. We may feel that their questions are ambiguous, biased, or unrelated to what is being tested.

Yet tests are a fact of life in our schools. All over the United States, from kindergarten to the twelfth grade and beyond, students are continually tested. Most of the tests are the informal, teacher-prepared kind that we will look at in the next section. But usually at least once every year in the elementary school, students take formal reading and math achievement tests.

Why is testing so basic a component of our educational system? One reason may be the American infatuation with quantification. If you can attach a number to an experience or a behavior, this somehow makes it a more objective and valid judgment. I can recall my own experience with this kind of thinking as a beginning teacher. I found that parents often had more confidence in the accuracy of a judgment of their child's performance when it was based on a test score rather than on my subjective assessment after weeks or even months of very careful observation. Moreover, educational programs consisting of hundreds of discrete skills that are meant to be mastered in a prescribed sequence lend themselves very nicely to testing programs designed to evaluate the mastery of the skills.

Thus, we have an interesting paradox: most of us dislike tests but nontheless choose to rely on them for making decisions. It seems likely that formal tests will be with us for a long time. Therefore, teachers and prospective teachers must change their perceptions from those of a test-taker to those of a test-giver. This means becoming informed about the nature of tests in order to understand their potential usefulness and avoid their misuse. Such knowledge is also important to help parents understand what test results mean both in and of themselves and in relation to other forms of assessment.

Test Standardization

A formal test is usually *standardized*, which means that it has been administered to large sample groups of children considered representative of children in general to determine the appropriateness of test items and to establish norms.

The standardization process actually begins much earlier, however, when the writer of the test composes the test questions. Drawing on her years of research and experience in the field for which the test is being designed (e.g., reading), the test writer constructs a large number of questions designed to test a child's knowledge of the subject. Then to get outside verification on the test items, she asks several other experts to evaluate them. When this is done, the test items may be said to have *face validity*; that is, they have a surface validity or accuracy (they appear to measure what they are intended to measure) because they have been reviewed by experts, although no detailed or statistical analysis has yet been made.

But face validity does not designate the kind of precise information about the quality of test items that is needed. To get this, the test must be administered to large, *representative* samples of children. *Representative* means that these samples must be similar in all the important variables to the children for whom the test is being constructed. Let us say that it is a test of reading readiness, which one should be able to administer to any child in the United States at the end of kindergarten or the beginning of first grade. The standardization samples must be similar to this total population on such significant variables as age, sex, ethnic group, geographical area, and socioeconomic status.

Once the sample groups have taken the test, the results are analyzed to evaluate each test item on its level of difficulty, discriminating capacity (how well it distinguishes between low- and high-scorers), and the progression of difficulty by age or grade (whether the percentage of students answering the item correctly increases with age or grade level). As a result of this item analysis, the test writer decides to discard some items because they are too easy, too difficult, or inappropriate. In addition, this preliminary try-out of the test yields additional information on test administration in the areas of directions, timing, and scoring.

Norms.   *Test norms* are also developed from the scores obtained by the standardization sample. Using the total number of correct answers (the *raw score*) achieved by the children in the sample, the test writer calculates the average score obtained by children at different ages or grade levels. These average scores are the norms against which the scores of children who are to take the test in the future will be compared.

The importance of the representativeness of the standardization sample becomes apparent here. Unless the standardization sample is comparable on the important variables to that group of children who will later take the test, measuring the latter's scores against the test norms may be unjustified. For example, one test of reading readiness indicates that its standardization sample was composed of children from families well above the median socioeconomic status for the United States. What significance does this fact have for use of the test? Since research usually finds a strong relationship between socioeconomic status and school achievement, we can expect that the norms derived from these children's scores on the test will be above average. Therefore, can we reasonably compare the scores of students from lower socioeconomic groups to these norms? Such a comparison is probably unfair.

In a situation where there is concern that the test norms are biased, it may be possible to develop *local norms* to be used as a standard of comparison. This process requires a school that does not have dramatic changes in its student population from year to year on important variables such as ethnic group and socioeconomic level. To establish local norms for your own school, use the scores that children in the school achieved on the test over the previous several years and calculate the average score achieved by the children in the school at various grade levels. Because these local norms are constructed from a population very similar to the children currently taking the test in the school, they provide a less biased standard of comparison than the test's national norms.[2] The local test norms can also be used to indicate how your school compares to the standardization sample, but it is important to familiarize yourself with the characteristics of the standardization sample (usually reported in the test manual), so that you can evaluate how valid a comparison with the sample would be for the children in your school.

Test norms are often reported as percentiles and grade-level equivalents. A *percentile rank* compares a student's score with others at the same grade level. A percentile rank of sixty for a child in the fifth month of second grade, for example, means that according to the test norms, sixty percent of the children in the fifth month of second grade scored at or below this child's score.

Likewise, raw scores are converted into *grade-level equivalents*. The test manual contains a chart that shows the conversions. Let us say that a raw score of seventy-five on the test converts to a grade level equivalent of 1.5 (fifth month of first grade). What this means is that the average score attained by children in the fifth month of first grade in the standardization sample was seventy-five.

Sometimes teachers misconstrue the meaning of a grade-level equivalent and equate it with the reading level in a basal reader. A teacher might mistakenly believe, for example, that a grade level equivalent of 1.5 on the test means that a child ought to be moved into the second level of the first-grade reader. Actually, grade-level equivalents on tests are entirely unrelated to the reading levels of books. No decisions on curriculum materials should be based on the results of this kind of standardized test.

Reliability and validity.   The standardization process also results in two other kinds of information about the test—its validity and its reliability. *Validity* in measurement has traditionally referred to whether or not the test actually measures what it is designed to measure. According to this definition, if a test of reading readiness is valid, then it will be a good predictor of reading achievement. That is, if we were to give this test to children *before* they learned to read, and then tested them again on reading achievement at the end of first grade, we would find a good correlation between the children's reading readiness and reading achievement scores. A more current definition of validity is concerned with the *interpretation* of a test's results. *Decision* or *discriminant* validity is determined by how valid (or invalid) the decision based on the test's results turns out to be.[3]

Reliability means that the results of a test are not significantly affected by chance variations. A reliable test is one that is stable or consistent in its measurement. If a child takes the test today and then takes it again in a week or two, we should find no great fluctuation in his two scores.[4]

Standard error.   Another important piece of information resulting from the standardization process, which you will find reported in the test manual, is the standard error of measurement. *Standard error* refers to how much fluctuation you could expect in a child's measured score on a test compared to his true score. The standard error is an index of how much the test is likely to be off in predicting the child's true score (the hypothetical score he would obtain on a perfect test).

Let us say that the manual reports a standard error for the test of four months (.4). This means that approximately sixty-eight percent of the time, a child's true score will be within .4 of his measured score. If his grade-level equivalent on the test is 3.5, then approximately sixty-eight percent of the time his true score will fall between 3.1 (3.5 − .4) and 3.9 (3.5 + .4). About ninety-five percent of the time, his true score will be within two standard errors (.8) of the measured score, making his range of grade-level equivalents from 2.7 (3.5 − .8) to 4.3 (3.5 + .8).[5] All standardized tests have standard errors of measurement, which indicate their imprecision and potential fallibility.

Criterion-referenced tests.   So far, we have been describing *norm-referenced* tests, those in which a child's performance is measured against the norms of a standardizing sample. Another kind of formal assessment is the *criterion-referenced* test. Instead of assessing achievement in relation to norms, criterion-referenced tests measure achievement against a set of behaviorally defined objectives. Such objectives specify the desired behavior precisely and indicate it in observable ways. For instance, a behavioral objective might require a student to identify all the compound words in a particular paragraph.

Criterion-referenced tests have predetermined levels of mastery rather than norms. A student may have to get at least seventy-five percent of the questions on such a test correct in order to be considered to have demonstrated mastery. One of the major criticisms of criterion-referenced tests is the arbitrary nature of the criterion levels that are set. Usually, there is no justification in research or theory for the particular levels that are chosen.

Criterion-referenced tests became popular as the schools accountability movement gathered momentum in the 1970s. The tests were used to measure the behaviorally defined skills for competencies that the schools were held accountable for teaching.

Survey tests. Most of the formal tests we see in schools can be classified as *summative assessment*; that is, they are given toward the *end* of instruction to evaluate its effectiveness: after a year in the first grade, for example, how well are children reading? Usually, these are called achievement tests, which is somewhat misleading since *all* tests indicate performance or achievement rather than native ability. A better name for these summative assessments is *survey tests*, since they are designed to yield general or rough estimates of *group* performance.

Please remember that it is group rather than individual performance that survey tests can be useful in assessing. This is so because in the standardization process, measures of central tendency (mean, median, mode) are used to *average* the separate scores of individuals into ranges of scores, which are reported as means or percentiles. An individual's score loses its separate identity as it is merged with the scores of others in the sample. Of course, this does not mean that a higher score does not correlate with higher achievement by a given child, merely that the percentiles are not accurate measures of individual performance. Diagnostic tests, on the other hand, are meant to give information on the performance of a single child.

Diagnostic tests. *Diagnostic tests* can be classified as *formative assessment* because they are given in the course of instruction or even before instruction begins. The information from a diagnostic test, therefore, is meant to help the teacher modify her instructional materials and methods to meet the child's needs more effectively.

Survey tests usually sample only broad areas of performance. A typical reading survey test in the primary grades might contain subtests on comprehension, word identification, and vocabulary. Diagnostic tests are much more specific and detailed. For example, the *Doren Diagnostic Reading Test of Word Recognition Skills* (American Guidance Service, Inc.) contains subtests for letter recognition, beginning sounds, whole word recognition, words within words, speech consonants, ending sounds, blending, rhyming, vowels, sight words, and discriminate guessing.

Once, diagnostic tests were administered to individual children almost exclusively by specially trained personnel. Now, many can be administered to the whole class by the regular teacher.

Problems with the Use of Standardized Tests

We have already noted some of the problems that may be associated with the use of standardized tests, such as equating a grade-level equivalent with the graded level of a reading text. This is a serious misuse of test results, not only because it is based on a nonexistent relationship but also because the reading content in a 3^2 (second level of the third grade) reader, let us say, is apt to be more difficult than the test material that results in a grade level equivalent of 3.5. A child who is given a 3^2 reader because of this erroneous notion is apt to be in for trouble, since the reading text may be too difficult for him.

Another problem already mentioned is potentially more serious, because it is so far-reaching. This is the use of a test with biased norms. Whether justified or not, many important decisions, such as promotion or retention, or selection for an accelerated or enrichment program, are based totally or partially on the results of standardized tests. If the test norms were developed on a standardization sample that differs significantly and in important ways from the group now taking the test, we have a right to question the validity of these decisions. It is very important, therefore, to make a careful check of a test's standardization process. This information should be available in the manual that accompanies the test.

There are other problems with the use of standardized or formal tests. They may have low *external* or *ecological validity*. Because so much attention is paid in standardized tests to controlling the design of the test materials (internal validity), the reading process being measured may no longer be representative of real reading in real contexts. The results of this kind of test, therefore, may have low generalizability (external validity).[6]

In addition, such tests may suffer from the same kinds of bias we often see in graded readers, such as underrepresentation of diverse ethnic groups, stereotyped male/female roles, and the portrayal of a predominantly rural or suburban environment. As we have already noted, the standard error of measurement is one indication that such tests predict imperfectly.

Sometimes a veritable gridlock of tests and curriculum occurs with the adoption of criterion-referenced tests and skills mastery reading programs. Children are taught hundreds of discrete skills, tested on these skills, and then retaught those which the tests indicate they have not yet mastered; or they move on to still others, on which they will be tested later. This kind of process represents a closed system that restricts change and development. Moreover, what appears on a test may be influenced more by how conveniently it fits a multiple-choice format than by its significance for assessing development in literacy.

A very serious problem in the use of standardized or formal assessment procedures arises from the interpretation or, sadly, misinterpretation of results. Teachers and other school personnel may interpret results rigidly, labeling some children "slow" or "gifted" and expecting them to live up to these labels. This is the well-known *Pygmalion Effect*, or *self-fulfilling prophecy*, in which test scores may unduly influence a teacher's expectations of a child's performance. Since the teacher's expectations are a major contribution to the child's subsequent achievement, this can create a vicious cycle.

Yet another problem is that the teacher can rarely administer formal assessment procedures when he feels they would be useful. Decisions on test selection and time of administration are generally made at the higher levels of school administration, which reduces the usefulness of such tests for the teacher.

Finally, we cannot ignore the negative impact such tests often have on children, parents, teachers, and administrators. When so much importance is invested in the results of tests, is it any wonder that children and their families approach them with fear? When the results of the annual survey tests are broadcast within a school, throughout a school district, and sometimes even in the local newspaper, we can appreciate the concern of school personnel about them. But is fear the best way to motivate students and teachers?

Ours is a "test-saturated" society, and I do not see any indications of a reversal in this situation. Tests are going to be with us for a while. What can we do? We can inform ourselves and our colleagues about both the potential usefulness and the limitations of tests. And we can be certain to employ many informal assessment procedures to refine and extend the information acquired from formal ones. We will consider these in the next section.

Informal Assessment

Good informal assessment procedures are based on careful observation and documentation. Almost any behavior that you observe contains important information about a child's performance: that Tanya only selects basal readers to read; that Lee's independent writing consists of copying charts and other written material from around the room; that Marcella carefully edits her stories several times before she meets you in conference; and that Kristen has no problem answering questions about what she has read but stumbles over many of the words when she reads aloud.

Most informal assessment does not require a separate time or a special technique. Instead, it is an integral part of your day-to-day interactions with the children, and it constitutes the primary basis for your decisions about modifying instruction. A few procedures, however, are somewhat more formal in that they have prescribed techniques for administration and interpretation. Four of the most widely used techniques of this kind are the informal reading inventory, miscue analysis, diagnostic survey, and cloze procedure.

Informal Reading Inventory

The purpose of an *informal reading inventory* is to determine a child's *instructional reading level*, the optimal level at which he should be taught to read. Generally, a child's instructional level is considered to be the highest level at which he can read comfortably, with good comprehension and word identification.[7]

Using research by Kilgallon,[8] the informal reading inventory was expanded by Betts,[9] and further popularized by Johnson and Kress.[10] It determines three functional reading levels based on the number of correct responses made by a child in word identification and comprehension: the *independent level*, at which reading for enjoyment and reading in the content areas should occur; the *instructional level*, at which the teaching of reading should occur; and the *frustrational level*, which should be avoided, because the reading material at this level is too difficult for the child.

Ironically, it has been found that content-area textbooks, such as those in science and social studies, are much more difficult to read than their grade-level designations would indicate. For most of these textbooks, grade level refers to the content covered not the difficulty of the reading material itself. Thus, a third-grade social studies text might contain information about agriculture, because in the textbook series this is a third-grade unit of study. However, the difficulty level of the reading material may be well above third grade. Therefore, rather than being at the child's independent level, the book may actually be at his frustrational level!

The following chart shows the percentage of correct responses required in word identification and comprehension for each of the three levels:

Level	Word Identification	Comprehension
Independent	99 percent + words pronounced correctly	90 percent + questions answered correctly
Instructional	95 percent + words pronounced correctly	75 percent + questions answered correctly
Frustrational	90 percent − words pronounced correctly	50 percent − questions answered correctly

These criterion levels, however, have been contested over the years: the percentages have been challenged as being arbitrary, or too stringent, or simply inaccurate.[11] Probably the most sensible solution is to use the informal reading inventory without rigidly adhering to the numerical standards and the criterion levels only as general guidelines.

To prepare an informal reading inventory, randomly select a passage of approximately a hundred words from each level of a graded series of basal readers starting with the primer. Preferably using a primer typewriter, record each passage on a separate sheet of paper, coding each so that you will know its level. Prepare four comprehension questions for each passage: two literal comprehension, one interpretation, and one critical evaluation. To make the sheets sturdier, use a stiff backing of some kind, such as oaktag, for each passage and cover it with clear adhesive paper.

Administer an informal reading inventory in a relaxed, unpressured manner. Have the child begin reading a passage that is at least one level *below* her current reading level. Tally as errors each word the child substitutes for another word, repeats, omits, or inserts. After she reads each passage, ask her the comprehension questions that go along with it. Have the child continue reading at successively higher levels until her score is about that of the instructional level: identification of about ninety-five percent of the words and correct answers to approximately seventy-five percent of the questions.

For children who are not yet reading at least at the level of a primer, randomly select fifteen different words, except proper nouns, from the series' preprimers. Type the words on separate cards. The child should read the words aloud. If the child cannot identify any of the words, continue with readiness work. Identification of between one and twelve words means that the preprimer is the appropriate level. A score above this may indicate that a move to the primer level is in order.

Added to the controversial nature of the criterion levels in the informal reading inventory are a number of other shortcomings. For one thing, it is a very time-consuming procedure. Second, its usefulness is reduced considerably if you do not use a particular basal reader series as the basis of your reading program. The vocabulary of different basal reader series, as well as that found in children's books and self-composed texts, may differ significantly from the particular basal reading series you use to construct the informal reading inventory. If the vocabulary is sufficiently unfamiliar to the child, you will not get an accurate estimate of his instructional reading level. Third, the informal reading inventory does not assess a number of important factors affecting a book's difficulty level, such as predictability of the language, the child's interest in the material, the physical layout of the text, and whether or not the child is already familiar with the story and concepts presented.[12] Fourth, asking a few questions about a very brief passage seems a rather superficial way to assess comprehension. Fifth, the *kind* of text used (narrative or expository) for the test passages, rather than merely the content, may affect their level of difficulty. Sixth, because they lack a beginning context, the passages may actually be more difficult than their graded readability level indicates.[13] Finally, the informal reading inventory merely *counts* errors. It does nothing to try to analyze what kinds of errors the child makes.

Miscue Analysis

Kenneth Goodman's research on strategies employed by readers indicates that analyzing reading errors might be a more productive procedure than merely counting them.[14] As we have seen, reading is an active process that involves sampling graphic, syntactic, and semantic cues; making predictions about the structure and meaning of a passage from selected cues; testing the predictions; and then either confirming or correcting them. In this process, both beginners and proficient readers make what are called *miscues*, which Goodman defines as actual responses in oral reading that do not match expected responses.[15] By observing and analyzing these miscues, the teacher can achieve insight into the nature of the reading process itself and be able to diagnose the specific areas of a child's strengths and weaknesses.

In Goodman's psycholinguistic model of reading, in which the goal is comprehension of meaning, only those miscues that alter the textual meaning intended by the writer are considered significant. The decision on whether or not to correct a miscue depends on how seriously it alters the meaning of the passage the child is reading and on the possibility of the child's own subsequent self-correction.

Qualitative miscue analysis involves presenting the child with new material approximately at the instructional level. The teacher audiotapes the child's oral reading of the selection so that she can later recheck the miscues she noted during the actual reading. She then analyzes each miscue. Those that do not alter the meaning of the passage are not considered for further study and follow-up.[16] For example, if the child reads, "All the *kids* went to the movies" when the text actually states "All the *children* went to the movies," there is no alteration in meaning. This miscue does not constitute an indication of reading weakness. Some miscues may only represent dialect differences, as when a child pronounces the word *pen* as *pin* but understands its correct meaning as *pen*, a writing implement.

Further analysis of the miscues in a child's oral reading may reveal some that are grammatically acceptable but violate the meaning of the passage. The implicit understanding of the structure of language among even beginning readers enables them to substitute for the correct word another that has a different meaning but is the same functional part of speech. For example, a child may read "The cat ran *over* the table" for "The cat ran *under* the table," which changes the meaning considerably; yet *under* and *over* are both prepositions and serve the same grammatical function in these two sentences. Deciding on whether to pursue this kind of miscue depends on the interaction of several factors: how seriously it changes the passage's meaning and the child's background and maturity.

Miscue analysis also evaluates the child's ability to retell what she has read. The teacher prepares for the retelling by having ready an outline of the text and a set of questions he can use to help the child expand the retelling. After she has finished reading aloud, the child is asked to close the book and tell everything she can remember about the material she has just read. The teacher may then ask the child questions on points from his outline if they were not covered sufficiently in the child's retelling. In their discussion of the reading miscue inventory, Yetta Goodman and Carolyn Burke describe in detail both the retelling procedure and the scoring of miscues.[17]

Finally, before deciding on whether instruction is called for because of meaning-altering miscues in the child's reading of the passage, the teacher should consider whether or not the child applied any self-correcting strategies to these miscues. Did the child make any attempts to correct these miscues through *regressing*, looking back over the previously read material and rereading it correctly? This self-correcting strategy is a mark of reading proficiency and represents the child's growth toward trying to extract more accurate meaning from the material read. As such, it constitutes a reading strength.

One difficulty in using the miscue analysis procedure is that it is extremely time-consuming. Weaver recommends a much more informal use of the miscue analysis using the child's regular oral reading, which can be checked for such characteristics as using preceding context to make predictions, making miscues that make sense in context, correcting miscues that do not make sense, and paying too much attention to graphophonic cues and too little attention to syntactic and semantic cues.[18] The miscue analysis has also been criticized for concentrating exclusively on oral reading, while ignoring the very important process of silent reading. However, you can get a sense of the child's silent reading comprehension skill if he first reads the material silently and then retells it in his own words.

Diagnostic Survey

Marie Clay's diagnostic survey is similar to the miscue analysis in that it goes well beyond the mere tallying of errors and concentrates instead on the strategies a child uses in reading.[19] It is a much more comprehensive procedure that consists of several different observation techniques and samples both reading and writing behaviors. Clay warns that no single observation technique used alone is adequate. The most reliable interpretations of a child's performance are drawn from a wide range of observations.

The pivotal observation technique in the diagnostic survey is the *running record* of text reading. No special material is required, and it is advisable to use texts that are part of the everyday program. Select three texts of one hundred to two hundred words each, at different reading levels—independent, instructional, and frustrational. Record everything the child says and does as he tries to read the text. Careful analysis of the running record will reveal important characteristics of the child's reading strategies. For example, you can see what kinds of cues the child uses—contextual, graphophonic, or structural. You can also observe whether the child uses any self-correction techniques (called *regressions* in miscue analysis). The running record is a dynamic assessment technique, since it captures the process of reading as it occurs.

In the United States, the most well-known part of the diagnostic survey is the Concepts about Print Test (*Sand* and *Stones*), which is designed for beginning readers. In this procedure, which takes five to ten minutes, the teacher reads the child a simple paperback book. As she reads, she asks the child to assist her by pointing out particular features of the book or printed passage, such as which side is the front of the book, where to start reading, where the teacher is reading, and which is the last part of the story.

Other techniques in the diagnostic survey focus on writing. One, a test of writing vocabulary, asks the child to write down all the words she knows, beginning with her name, in a ten-minute period. Administering this procedure at the beginning, middle, and end of the school year provides a revealing developmental record of the child's progress.

Clay also provides this scale for rating the language level, message quality, and directional principles in beginning writing samples:[20]

Language Level

Record the number of the highest level of linguistic organization used by the child.

1. Alphabetic (letters only).
2. Word (any recognizable word).
3. Word group (any two-word phrase).
4. Sentence (any simple sentence).
5. Punctuated story (of two or more sentences).
6. Paragraphed story (two themes).

Message Quality

Record the number below for the best description of the child's sample.

1. He has a concept of signs (uses letters, invents letters, uses punctuation).

2. He has a concept that a message is conveyed.

3. A message is copied.

4. Repetitive use of sentence patterns like "Here is a . . ."

5. Attempts to record own ideas.

6. Successful composition.

Directional Principles

Record the number of the highest rating for which there is no error in the sample of the child's writing.

1. No evidence of directional knowledge.

2. Part of the directional pattern is known:
   Either start top left
   Or move left to right
   Or return down left.

3. Reversal of the directional pattern (right to left and return down right).

4. Correct directional pattern.

5. Correct directional pattern and spaces between words.

6. Extensive text without any difficulties of arrangement and spacing of text.

Because the diagnostic survey is so comprehensive, it could be very time-consuming. However, many of its techniques can easily by incorporated into the child's regular reading/writing conferences. For example, taking a running record every once in a while as the child reads aloud in the conference should not add substantially to the time required, and the valuable information revealed should more than compensate for the added effort. Likewise, you can easily get an index of the child's knowledge of print jargon and concepts as she reads aloud by asking her to point out various features of the text.

Cloze Procedure

The *cloze procedure* is another technique in which the reader derives meaning from a passage by using its semantic and syntactic cues.[21] The cloze procedure is an extension of the principle of *closure*, which is the tendency to perceive incom-

Figure 7–1   An incomplete object perceived as whole

plete objects as whole entities by filling in the gaps in the actual sensory input. Thus, the object in Figure 7–1, though it is not a complete figure, would probably be perceived as an apple. Similarly, we tend to close or complete psychological experiences in order to maintain a sense of psychological balance or well-being. In applying this principle to reading, the cloze procedure requires the child to fill in, by use of contextual clues, words that have been deleted at regular intervals from a selected passage.

To prepare a cloze procedure, select a passage of at least 275 words from near the beginning of the book or chapter you are going to use, so that comprehension will not depend too heavily on prior material. Starting with the second sentence and proceeding through the sentence just before the last, delete words at regular intervals. The shorter the interval between deleted words, the more difficult it is to fill in the missing words correctly. The typical range of deleted words used in this procedure is between every fifth and every twelfth word; I suggest that you delete every tenth word. Type the passage with lines of equal length for deleted words. Number the lines in order and list the deleted words on a separate sheet. Give the child the passage and ask him to write in the deleted words. Do not time the procedure and encourage the child to fill in every deletion. The child's score is simply the total number of missing words he fills in correctly.

Although there is some research to indicate that accepting only the *exact* words for deletions makes the cloze procedure a more effective diagnostic tool,[22] I would recommend that you also accept good synonyms as correct responses, since they do not alter the meaning of the passage significantly. In addition, accepting synonyms will prevent the child from becoming frustrated by having an essentially correct response rejected.

Because the cloze procedure requires some sophistication in both the use of contextual cues and the writing out of correct responses, it is usually used with children from the third grade on. Balyeat and Norman, however, describe a cloze procedure employing language experience stories that can be used successfully with children in the early primary grades.[23]

Research and practical experience demonstrate the usefulness of the cloze procedure as a diagnostic tool and as a teaching device for improving comprehension skills (see chapter 6).[24] As with all procedures, however, it has certain limitations. For example, contextual cues alone may be insufficient for identifying some deleted words. And the procedure does not analyze the specific strategies the child uses to identify deleted words.

Ongoing Informal Assessment

The informal reading inventory, miscue analysis, the diagnostic survey, and cloze procedure are systematic and specialized techniques with prescribed methods for administering and scoring. They will comprise only a very small percentage of your informal assessment program. The bulk of the diagnostic information you collect will come from daily informal observations of children and interactions with them. Diagnosis is as much a state of mind as it is a series of procedures. What you need is the kind of mental set that heightens and sensitizes your awareness of the diagnostic potential in children's activities. As we have noted earlier, keen observaton and careful documentation are essential.

Response to print.   One exceedingly rich source of information on children's status in literacy is their response to books and other reading matter. You can look for these kinds of behaviors in preschoolers as young as three: an interest in being read to as shown by such things as enthusiasm and involvement during reading and requests that they be read to and that a favorite story be reread again and again; the ability to retell favorite stories and make up stories of their own; and the ability to simulate the act of reading in such ways as holding the book correctly, looking at the print, and proceeding from left to right.

Knowledge of books and print.   Another significant source of information is children's knowledge of books and print. Marie Clay's *Concepts About Print Test*, described earlier, which you can modify to meet the needs of your own children, can be useful here. These or similar procedures can help you find out if a child knows about the physical format of a book, that the story is conveyed through the print, and the correct directional orientation in reading.

Familiarity with environmental print.   Children's familiarity with and ability to read environmental print is still another area to look at. Much of this assessment should occur incidentally, as children come into contact with environmental print each day. For example, in preparing a batch of play dough with a small group of children, note who is able to identify the salt and flour package labels. Can they read the brand names (e.g., Red Cross or Morton Salt) or simply identify what *kinds* of products they are? When you are out for a walk with the children, do they recognize the stop sign at the corner, can they read the street signs, and do they know what the sign by the fast food restaurant says?

Another more formal way to assess children's knowledge of environmental print is to use a procedure similar to one developed by Harste, Woodward, and Burke.[25] They presented familiar packaged products, like Crest Toothpaste and Jell-O, to children under three different conditions: with the package intact; with the package's two-dimensional graphics removed; and without the package, using only a typed print of the product label. The children were asked under each condition what they thought the stimulus said, and for the first two conditions, what things helped them know what it said.

Involvement in story dictation and reading.   How actively do children participate in story dictation and reading? Certainly, this is another index of their development in literacy. Does a child offer his ideas to group dictated accounts? Does he enjoy dictating and rereading his own stories? When rereading a dictated story, does he look at the words or the illustration, try to recall the exact words or paraphrase, read left to right and top to bottom, and pronounce separate words as he looks at them? How many key words has he learned? Does he look for and take pleasure in finding these words in other places, such as magazines and newspapers? Does he also enjoy reading nondictated material, such as books? What particular kinds of books is he especially interested in?

Writing.   Of course, you will also want to observe children's writing. Even if her writing is not yet conventional, a child may understand that the scribbles or pictures she has made symbolize meaning. Give children paper and ask them to write something, just as you yourself will do at your desk. Afterward, everyone (including you) who wants to can read their stories. Which children use pictures or some combination of pictures and other symbols, such as letters and numerals? Do you see instances of the letter-name strategy in spelling (e.g., *U* for the word *You*) or other kinds of invented spelling (e.g., *skwrl* for *squirrel*)? What is the child's attitude about writing: enthusiastic, cautious, fearful, or disinterested? Does the child spontaneously seek opportunities to write—does she copy the charts and signs that are hanging around the room, does she enjoy using the primer typewriter and microcomputer? What strategies does the child employ when she does not know how to spell a word she needs—does she seek your help, use her picture dictionary, spell the word as best she can, or leave a space for it to come back to later on?

Donald Richgels describes an informal procedure for assessing a child's development in spelling by looking at the child's invented spelling.[26] The child is asked to spell ten familiar words from orally presented meaning clues: For the word *kitten*, the clue is *A baby cat is called a* ———. The child spells the word using plastic uppercase letters. The directions for scoring the procedure allow for nonconventional spellings. For example, the child is given credit for each of the thirty-one required phonemes in the ten words that she represents either conventionally or by showing an awareness of sounds in letter names. In addition, Richgels provides a checklist for interpreting the child's performance, which looks at such features as whether the child experiments with the plastic letters as symbols of sound, whether a letter-name strategy dominates, and whether some elements of conventional spelling have appeared.

Reading/writing folders.   Once the literacy program is going full speed, the focal points of your formal assessment plan will be the child's reading and writing folder and your individual conferences with him. The dated samples of the child's work, combined with your own comments, provide a continuous, longitudinal, and complete record of his development in literacy.

Perhaps three times a year you might want to review all the folders to get a picture of the progress of your entire class. At these times you would check to see how well children are faring in the development of reading proficiency in the areas of comprehension, word identification, interest, and fluency. Likewise, you would look for growth in writing proficiency as demonstrated by their interest in and desire to write; knowledge of the conventions of different forms of writing, such as a shopping list and a letter; spelling progression from unconventional to conventional; ability to edit and revise; development of story structure and cohesion; and ability to write in different kinds of discourse and for different purposes.

Naturally, evaluation of the children's progress in these areas would be tempered by both their level of development and their abilities. Always remember that growth is *not* linear. Children may draw one day, use letters the next, and go back to drawing on the third. Or they may write the letters in their names conventionally today and backward tomorrow. What you are looking for is development over time, with its normal progressions and regressions.

Occasionally, you might want to add somewhat special kinds of data. For example, you can audiotape several instances of a child's story retellings over time. This provides a firsthand record of the child's growing sense of story structure and of his development in controlling various features such as cohesion. You can also note growth in vocabulary, fluency, and complexity of language.

For the information you collect on children's development to be really useful, you need to have a simple, practical, and efficient way to record it. Otherwise, the information will be lost or inaccessible, and your purpose for assessment, to determine children's progress so that you can better meet their needs, will have failed. In the next section, we will consider record-keeping.

Record-Keeping

In the following discussion, we will look at anecdotal records, vignettes, logs, diaries, and checklists.

Anecdotal Records

Anecdotal records are among the most useful kinds of data collection procedures. By highlighting specific, yet representative samples of a child's behavior, anecdotal records add both depth and clarity to the picture of the child's development over time.

An anecdotal account is characterized by its objectivity, specificity, brevity, and selectivity. The teacher does not record random samples of the child's behavior; rather, she selects those that are *characteristic* of the child's writing and reading performance. The teacher does not include subjective impressions in the account itself but limits the statement to what she has actually observed. Comments about the observation are kept separate from the record of the observation itself. For example, instead of noting that "John became highly frustrated with the reading passage," the statement might read, "John's response to the reading passage was marked by fidgeting, frequent looking away from the book, and stumbling over several words." The anecdote describes briefly and succinctly the child's specific behavior and includes information on all pertinent factors.

Anecdotal records can be recorded on separate three-by-five inch or four-by-six inch index cards:

Name _____   Class _____   Teacher _____
Date _____
Observation:

The reverse side of the card can be reserved for the teacher's comments about the observation.

Another way to record anecdotes is to use a separate eight-and-a-half-by-eleven inch sheet of paper for each child, with room for entries as follows:

Name _____   Class _____   Teacher_____

Date   Observation   Comment

_____   _____   _____

The separate, dated anecdotal accounts are noted and commented upon on this one sheet of paper. The advantage of this format is that it provides, at a glance, a chronological record of a given child's behavior, although it does not allow as much space for observations and comments as the index card format.

Vignettes, Logs, and Diaries

A variation of the anecdotal record is the *vignette*. This is the teacher's written account of what she considers to be a rather special moment in the child's development. A teacher might want to record the circumstances surrounding a child's first individually dictated story, for example, or how another child started to edit and revise written work on his own.

Some teachers prefer to keep continuous, open-ended records in the form of *logs* or *diaries*. Each day they record in a small, handy notebook and with as much detail as they can, what they observed to be particularly significant about the day's events.

Whichever approach you select, it is essential to set aside time each week to review the information you have collected. This information can help you make *informed* decisions about possible modifications in your teaching plan to further the children's progress.

Checklist

Another kind of record-keeping system is a special form or checklist of specific behaviors, which can be a quick and efficient way to note development. However, unless the categories to be noted are especially designed to meet the needs of *your own program*, such a system may yield little or no useful information. This kind of record-keeping system should not be elaborate. As a matter of fact, the simpler and easier it is to use, the more efficient it will be.

Characteristics of a good checklist.   The criteria I would use in selecting or designing a recording format of the checklist type are:

- It would be clear.
- It would be easy to record and retrieve information.
- It would be appropriate for children's needs.
- It would use behavioral terms.

- It would have room for comments.
- It would be reusable.

By *clarity* and *uses behavioral terms*, I mean that the words you select should be precise and that, whenever possible, you should define performance criteria behaviorally. When you place a check next to a particular behavior, what that check signifies should be readily apparent. Rather than noting "Shows an interest in reading," which is rather vague, you might include other more specific and observable behaviors such as "Selects books to read independently" and "Listens attentively when books, etc. are read aloud."

Either a series of symbols or a rating scale can be useful in indicating whether or not a child has demonstrated competence in a skill or to what degree he has exhibited a particular behavior. In the former case, perhaps three symbols (such as a plus sign, a check, and a minus sign) can indicate respectively that the child demonstrates the skill or behavior frequently, sometimes, or rarely. A rating-scale design, on the other hand, usually incorporates five points or levels—never, infrequently, sometimes, frequently, and always—which you check off as appropriate for each behavior.

A recording format in which it is *easy to record and retrieve information* is one pared down to its simplest form and containing no gimmickry or distracting features. This means *not* having so much information on a page that you have to plow through a visual maze to find what you are looking for. Limiting the information to a single page is a good time-saver too, especially when you consider that you will have a separate form for each child in your group. The symbol key that designates the meaning of each numeral or symbol (e.g., a check means frequently, the numeral 3 means sometimes) should also be included on the same page. Use horizontal and vertical lines sparingly to divide the space on the page into separate skills and different dates of entry. Too many lines can be visually confusing.

A format for recording literacy development that is *appropriate for children's needs* should include items that are both significant and representative of the literacy process of the children in your group. For example, if you were considering the reading process, then you would want to observe important behaviors under the categories of comprehension, word identification, interest, and fluency. For children in the primary grades, fluency would be the least significant category, while the ability to employ word identification strategies would be more significant.

You should list specific behaviors under each category neutrally as well as behaviorally. Sometimes, recording formats suffer from the "pathologist's syndrome" by concentrating exclusively on weaknesses and designating behaviors negatively (the child "mispronounces," or "cannot").

For writing, you might want to observe a child's performance in such areas as writing interest, knowledge and use of the conventions of written language, independence in writing, editing and revising, and writing in different styles and for different purposes.

It is always possible, even desirable, to modify the behaviors you list as children develop. For example, at the start of the primary grades, you would be less concerned about a child's ability to spell conventionally than about his understanding of the sound/symbol relationship, as shown by his invented spelling. Later on, you would be more interested in whether the child is using more visual cues in spelling words.

Your selection of specific skills and behaviors for a recording format should be based on the goals and characteristics of your literacy program and the needs and capacities of the children in your class. If comprehension of meaning and interest in reading constitute your primary goals in reading instruction, then you should observe and diagnose these two categories most acutely, and your recording format should reflect their predominance in the number and specificity of behaviors noted in these areas. In addition, although curriculum guides and published checklists may indicate that children in a particular grade should master a given skill, if your own experience and philosophy of teaching do not agree, then you should not include the skill in your recording format.

The recording format should allow you to get a picture of the flow of a child's development in literacy—progressing, regressing, and leveling off in plateaus. For this to be possible, the format must *provide space for several entries* so you can see whether or not there has been a change in performance, and if so, what kind of change.

You can make anywhere from three to ten entries a year, depending on how much time you are able to devote to this kind of record-keeping, and each entry should be dated. Actually, you can have too many entries; adding more and more information makes it difficult to record and retrieve data; a law of diminishing returns operates. The interval of time between entries should not be so short as to prevent the possibility of observing noticeable increments or changes in performance. If it is, then the effort you have expended in observation and recording will be ill-spent. On the other hand, it should not be so long as to preclude making appropriate changes in instruction based upon the information recorded.

Most teachers find that adding *written-out comments* increases the effectiveness of a checklist, because it permits a wider latitude of observation than the more precise but constraining symbols or rating scale. In the interests of time and space, however, try to develop a terse, telegraphic kind of code to convey your observations and impressions in single words and brief phrases. If possible, allow space for such comments in each category of reading and writing performance. You can use the reverse side of the recording format for more global or summary comments on the child's total literacy performance, each of which should also be dated. This combination of both subjective comments and objective observations provides a well-rounded assessment format.

A sample reading profile. Following the criteria for developing a checklist listed above, a sample reading profile might look like the one shown in Figure 7–2. (Only one specific behavior is included for illustrative purposes under each category.)

Child _____ Year _____ Teacher _____
                          Dates

				Comments
Comprehension				
1. Recalls facts and details				
2. . . .				
Word identification				
1. Uses contextual cues				
2. . . .				
Interest				
1. Listens attentively during story reading				
2. . . .				
Fluency				
1. Reads phrases as units				
2. . . .				

Symbol Key
+ = Frequently
✓ = Sometimes
− = Rarely

Figure 7–2   A reading profile

Fundamental Considerations

Some would say that tests by their very nature are bad. I would say rather that some tests are by their nature poor. That is, they are so poorly constructed that they fail to serve any good purpose. What is even more significant, however, is the way in which tests are used. It is not so much that tests themselves are bad, but that they are selected, administered, and interpreted inappropriately.

Misuse is probably most blatant with formal assessment procedures, but even a casual examination of classrooms will often reveal a misuse of the results of informal assessment procedures. I can recall seeing a very attractive bookworm display posted along the top of a bulletin board in a first-grade room. The placement of children's names on the bookworm was determined by how many books they had read. Names of advanced readers were clustered toward the bookworm's head, while slowpokes, those who had completed just three or four books, were straggling near the bookworm's tail. As attractive as the display was, there were at least two things wrong with it. First, I can tell you from my own experience as a first-grade teacher that for some children reading just three or four books may represent a greater accomplishment than other children's reading of thirty or forty. Some children come to first grade having mastered much of what they need to know and do in order to read. Some of them are already reading. For those who find reading a slow and difficult process, however, being able to read just a few books is a genuine achievement. Yet the message these children received when they saw their names at the end of the bookworm was just the opposite. What good purpose is served by this kind of reinforcement?

The second problem with this display was its *public nature*. As we have noted all along in this book, there are many appropriate opportunities to display children's work: hanging group stories on a chart rack, displaying projects on bulletin boards and tables, and setting out class and individually composed books in the language arts area. But work that is being used in some way as an assessment of a child's performance should be considered confidential. It belongs in his reading/writing folder, where he can use it with the teacher to make decisions on how to proceed. The child's parents and other appropriate school personnel should also have access to this material, but it is unfair to make it a public display.

As mentioned earlier in this chapter, it is quite unlikely that there will be an end to the use of tests. Moreover, informal assessment procedures lie at the heart of diagnostic teaching and can provide the teacher with much valuable information. Thus, the answer to problems associated with assessment must come from knowledge and ethics.

Some misuse of assessment procedures arises from ignorance. An example of this is the equation of a standardized test's grade level equivalent with the grade level of a basal reader. It is important, therefore, for teachers to become informed about tests, what they are designed to do, and how they are meant to be used. The references by Schreiner, Schwartz, and Schell in the suggestions for Further Reading at the end of this chapter are particularly useful for this purpose.

Equally important is the assurance that the selection, administration, and interpretation of assessment procedure results are guided by high standards of professional ethics. Good assessment demands that teachers be flexible, honest, discreet, and open-minded. To act otherwise is to violate their role and purpose. Following are some guidelines that can help in selecting, administering, and interpreting assessment procedures:[27]

Test Selection

1. A standardized test should report information on its standardization process fully, including how and on what samples its norms were developed and its estimates of reliability and validity.

2. The standardization sample should be similar to the children who are going to take the test on all important variables.

3. When there are significant differences between the standardization sample and the children who are going to take the test, establishment of local norms may be in order.

4. Selection of a particular test should be made only after a thorough review and evaluation of all tests available for the given purpose.

5. Tests that are selected should undergo a periodic review of their potential usefulness.

Test Administration

1. Directions for administering and scoring a test should be clear and easy to follow.

2. The process of converting scores should be simple and efficient.

3. Directions for administering and scoring a standardized test should be followed precisely as indicated because the test's norms were developed from these specific procedures.

4. Test sessions should be relaxed and comfortable.

5. Preparation for tests should not be unduly lengthy or involve material that is too similar to actual test content.

Test Interpretation

1. For the conclusions on a child's achievement to be valid, they must be drawn from the results of a variety of different assessment procedures.

2. The assessment process should be ongoing with continuous inputs on the child's performance over time.

3. The child who is being assessed should play an important cooperative role in the assessment process.

4. Assessment data should be considered confidential.

5. Conclusions on a child's performance should be considered tentative and subject to continuous review.

6. Children should not be labeled and categorized on the basis of assessment.

7. Tests should be considered just one of many ways to assess a child's performance, none of which is inherently and uniformly superior to the others.

Summary

This chapter has considered assessment as an integral component of the literacy program. We have seen that most assessment information should come from careful daily observation. But, occasionally, the results of a standardized test can add to your information on a child's performance, provided that the test is appropriate and that the results are interpreted correctly. Effective assessment also requires an efficient system for keeping records. Especially important to the success of the assessment plan is your understanding of the nature of tests and your application of high ethical standards in the assessment process. To realize their full potential in the literacy program, assessment procedures should:

- Comprise a functional and regular component of the program.
- Be understood by the children as to their purpose and use.
- Be administered in a relaxed and informal manner.
- Be used prudently in decision making.

Activities

1. Arrange to examine a standardized primary-grade reading survey test at your college/university library. Review the test itself and its accompanying instruction manual. Evaluate the test on these criteria: clarity of directions for administering and scoring, ease of administering and scoring, ambiguity of test items, evidence of bias in test items, and representativeness of the standardization sample. Identify the test you have reviewed and cite specific examples from it to support your findings.

2. Select books at a second or third grader's independent, instructional, and frustrational levels from the regular reading material in his class. Make a running record of a child's oral reading of a short passage (100–200 words) from each book. What does the record indicate about the kinds of cues the child was using? Did he self-correct? Based on this assessment, what recommendations would you make for future instruction?

3. Have a child read aloud from a passage at her or his instructional level. What kinds of miscues does the child make? What percentage of the miscues interfere with meaning? How many may be attributable to dialect? Does the child make any regressions? Based on this child's oral reading performance, what teaching strategies would you use? Why would you use these strategies?

4. Construct a cloze procedure using a group-dictated story. Administer it to a

child in a first-grade class. Analyze the results and compare them with information on this child's reading performance obtained from other kinds of assessments that the teacher gives you. (See the article by Balyeat and Norman listed in the Notes for further information on this technique.)

5. Arrange to observe a second- or third-grade class for an entire morning session. Select one child as the focus of your observation. Make a list of the child's behaviors and activities that you could use as a teacher for informal assessment purposes. Note each behavior briefly and objectively. Afterward, go over your list and indicate what *potential* diagnostic data on the child's reading and writing performance you might be able to infer from each item.

Further Reading

Almy, M., and Genishi, C. *Ways of Studying Children*, rev. ed. New York: Teachers College Press, 1979.

Farr, R., and Carey, R. F. *Reading—What Can Be Measured?* 2d ed. Newark, Del.: International Reading Association, 1986.

Genishi, C., and Dyson, A. H. *Language Assessment in the Early Years*. Norwood, N.J.: Ablex, 1984.

Schreiner, R., ed. *Reading Tests and Teachers: A Practical Guide*. Newark, Del.: International Reading Association, 1979. See also another publication of the International Reading Association, *Diagnostic and Criterion-Referenced Tests: Review and Evaluation*, ed. L. Schell. 1981.

Schwartz, J. I. "Standardizing a Reading Test." *The Reading Teacher* 30 (1977): 364–68.

Note as well that reviews of recently published tests are a regular feature of the journal, *The Reading Teacher*.

APPENDICES

APPENDIX A

Some Characteristics of Black Vernacular English

I. Syntactical Characteristics of Black Vernacular English

    A. Verb Forms and Verb Markers

        1. Dialect usages of the form *to be*

            a. The form *be* is often used in place of other forms of the auxiliary, regardless of the subject

                (1) He be doing that.

                (2) They be messing around.

                (3) I be here this afternoon.

            b. The forms *is* and *are* of the verb "to be" are omitted; the *am* (or its contraction *'m*) is almost always present

                (1) He tired.

                (2) They with us.

                (3) I'm happy.

            c. No conformity exists in person-number agreement when full forms of *to be* are used; generally, the past tense form is *was* and the present tense form is *is*

                (1) They was there.

                (2) The boys is there.

Adapted from: Fasold, R. W., and Shuy, R., Editors. (1970). *Teaching Standard English in the Inner City* (Urban Language Series #6). Washington, D.C.: Center for Applied Linguistics. (ERIC Document Reproduction Service No. ED037720). And National Council of Teachers of English. (1968). *Nonstandard Dialect*. Champaign, Illinois: National Council of Teachers of English. (ERIC Document Reproduction Service No. ED021248)

2. The third person singular present tense marker

    a. The suffix *-s* or *-os*, used in standard English to identify the present tense of a regular third person singular verb, is absent in black dialect

        (1) He do.

        (2) It know.

    b. The *-s* suffix is absent from the auxiliary *don't* in the present tense when the subject is in the third person singular

        (1) He don't go.

        (2) He don't walk.

    c. Since the *-s* suffix does not exist in black dialect, the verbs *have* and *do* remain so in the third person singular, present tense, rather than becoming *has/does*

        (1) He have a bike.

        (2) He always do silly things.

3. The four perfective constructions in black dialect

    a. Present—the forms of *have*, often contracted in standard English (*'ve; 's*), are often omitted

        (1) I been here for hours.

        (2) He gone home already.

    b. Past—this construction with *had* is more common in black dialect narratives than in standard English

        (1) He had found the money.

        (2) He had gone back home.

    c. Completive—formed from the verb *done* plus a past form of the verb

        (1) They done came.

        (2) I done forgot what you call it.

    d. Remote time—indicates that the speaker conceives of the action as taking place in the distant past

        (1) I been had it there for about three years.

        (2) You won't get your dues that you been paid.

4. Nonstandard forms involving future tense

    a. *Gonna* is frequently a future indicator in black dialect

        (1) He gonna go.

        (2) He gonna get in trouble.

    b. The use of *will* to indicate future is frequently contracted (*'ll*) or eliminated, particularly when the next word begins with a labial consonant

        (1) He'll go tomorrow.

        (2) He miss you tomorrow.

B. Nouns, Pronouns, Adjectives, Adverbs

1. The formation of plurals with *-s* or *-es* markers

    a. The *-s* or *-es* suffixes that mark most plurals in standard English are occasionally absent in black dialect

        (1) He took five book.

        (2) The other teacher, they'll yell at you.

    b. The plurals of irregular nouns are frequently formed with the regular
       -s suffix

       (1) one foot/two foots
       (2) one deer/two deers

    c. Black dialect may add the *-s* suffix to the irregular plural of standard
       English words to form "double plurals" (mens, womens, teeths, mices,
       peoples)

2. The possessive construction in black English

       (In forming the possessive with common nouns, no marker is used if
       the word for the possessor precedes the word for the thing possessed)
       (1) The boy hat
       (2) John old lady house

3. Usages of personal, demonstrative, and relative pronouns

    a. Prenominal Apposition is the construction in which a pronoun, usually
       the nominative form, is used in apposition to the noun subject

       (1) My brother, he bigger than you.
       (2) That teacher, she yell all the time.

    b. In an existential or expletive function, black dialect uses *it*

       (1) It's a boy in my room name Robert.
       (2) It was one in the hall this morning.

    c. The personal pronouns *they* and *you* may be substituted for the pos-
       sessive pronouns *their* and *your*

       (1) They brought it on they own selves.
       (2) I like you coat.

    d. The pronoun *them* often replaces the demonstrative pronoun *those*;
       this is often reinforced by *here*

       (1) I want them books.
       (2) I want this here book.

    e. The pronoun *which* often replaces the standard form *who*

       (Linda, which is my sister . . .)

C. Negation in Black Dialect

1. The use of *Ain't*

    a. *Ain't* is a common negative form of *is, are, am* and auxiliary *have* and
       has

       (1) He ain't here.
       (2) I ain't goin'.

    b. *Ain't* is often used as a past tense signal, having merged with *int* for
       didn't

       (1) He ain't start it.
       (2) He ain't touch me.

2. Multiple Negation

    a. A negative may be attracted to every indefinite pronoun or adverb so
       that a single element, instead of being represented by one negative
       form, is expressed by two or more

(1) He doesn't know nothing.

(2) I ain't never had no trouble wit' none of them.

b. Negation can be expressed with negative adverbs

(He doesn't hardly come to see us.)

c. If a sentence has an indefinite noun phrase containing a negative marker (*nobody, nothing, no dog*) before the verb, the negativized form of the verbal auxiliary (*can't, wasn't, didn't*) may appear at the beginning of the sentence

(1) Can't nobody do it.

(2) Wasn't nothing wrong.

D. Sentence Patterns: The formation of questions

a. Direct questions may not be expressed in inverted form, and may omit *do* or *does*

(1) He fixes that?

(2) How it taste?

b. The inverted form of the question is used for indirect questions but without the forms *if* or *whether*

(1) I want to know where did he go?

(2) I want to know did he go somewhere?

II. Phonological Characteristics of Black Vernacular English

A. Consonants and Consonant Clusters

1. The final member of consonant clusters

a. A single consonant for a word-final cluster occurs only when both members of a cluster are either voiced or voiceless (see table)

Consonant Sounds

Voiced	b	d	g	j	v	w	z	th (this)
Voiceless	p	t	k c	ch	f	wh	s	th (things)
Voiced	—	l	m	n	ng	r	y	zh (azure)
Voiceless	h	—	—	—	—	—	—	sh

(1) Voiced—(nd) mind; (ld) cold

(2) Voiceless—(st) test; (sp) wasp; (ft) left; (pt) adept; (ct) act

b. When one of the members of the cluster is voiced and one is silent, the reduction does not occur

(1) (mp) jump—*m* is voiced; *p* voiceless

(2) (nt) count—*n* is voiced; *t* voiceless

(3) (lt) belt—*l* is voiced; *t* voiceless

c. As a result of the consonant cluster rule, certain pairs of words in black dialect have the same pronunciation

(1) bill/build

(2) coal/cold

(3) west/Wes

2. Pluralization in relation to the consonant reduction rule

(Words ending in -s plus -p, -t or -k add the -es plural, forming the plural as if the word ended in -s rather than in -sk, -st, or -sp)

(1) desk/desses

(2) ghost/ghoses

(3) wasp/wasses

3. The -ed suffix as a past tense, past participle, and derived adjective marker

(When the addition of the -ed suffix results in either a voiced or voiceless cluster, the cluster may be reduced)

(1) Past tense marker—Yesterday he mov' away. (vd)

(2) Participle—The boy was mess' up. (st)

(3) Adjective—He had a scratch' arm. (st)

B. The *th* Sounds: The sounds for *th* in black dialect are dependent on where *th* occurs in a word and/or what sounds occur next to it.

1. Word Initial—at the beginning of a word, the *th* is pronounced in one of three ways:

(1) Voiced interdental fricative—the *th* is pronounced as a *d*
the/de; they/dey; that/dat

(2) Voiceless interdental fricative—the *th* is sometimes pronounced as *t*
thought/tought; think/tink; thin/tin

(3) *th* followed by *r*—such words may be pronounced with an *f*
three/free; throat/froat

2. Within a word, three main pronunciations are possible for *th*

(1) for the Voiceless sound, *th* is pronounced as *f*
nothing/nuf'n; author/ahfuh; ether/eefuh

(2) for the Voiced sound, *th* is pronounced as *v*
brother/bruvah; rather/ravah; bathing/bavin'

(3) for *th* followed by a nasal sound, *th* is pronounced *t*
arithmetic/'ritmetic; nothing/nut'n; monthly/montly

3. Word Final—three main pronunciations are apparent for *th* when it comes at the end of a word

(1) The predominant sound for final *th* is *f*
Ruth/Ruf; tooth/toof; south/souf

(2) When the preceding sound is the nasal sound *n*, a *t* sound may occur
tenth/tent'; month/mont'

(3) The stop *t* or *d* may also be used with the preposition *with*
wit, wid

C. Controlled Vowels: The pronunciation rule for *r* and *l* in black dialect depends on whether they appear 1) after a vowel; 2) between the vowels; or 3) after initial consonants

1. After a Vowel (postvocalic)—only a "phonetic vestige" of *r* or *l* is pronounced unless it precedes a consonant, in which case no phonetic vestige is evident at all

(1) sister/sistuh; steal/steauh; nickel/nickuh; bear/beauh

(2) help/hep

2. Between Vowels—*r* or *l* may be absent when followed by another word beginning with a vowel and also between two vowels within a word

    (1) fouh apples

    (2) Carol/Ca'ol; story/sto'y; marry/ma'y

3. After Initial Consonants—*r* may be absent when the following vowel is either *o* or *u* or in unstressed syllables

    (1) throw/th'ow; through/th'ough

    (2) protect/p'otect; professor/p'ofessuh

D. Nasalization: There are several aspects of the nasals *-m*, *-n*, and *-ng*, some characteristic to all nonstandard dialects, others unique to black English:

1. The use of *-in* for the suffix *-ing* (e.g., singin', buyin', swimin')

2. At the end of a syllable, the final nasal consonant is sometimes not pronounced; rather a nasalization of the preceding vowel occurs, causing such words as *rum*, *run*, and *rung* to sound alike

3. Before a nasal consonant, *i* and *e* do not contrast, making such words as *pin* and *pen*, and *tin* and *ten* sound identical

E. Rules Concerning Final *b*, *d*, and *g*

1. Devoicing

    a. At the end of a syllable, the voiced stops *b*, *d*, and *g* are often pronounced as the corresponding voiceless stops *p*, *t*, and *k*

    NOTE: The above rule does not mean that such words as *pig/pick*, *bud/butt*, and *cab/cap* are pronounced alike. They are distinguished by the length of the vowel. The vowel is lengthened before sounds such as *d* in *bud*, even though the *d* is actually pronounced *t*

    b. "Devoicing" can take place in an unstressed syllable (e.g., *salat* for *salad*, *hundret* for *hundred*) as well as a stressed syllable (*mut* for *mud*, *goot* for *good*, *loat* for *load*)

2. Deletion of *d*: Some black dialect speakers may show the complete absence of the stop *d*; more frequently, however, when *d* is followed by a consonant rather than a vowel; its absence is most common before *s* or *z*

    (1) goo' man; ba' soldier

    (2) kiz for kids; boahz for boards

F. Other Pronunciation Features of Black English

1. Vocal Glides: The vocal glides represented as *ay* (e.g., side, time) and *oy* (e.g., boy, toy) are generally pronounced without the glide, particularly when followed by a voiced sound or a pause rather than by a voiceless sound

    (1) side/sahd; time/tahm

    (2) toy/toah BUT kite, bright, fight, not kaht, braht, faht

2. Indefinite Articles *a* and *an*

    a. The article *a* is used regardless of how the following word begins

    b. With a selected group of words (of more than one syllable), which may begin with a vowel similar to *a*, the article may be completely absent

(1) He had eraser.

(2) He had erector set.

3. Stress: In black vernacular English, certain words of more than one syllable may be stressed on the first syllable rather than on the second syllable as in standard English

(1) police for police

(2) hotel for hotel

(3) July for July

4. *str* clusters

a. In certain words such as *string* and *street*, the *str* cluster may be pronounced as *skr*, producing *skring* and *skreet*

b. At the end of a word, *st* may be changed to *sk*, producing *wrisk* for *wrist*, *twisk* for *twist*

APPENDIX B

Directions
for Book Binding

1. Stack eight to ten sheets of wide paper very carefully, so that all edges are even. Fold in half to form the leaves of the book, pressing the creased edge firmly. Then cut the inside cover sheet, which can be colored or plain depending on your desire. The cover sheet should be one-half inch smaller than the regular leaves. Center the cover around the folded leaves and press down creased edge firmly.
2. Open leaves so that the center fold can be stitched. Start sewing from the center of the page with one-half-inch stitches, moving to either edge and returning to center following the same holes. Continue again from center to opposite edge, stitch back to center and tie off at the back of the fold.
3. Cut two pieces of cardboard, approximately one-fourth inch larger than the folded leaves.
4. Cut one large piece of paper or cloth approximately one-and-one-half to two inches larger than the two pieces of cardboard when laid side by side. If you are using contact paper, take off the inner lining. Laying the paper with sticky side up, arrange the two pieces of cardboard on the contact paper so that you have about one-fourth inch separating them in the middle of the page. This separation will form the back binding of your book. (Depending on the thickness of your leaves, adjust to allow sufficient space between the two cardboard covers.) Press the cardboard down firmly, cut mitered (V-cut) corners, and fold down firmly over the cardboard. If you are using cloth or nonsticky paper, cover the back side of the two pieces of cardboard with paste before placing them on your covering material.
5. Place the sewn edge of the folded leaves in the middle of the open area between the cardboard covers. Ease in and fold the covers around the leaves, pressing firmly over the stitched area.
6. Open front cover, folding back the cardboard; put paste around edge of your inside cover sheet and press down firmly on the cardboard. Flip book over and repeat on the back side. If you have covered carefully and followed directions you now have a bound book. Congratulations!

(Directions Courtesy of Professor L. Perryman, Queens College, City University of New York)

NOTES

Section One. Foundations of Instruction

1. J. A. Langer, "Musings . . . A Sociocognitive View of Language Learning," *Research in the Teaching of English* 19 (1985): 325–27.

Chapter 1. Knowing Children

1. M. C. Robeck, *Infants and Children: Their Development and Learning* (New York: McGraw-Hill, 1978).

2. M. Almy, *Young Children's Thinking: Studies of Some Aspects of Piaget's Theory* (New York: Teachers College Press, 1966).

3. C. Kamii, *Number in Preschool and Kindergarten* (Washington, D.C.: National Association for the Education of Young Children, 1982).

4. B. J. Wadsworth, *Piaget's Theory of Cognitive and Affective Development*, 3d ed. (New York: Longman, 1984).

5. S. Isaacs, *Intellectual Growth in Young Children* (London: Routledge & Kegan Paul, 1930).

6. J. Piaget, *The Language and Thought of the Child* (London: Routledge & Kegan Paul, 1959).

7. J. Piaget, *The Origins of Intelligence in Children* (New York: International Universities Press, 1952).

8. J. Piaget, *Six Psychological Studies* (New York: Vintage Books, 1967).

9. See for example M. Donaldson, *Children's Minds* (New York: Norton, 1978).

10. L. S. Vygotsky, *Thought and Language* (Cambridge, Mass.: MIT Press, 1962).

11. J. C. Harste, C. L. Burke, and V. A. Woodward, *Children, Their Language and World:*

Initial Encounters with Print (Bloomington, Ind.: University of Indiana, Department of Language Education, 1981).

12. G. Wells, *Learning through Interaction* (Cambridge: Cambridge University Press, 1981).

13. Almy, *Young Children's Thinking*, p. vi.

14. C. B. Cazden, "Suggestions from Studies of Early Language Acquisition," *Childhood Education* 46 (1969): 128.

15. B. J. Wadsworth, *Piaget for the Classroom Teacher* (New York: Longman, 1978).

16. C. R. Snow, "The Conversational Context of Language Acquisition," in *Recent Advances in the Psychology of Language—Language Development and Mother-Child Interaction*, ed. R. N. Campbell and P. T. Smith (New York: Plenum, 1978).

17. L. J. Stone, H. T. Smith, and L. B. Murphy, eds. *The Social Infant* (New York: Basic Books, 1978).

18. D. Durkin, *Children Who Read Early* (New York: Teachers College Press, 1966).

19. R. Weir, "Some Questions on the Child's Learning of Phonology," in *The Genesis of Language: A Psycholinguistic Approach*, ed. F. Smith and G. E. Miller (Cambridge, Mass.: MIT Press, 1966).

20. W. Condon and L. Sander, "Neonate Movement Is Synchronized with Adult Speech," *Science* 183 (1974): 99–101.

21. J. S. Bruner, "Nature and Uses of Immaturity," in *Play—Its Role in Development and Evolution*, ed. J. S. Bruner, A. Jolly, and K. Sylva (New York: Basic Books, 1976).

22. E. V. Clark, "What's in a Word? On the Child's Acquisition of Semantics in His First Language," in *Cognitive Development and the Acquisition of Language*, ed. T. E. Moore (New York: Academic Press, 1973).

23. J. Berko, "The Child's Learning of English Morphology," *Word* 14 (1958). 150–177.

24. S. M. Ervin, "Imitation and Structural Change in the Child's Language," in *New Directions in the Study of Language*, ed. E. H. Lenneberg (Cambridge, Mass.: MIT Press, 1964).

25. N. Chomsky, *Aspects of the Theory of Syntax* (Cambridge, Mass.: MIT Press, 1965).

26. C. Cazden, "Play with Language and Metalinguistic Awareness: One Dimension of Language Experience," *OMEP, International Journal of Early Childhood* 6 (1974): 12–24.

27. E. H. Hiebert, "Developmental Patterns and Interrelationships of Preschool Children's Print Awareness," *Reading Research Quarterly* 16 (1981): 236–60.

28. J. Downing and P. Oliver, "The Child's Conception of a Word," *Reading Research Quarterly* 9 (1973–1974): 568–82. Hare, V. C. "What's in a Word? A Review of Young Children's Difficulties with the Construct 'Word,'" *The Reading Teacher* 37 (1984): 360–64.

29. B. Bernstein, "A Sociolinguistic Approach to Social Learning," in *Penguin Survey of the Social Sciences*, ed. J. Gould (Baltimore: Penguin, 1965). S. B. Heath, *Ways with Words: Language, Life and Work in Communities and Classrooms* (New York: Cambridge University Press, 1983).

30. B. G. Heald-Taylor, "Scribble in First Grade Writing," *The Reading Teacher* 38 (October, 1984): 4–8.

31. J. Schickedanz, *More than the ABC's: The Early Stages of Reading and Writing* (Washington, D.C.: National Association for the Education of Young Children, 1986).

32. M. Clay, *What Did I Write?* (Portsmouth, N.H.: Heinemann, 1975).

33. A. H. Dyson, "Research Currents: Young Children as Composers," *Language Arts* 60 (1983): 884–91.

34. M. L. King and V. M. Rentel, "Conveying Meaning in Written Texts," *Language Arts* 58 (1981): 721–28.

35. Harste, Burke, and Woodward, *Children, Their Language and World*.

36. L. L. Lamme and N. M. Childers, "The Composing Processes of Three Young Children," *Research in the Teaching of English* 17 (1983): 31–50.

37. J. Britton, "The Student's Writing," in *Explorations in Children's Writing*, ed. E. Everetts (Urbana, Ill.: National Council of Teachers of English, 1970). J. Tough, *The Development of Meaning* (New York: Wiley, 1977).

38. M. Clay, *What Did I Write?* (Auckland, N.Z.; Portsmouth, N.H.: Heinemann, 1975).

39. G. L Bissex, *Gnys at Wrk: A Child Learns to Write and Read* (Cambridge, Mass.: Harvard University Press, 1980).

40. W. B. Gillooly, "The Influence of Writing-System Characteristics on Learning to Read," *Reading Research Quarterly* 8 (1973): 167–99.

41. J. R. Gentry, "Learning to Spell Developmentally," *The Reading Teacher* 34 (1981): 378–81. J. R. Gentry, "An Analysis of Developmental Spelling in *Gnys at Wrk*," *The Reading Teacher* 36 (1982): 192–200.

42. C. Read, "Pre-school Children's Knowledge of English Phonology," *Harvard Educational Review* 41 (1971): 1–34. J. W. Beers, "Developmental Strategies of Spelling Competencies in Primary School Children," and E. Henderson, "Developmental Concepts of Word," both in *Developmental and Cognitive Aspects of Learning to Spell: A Reflection of Word Knowledge*, ed. E. Henderson and J. Beers (Newark, Del.: International Reading Association, 1980).

43. In the production of speech sounds, affrication means that the sound is produced when the breath stream is stopped completely and then released at articulation like the /j/ in *jump*.

44. For an excellent summary of invented spelling, see S. Sowers, "Six Questions Teachers Ask about Invented Spelling," in *Understanding Writing*, 2d ed., T. Newkirk and N. Atwell (Portsmouth, N.H.: Heinemann, 1988).

45. Bissex, *Gnys at Wrk*.

46. M. L. King and V. M. Rentel, *How Children Write: A Longitudinal Study* (Washington, D.C.: National Institute of Education, 1981).

47. A. N. Applebee, *The Child's Concept of Story: Ages 2 to 17* (Chicago: University of Chicago Press, 1978).

48. J. M. Golden, "Children's Concept of Story in Reading and Writing," *The Reading Teacher* 37 (1984): 578–84.

49. C. R. Snow, "Literacy and Language: Relationships During the Preschool Years," *Harvard Educational Review* 55 (1983): 165–89.

50. Berko, "The Child's Learning of English Morphology"; C. Chomsky, *The Acquisition of Syntax in Children from 5 to 10* (Cambridge, Mass.: MIT Press, 1969).

Chapter 2. Understanding the Written Code

1. H. G. Commager, "McGuffey and His Readers," *Saturday Review*, June 16, 1962, 50–51, 69–60.

2. J. Flood and D. Lapp, *Language/Reading Instruction for the Young Child* (New York: Macmillan, 1981).

3. D. M. Willows, D. Borwick, and M. Hayvren, "The Content of School Readers," in *Reading Research: Advances in Theory and Practice*, vol. 2, ed. G. E. MacKinnon and T. G. Waller (New York: Academic Press, 1981).

4. L. V. Rodenborn and E. Washburn, "Some Implications of the New Basal Readers," *Elementary English* 51 (1974): 885–88.

5. H. M. Popp, "Current Practices in the Teaching of Beginning Reading," in *Toward a Literate Society*, ed. J. Carroll and J. S. Chall (New York: McGraw-Hill, 1975).

6. J. Britton, *Language and Learning* (Coral Gables, Fla.: University of Miami Press, 1970).

7. M. A. K. Halliday, *Explorations in the Functions of Language* (London: Edward Arnold, 1973).

8. S. Langer, "Expressive Language and the Experience of Poetry," in *An Expressive Language*, ed. H. Werner (Worcester, Mass.: Worcester Press, 1955).

9. W. Labov, *The Study of Nonstandard English* (Urbana, Ill.: National Council of Teachers of English, 1970).

10. D. D. Steinberg and J. Yamada, "Are Whole Word Kanji Easier to Learn than Syllable Kana?" *Reading Research Quarterly* 14 (1978–1979): 88–99.

11. N. Chomsky, *Aspects of the Theory of Syntax* (Cambridge, Mass.: MIT Press, 1965).

12. D. R. Hittleman, with C. G. Hittleman, *Developmental Reading, K–8: Teaching from a Psycholinguistic Perspective* 2d ed. (Boston: Houghton Mifflin, 1983).

13. K. S. Goodman, "Unity in Reading," in *Becoming Readers in a Complex Society*, Eighty-third Yearbook of the National Society for the Study of Education, part 1, ed. A. C. Purves and O. Niles (Chicago: National Society for the Study of Education, 1984).

14. C. Weaver, *Psycholinguistics and Reading: From Process to Practice* (Cambridge, Mass.: Winthrop, 1980).

15. Hittleman, *Developmental Reading, K–8*.

16. L. M. Rosenblatt, *The Reader, the Text, the Poem* (Carbondale, Ill.: Southern Illinois University Press, 1978).

17. Goodman, "Unity in Reading."

18. Hittleman, *Developmental Reading K–8*.

19. Goodman, "Unity in Reading."

20. D. E. Rumelhart, "Towards an Interactive Model of Reading," in *Attention and Performance VI*, ed. S. Dornic (Hillsdale, N.J.: Lawrence Erlbaum, 1977).

21. K. S. Goodman and O. S. Niles, *Reading Process and Program* (Champaign, Ill.: National Council of Teachers of English, 1970).

22. Goodman and Niles, *Reading Process and Program*.

23. F. Smith, *Understanding Reading: A Psycholinguistic Analysis of Reading and Learning to Read* (New York: Holt, Rinehart & Winston, 1971).

24. K. S. Goodman, "Reading: A Psycholinguistic Guessing Game," in *Theoretical Models and Processes of Reading*, ed. H. Singer and R. Ruddell (Newark, Del.: International Reading Association, 1976).

25. Smith, *Understanding Reading*.

26. E. J. Gibson, "Reading for Some Purpose," in *Language by Ear and by Eye*, ed. J. F. Cavanagh and I. G. Mattingly (Cambridge, Mass.: MIT Press, 1972).

27. Smith, *Understanding Reading*.

28. Goodman, "Reading: A Psycholinguistic Guessing Game."

29. A. C. Graesser, *Prose Composition: Beyond the Word* (New York: Springer-Verlag, 1981).

30. J. Rash, T. D. Johnson, and N. Gleadow, "Acquisition and Retention of Written Words by Kindergarten Children Under Varying Learning Conditions," *Reading Research Quarterly* 19 (1984): 452–460.

31. N. Modiano, "Bilingual Education for Children of Linguistic Minorities," *America Indigena* 28 (1968): 405–14.

32. R. J. Rodrigues and R. H. White, *Mainstreaming the Non-English Speaking Student* (Urbana, Ill.: National Council of Teachers of English, 1981).

33. J. W. Lindfors, *Children's Language and Learning* (Englewood Cliffs, N.J.: Prentice-Hall, 1980).

34. Labov, *The Study of Nonstandard English*.

35. V. C. Hall and R. R. Turner, "The Validity of the 'Different Language Explanation' for Poor Scholastic Performance by Black Students," *Review of Educational Research* 44 (1974): 69–81; J. I. Schwartz, "Dialect Interference in the Attainment of Literacy—A Review of the Research," *Journal of Reading* 25 (1982): 44–46; V. Seitz, *Social Class and Ethnic Group Differences in Learning to Read* (Newark, Del.: International Reading Association, 1977).

36. K. S. Goodman, with C. Buck, "Dialect Barriers to Reading Comprehension Revisited," *The Reading Teacher* 26 (1973): 6–12.

Section Two. The Program in Action
Chapter 3. Emergent Literacy

1. R. Weir, *Language in the Crib* (The Hague: Mouton, 1962).

2. E. Ferreiro and A. Teberosky, *Literacy before Schooling* (Portsmouth, N.H.: Heinemann, 1982).

3. J. Downing and P. Oliver, "The Child's Acquisition of a 'Word,'" *Reading Research Quarterly* 9 (1973–1974): 568–82.

4. S. Ashton-Warner, *Teacher* (New York: Simon & Schuster, 1965).

5. For a useful bibliography of predictable books, see L. K. Rhodes, "I Can Read! Pre-

dictable Books as Resources for Reading and Writing Instruction," *The Reading Teacher* 34 (1981): 511–18.

6. B. Park, "The Big Book Trend—A Discussion with Don Holdaway," *Language Arts* 59 (1982): 815–21.

7. M. Cochran-Smith, *The Making of a Reader* (Norwood, N.J.: Ablex, 1984); E. Sulzby, "Children's Emergent Reading of Favorite Storybooks: A Developmental Study," *Reading Research Quarterly* 20 (1985): 458–81.

8. J. Schickedanz, *More than the ABC's: The Early Stages of Reading and Writing* (Washington, D.C.: National Association for the Education of Young Children, 1986).

9. D. Holdaway, *The Foundations of Literacy* (Sydney, Australia: Ashton Scholastic, 1979).

10. C. A. Temple, R. G. Nathan, and N. A. Burris, *The Beginnings of Writing* (Boston: Allyn and Bacon, 1982).

11. Adapted from J. C. Harste, V. A. Woodward, and C. L. Burke, *Language Stories & Literacy Lessons* (Portsmouth, N.H.: Heinemann, 1984).

Chapter 4. Reading and Writing More Conventionally

1. B. Veitch and M. Carasso, *A Child's Cookbook* (Orinda, Calif.: Orinda Cooperative Nursery School, 1974).

2. M. V. Morphett and C. Washburne, "When Should Children Begin to Read?" *Elementary School Journal* 31 (1931): 496–503.

3. D. H. Graves, *Writing: Teachers and Children at Work* (Portsmouth, N.H.: Heinemann, 1983); L. McC. Calkins, *The Art of Teaching Writing* (Portsmouth, N.H.: Heinemann, 1986).

4. S. Ashton-Warner, *Teacher* (New York: Simon & Schuster, 1965).

5. M. Hall, *Teaching Reading as a Language Experience*, 3d ed. (Columbus, Ohio: Merrill, 1981).

6. Hall, *Teaching Reading as a Language Experience*.

7. A. P. Hunt and J. R. Reuter, "Readability and Children's Picture Books," *The Reading Teacher* 32 (1978): 23–27.

8. D. W. Ellis and F. W. Preston, "Enhancing Beginning Reading Using Wordless Picture Books in a Cross-Age Tutoring Program," *The Reading Teacher* 37 (1984): 692–98.

9. C. Lauritzen, "Oral Literature and the Teaching of Reading," *The Reading Teacher* 33 (1980): 787–90.

10. D. Holdaway, *The Foundations of Literacy* (Sydney, Australia: Ashton Scholastic, 1979).

11. D. Yarington, *The Great American Reading Machine* (Rochelle Park, N.J.: Hayden Book Company, 1978).

12. R. A. McCracken, "Initiating Sustained Silent Reading," *Journal of Reading* 14 (1971): 521–24, 582–83.

13. M. A. K. Halliday and R. Hasan, *Text and Context: Aspects of Language in Social-Semiotic Perspective* (Tokyo: Sophia University Press, 1980).

14. R. W. Shuy, "Finding a Sense of Wonder in Language and Literacy," in *Resource: College Reading: Response to the CUNY Reading Seminars*, publication of the Institutional Resource Center, Office of Academic Affairs, City University of New York, Fall 1983, pp. 23–34.

15. D. H. Graves, "An Examination of the Writing Processes of Seven-Year-Old Children," *Research in the Teaching of English* 9 (1975): 227–41.

16. J. C. Harste, V. A. Woodward, and C. L. Burke, *Language Stories & Literacy Lessons* (Portsmouth, N.H.: Heinemann, 1984).

17. M. A. K. Halliday, *Explorations in the Functions of Language* (London: Edward Arnold, 1975).

18. D. H. Graves, *Balance the Basics: Let Them Write* (New York: Ford Foundation, 1978).

19. C. M. Hauser, "Encouraging Beginning Writers," *Language Arts* 59 (1982): 681–86.

20. M. Hall, *The Language Experience Approach for Teaching Reading: A Research Perspective* (Newark, Del.: International Reading Association, 1978).

21. A. T. Burrows, D. C. Jackson, and D. O. Saunders, *They All Want to Write*, 3d ed. (New York: Holt, Rinehart and Winston, 1964).

Chapter 5. Becoming Proficient in Reading and Writing

1. D. H. Graves, *Writing: Teachers and Children at Work* (Portsmouth, N.H.: Heinemann, 1983).

2. J. Moffett and B. J. Wagner, *Student-Centered Language Arts and Reading, K–13*, 2d ed. (Boston: Houghton Mifflin, 1976).

3. K. Tobin, "Effects of Teacher Wait Time on Discourse Characteristics in Mathematics and Language Arts Classes," *American Educational Research Journal* 23 (1986): 191–200.

4. Graves, *Writing*.

5. A. T. Burrows, D. C. Jackson, and D. O. Saunders, *They All Want to Write*, 3d ed. (New York: Holt, Rinehart and Winston, 1964).

6. R. G. Stauffer, *Teaching Reading as a Thinking Process* (New York: Harper & Row, 1969).

7. P. M. Cunningham, S. A. Moore, J. W. Cunningham, and D. W. Moore, *Reading in Elementary Classrooms: Strategies and Observations* (New York: Longman, 1983).

8. Cunningham et al., *Reading in Elementary Classrooms*.

9. D. G. Hennings, "A Writing Approach to Reading Comprehension—Schema Theory in Action," in *Composing and Comprehending*, ed. J. M. Jensen (Urbana, Ill.: ERIC Clearinghouse on Reading and Communication Skills, 1984).

10. Burrows et al., *They All Want to Write*.

11. D. Durkin, *Teaching Young Children to Read*, 3d ed. (Boston: Allyn and Bacon, 1980).

12. C. J. Fisher and C. A. Terry, *Children's Language and the Language Arts* (New York: McGraw-Hill, 1977).

13. Burrows et al., *They All Want to Write*, p. 112.

14. Nebraska Curriculum Development Center, *A Curriculum for English* (Lincoln, Neb.: University of Nebraska Press, 1966).

15. J. W. Stewig, "Choral Speaking—Who Has the Time: Why Take the Time?" *Childhood Education* 58 (1981): 25–29.

16. Burrows et al., *They All Want to Write*.

17. M. R. Donoghue, *The Child and the English Language Arts*, 3d ed. (Dubuque, Iowa: Wm. C. Brown, 1979).

18. Donoghue, *The Child and the English Language Arts*.

19. L. Quant, "Factors Affecting the Legibility of Handwriting," *Journal of Experimental Education* 14 (1946): 297–316.

20. D. M. Lee and J. B. Rubin, *Children and Language: Reading and Writing; Talking and Listening* (Belmont, Calif.: Wadsworth, 1979).

21. L. S. Davis, "The Applicability of Phonic Generalizations to Selected Spelling Programs," *Elementary English* 49 (1972): 706–13.

22. P. R. Hanna and J. S. Hanna, "The Teaching of Spelling," *The National Elementary Principal* 45 (1965): 19–28.

23. Graves, *Writing*.

24. P. Coburn et al. *Practical Guide to Computers in Education* (Reading, Mass.: Addison-Wesley, 1982).

25. Other word processing programs have been developed for use with children as young as first graders. See, for example, J. Phenix and E. Hanna, "Word Processing in the Grade One Classroom," *Language Arts* 61 (1984): 804–12.

Section Three. Specifics of Instruction
Chapter 6. Comprehension

1. E. L. Thorndike, "Reading as Reasoning: A Study of Mistakes in Paragraph Reading," *Journal of Educational Research* 8 (1917): 323–33.

2. D. Durkin, *Teaching Them to Read*, 4th ed. (Boston: Allyn and Bacon, 1983).

3. K. S. Goodman, "Effective Teachers of Reading Know Language and Children," *Elementary English* 51 (1974): 823–28.

4. B. Bettleheim and K. Zelan, "Why Children Don't Like to Read," *Atlantic Monthly*, (1981): 25–31.

5. B. Park, "The Big Book Trend—A Discussion with Don Holdaway," *Language Arts* 59 (1982): 815–21.

6. L. C. Ehri and L. S. Wilce, "Do Beginners Learn to Read Function Words Better in Sentences or in Lists?" *Reading Research Quarterly* 15 (1980): 451–76.

7. D. Elkind, "We Can Teach Reading Better," *Today's Education* 64 (1975): 34, 36–38.

8. In English, word forms change to indicate different syntactical relationships and meaning. Structural cues are cues to the units of meaning, or *morphemes*, that comprise a word. There are two kinds of morphemes: *free morphemes*, which can stand by themselves; and *bound morphemes*, which cannot stand alone, and thus must be affixed to other morphemes.

9. Durkin, *Teaching Them to Read*.

10. F. G. Guszak, "Teachers' Questions and Levels of Reading Comprehension," in *The Evaluation of Children's Reading Achievement*, ed. T. Barrett. (Newark, Del.: International Reading Association, 1967); J. P. Ives, "The Improvement of Critical Reading Skills," in *Problem Areas in Reading—Some Observations and Recommendations*, ed. C. Morrison (Providence, R.I.: Oxford Press, 1966).

11. J. A. Langer, "Examining Background Knowledge and Text Comprehension," *Reading Research Quarterly* 19 (1984): 468–81.

12. L. Christenbury and P. P. Kelly, *Questioning—A Path to Critical Thinking* (Urbana, Ill.: ERIC/NCTE, 1983).

13. M. V. Zintz, *The Reading Process: The Teacher and the Learner*, 2d ed. (Dubuque, Iowa: Brown, 1975).

14. D. Durkin, "What Classroom Observations Reveal About Reading Instruction," *Reading Research Quarterly* 14 (1978–1979): 481–533.

15. B. J. Guzzetti, "The Reading Process in Content Fields: A Psycholinguistic Investigation," *American Educational Research Asosociation Journal* 21 (1984): 659–68.

16. Durkin, *Teaching Them to Read*.

17. P. M. Cunningham, S. A. Moore, J. W. Cunningham, and D. W. Moore, *Reading in Elementary Classrooms: Strategies and Observations* (New York: Longman, 1983).

18. M. L. Lake, "Improve the Dictionary's Image," *Elementary English* 48 (1971): 363–65.

19. Cunningham et al., *Reading in Elementary Classrooms*.

20. D. Johnson and P. D. Pearson, *Teaching Reading Vocabulary* (New York: Holt, Rinehart and Winston, 1978).

21. D. R. Hittleman with C. G. Hittleman, *Developmental Reading, K–8: Teaching from a Psycholinguistic Perspective*, 2d ed. (Boston: Houghton Mifflin, 1983).

22. A. D. Pellegrini and L. Galda, "The Effects of Thematic-Fantasy Play Training on Development of Children's Story Comprehension," *American Educational Research Journal* 19 (1982): 443–52.

23. D. Durkin, *Teaching Young Children to Read*, 3d ed. (Boston: Allyn and Bacon, 1980).

24. Hittleman, *Developmental Reading, K–8*.

25. Adapted from C. Weaver, *Psycholinguistics and Reading: From Process to Practice* (Cambridge, Mass.: Winthrop, 1980).

Chapter 7. Assessment

1. M. Almy and C. Genishi, *Ways of Studying Children*, rev. ed. (New York: Teachers College Press, 1979).

2. M. Deutsch and J. S. Fishman, "Guidelines for Testing Minority Group Children," *Journal of Social Issues* 20 (1964): 129–45.

3. P. H. Johnston, "Assessment in Reading," in *Handbook of Reading Research*, ed. P. D. Pearson (New York: Longman, 1984).

4. J. I. Schwartz, "Standardizing a Reading Test," *The Reading Teacher* 30 (1977): 364–68.

5. On a normal (bell-shaped) distribution of scores, approximately sixty-eight percent

of the scores will fall within one standard error of the mean of the distribution. Likewise, approximately ninety-five percent of the scores will fall within two standard errors of the mean.

6. Johnston, "Assessment in Reading."

7. P. M. Cunningham, S. A. Moore, J. W. Cunningham, and D. W. Moore, *Reading in Elementary Classrooms: Strategies and Observations* (New York: Longman, 1983).

8. P. Kilgallon, "A Study of Relationships among Certain Pupil Adjustments in Language Situations." Ph.D. diss., Pennsylvania State College, 1942.

9. E. A. Betts, *Foundations of Reading Instruction* (New York: American Book, 1946).

10. M. S. Johnson and R. A. Kress, *Informal Reading Inventories* (Newark, Del.: International Reading Association, 1965).

11. L. Hunt, "The Effect of Self-Selection, Interest and Motivation upon Independent, Instructional, and Frustrational Levels of Reading." Paper presented at the International Reading Association Conference, Kansas City, 1969; C. Pennock, "IRI—Dogma or Data," *The Reading Teacher* 28 (1975): 782–83; W. R. Powell, "Reappraising the Criteria for Interpreting Informal Inventories." Paper presented at the International Reading Association Conference, Boston, 1968; G. Spache and E. Spache, *Reading in the Elementary School*, 2d ed. (Boston: Allyn and Bacon, 1969).

12. C. Genishi and A. H. Dyson, *Language Assessment in the Early Years* (Norwood, N.J.: Ablex, 1984).

13. J. A. Caldwell, "A New Look at the Old Informal Reading Inventory," *The Reading Teacher* 39 (1985): 168–73.

14. K. S. Goodman, "Analysis of Oral Raeading Miscues: Applied Psycholinguistics," *Reading Research Quarterly* 6 (1969): 9–30.

15. K. S. Goodman, "Miscues: Windows on the Reading Process," in *Miscue Analysis*, ed. K. S. Goodman and O. S. Niles (Urbana, Ill.: National Council of Teachers of English, 1973).

16. Y. M. Goodman, "Qualitative Reading Miscue Analyses for Teacher Training," in *Language and Learning to Read: What Teachers Should Know about Language*, ed. R. E. Hodges and E. H. Rudorf (Boston: Houghton Mifflin, 1972).

17. Y. M. Goodman and C. Burke, *Reading Miscue Inventory—Alternative Procedures* (New York: R. C. Owen, 1987).

18. C. Weaver, *Psycholinguistics and Reading: From Process to Practice* (Cambridge, Mass.: Winthrop, 1980).

19. M. M. Clay, *The Early Detection of Reading Difficulties*, 3d ed. (Auckland, New Zealand: Heinemann, 1985).

20. Clay, *What Did I Write?*, p. 35.

21. W. Taylor, "Cloze Procedure: A New Tool for Measuring Readability," *Journalism Quarterly* 40 (1953): 414–38.

22. J. R. Bormuth, "The Cloze Procedure," in *Help for the Reading Teacher—New Directions in Research*, ed. W. D. Page (Urbana, Ill.: ERIC Clearinghouse on Reading and Communication Skills, 1975).

23. A. Balyeat and D. Norman, "LEA – cloze—Comprehension Test," *The Reading Teacher* 28 (1975): 555–60.

24. R. Bloomer, "The Cloze Procedure as a Remedial Reading Exercise," *Journal of De-*

velopmental Reading 10 (1962): 173–81; J. R. Bormuth, "Factor Validity of Cloze Tests as Measures of Reading Comprehension Ability," *Reading Research Quarterly* 4 (1969): 358–65; E. F. Rankin, "The Cloze Procedure—A Survey of Research," in *The Philosophical and Sociological Bases of Reading*, ed. E. L. Thurston and L. E. Hafner (Milwaukee, Wis.: National Reading Conference, 1965); J. W. Schneyer, "Use of Cloze Procedure for Improving Reading Comprehension," *The Reading Teacher* 19 (1965): 174–79.

25. J. C. Harste, V. A. Woodward, and C. L. Burke, *Language Stories and Literacy Lessons* (Portsmouth, N.H.: Heinemann, 1984).

26. D. J. Richgels, "Beginning First-Graders Invented Spelling Ability and Their Performance in Functional Classroom Writing Activities," *Early Childhood Research Quarterly* 1 (1986): 85–97.

27. J. I. Schwartz, "Testing: Some Caveats and Some Suggestions," *Kappa Delta Pi Record* 14 (December 1976): 49, 52.

INDEX